A PRISON OF EXPECTATIONS

A Prison of Expectations

The Family in Victorian Culture

STEVEN MINTZ

New York University Press
New York & London
1983

Copyright © 1983 by New York University

Library of Congress Cataloging in Publication Data
Mintz, Steven, 1953–
A prison of expectations.

Bibliography: p.
Includes index.
1. Family—England—History—19th century—Case
studies. 2. Family—United States—History—19th
century—Case studies. 3. Middle classes—England
—History—19th century—Case studies. 4. Middle
classes—United States—History—19th century—
Case studies. 5. Authors, English—19th century
—Political and social views. 6. Authors, American
—19th century—Political and social views.
I. Title.
HQ613.M56 1983   306.85   82-14481
ISBN 0-8147-5388-4

Manufactured in the United States of America

Clothbound editions of New York University Press books are Smyth-
sewn and printed on permanent and durable acid-free paper

To Susan M. Kellogg

Contents

viii   *Contents*

Illustrations

Preface

THE image is a vivid one, even though it is constructed of a mosaic of half-remembered novels, two-volume life and letters, and gilded framed paintings. It is a picture of a Victorian family, dominated by a bewhiskered father, surrounded by his submissive wife, his respectful children, and perhaps a spinster aunt and an aging grandparent. It is not difficult to account for the lasting appeal of this Victorian icon. To generations that have witnessed stunning upheavals in family patterns, gender roles, and sexual mores, the image of the Victorian family suggests a more stable and ordered past, a model of hierarchical organization, deference, and discipline contrasting sharply with our own disordered times.

The stereotype of the Victorian family—even though represented in innumerable daguerreotypes—is as much fantasy as reality. There was, of course, no single Victorian family type. Even a minimal familiarity with nineteenth-century culture calls to mind the enormous diversity of the Victorian family, ranging from the unforgettable image of Friedrich Engels's Manchester working-class family, in which filial discipline and moral order have broken down under the effects of the factory system, to Alexis de Tocqueville's portrait of the "democratic family" bound together by "natural affection" rather than by paternal discipline. The Victorian family took many forms. Yet in this book we shall enter only five Victorian homes in order to shed light

on crucial aspects of middle-class character and family life during the Victorian era.

By investigating the private lives of five of the most famous
and influential Victorian novelists—Robert Louis Stevenson,
George Eliot, Harriet Beecher Stowe, Catharine Sedgwick, and
Samuel Butler—this study traces patterns of intersection between family dynamics and larger cultural problems of authority, legitimacy, and discipline in nineteenth-century Britain and
America; between struggles to achieve a personal independence
within a Victorian home and the larger historical struggle to
adapt older traditions of deference, authority, and responsibility
to the emerging realities of a democratic age.

The book's method is to develop a series of case studies against
a background of social history, which includes discussion of the
changing social and demographic characteristics of the middle-
class home, the psychology of Victorian love and marital relationships, and beliefs about the socialization of children. Although the study draws extensively upon the social history of
the family, its approach is essentially cultural, in that it deals
primarily with issues relating to perception, belief, language, and
psychology. Instead of focusing on the measurable and quanti-
fiable dimensions of family life, this book concentrates on the
Victorian family's emotional patterns. By showing how family
conflicts take on more general cultural strains and illustrating
how the resolution of family problems reflects wider changes in
Victorian religious and philosophic thought, this study seeks to
provide a bridge between the lives of individuals and larger cultural patterns, between individual personality and larger patterns of religious, legal, and institutional change.

David Brion Davis helped to shape the aims and spirit of this
book. From him, I learned about an approach to history that
draws upon the empirical findings of the "new" social history
but that is primarily interested in the psychological, cognitive,
and moral implications of social change. Davis has shown that
history is not simply a time line or a calendar of events but an

attempt to confront existential questions and to explore human consciousness across time.

I was also fortunate to study with Dr. Ernst Prelinger, who introduced me to psychoanalytic theory and who influenced my interpretation of family interaction and dynamics. I am indebted to the Kanzer Fellowship for Psychoanalytic Studies in the Humanities for the generous support that made it possible for me to study with Dr. Prelinger.

Not least, I am grateful to the advice and criticism of family and friends, without which this book could not have been written. To Charles Dellheim I owe a debt of gratitudes that goes far beyond his willingness to put his knowledge of English history and literature at my service. He is all one could ask for in a graduate school friend. I was also fortunate in having the support of Alan Heppel, Robin Kaufman, and Carol Mostow, who taught me to appreciate the inner struggles of value and impulse that underlie behavior that too often appears to be without pattern or meaning. My debt to my parents and sisters is equally great. Their encouragement, support, and enthusiasm contributed immeasurably to this book. Colin Jones, Director of New York University Press, offered support and guidance in transforming my manuscript into a book. My greatest debt is to Susan M. Kellogg, to whom this book is dedicated, who sacrificed enormous amounts of time from her work in order to read and criticize the manuscript, to discuss the basic themes and organization of the study, and to share her knowledge on the social theory of the family. I cannot express sufficient gratitude for her patience, encouragement, and counsel.

During the period when this book was written, the death of my grandmother occurred. And this event, which was the most severe incident in the life of my family, brought home the reason we need to study history: to come to terms with a still felt past.

Acknowledgments

GRATEFUL acknowledgment is made to the following for permission to quote material under copyright:

The Beinecke Rare Book and Manuscript Library, Yale University: For material from the papers of Robert Louis Stevenson.

Jonathan Cape Ltd.: Excerpts from Arnold Silver, ed., *The Family Letters of Samuel Butler* (Stanford, California, 1962).

The Schlesinger Library, Radcliffe College: For material from the papers of Harriet Beecher Stowe.

The Stowe-Day Foundation: For material from the papers of Harriet Beecher Stowe.

Yale University Press: Excerpts from Gordon S. Haight, ed., *The George Eliot Letters* (9 vols., New Haven, 1954–1955, 1978).

A PRISON OF EXPECTATIONS

CHAPTER 1

Introduction

D URING the past decade few fields of history have generated
such excitement or occasioned such lively debate as the
history of the family. The research on the family, which reflects
a growing concern among historians with the analytic methods
and concepts of sociology and anthropology, has led to the sys-
tematic use of new sources of data, such as parish records and
manuscript censuses, and to the application of new methods of
inquiry, such as the demographic technique of "family reconsti-
tution." By reaching into areas that were previously the domain
of such disciplines as social psychology, cultural anthropology,
law, and demography, the study of the family has led to a vital
reshaping and broadening of the meaning of history.

The explanation for this burgeoning interest in the history of
the family is not simple. There can be no doubt that part of the
concern with family history is related to recent abrupt demographic, economic, and ideological changes buffeting the institution. In the United States, these changes are manifest in the
doubling of the divorce rate in the course of a decade; a doubling of the number of female-headed households in a generation; a sharp influx of women into the wage labor force, so that
today more than half of all mothers with school-aged children
work outside the home; and a precipitous decline in the number
of children per family, from 3.8 in 1957 to slightly less than 2.0
now. These changes aside, an apparent increase in sexual activity

outside marriage, proliferation of complex kinship patterns as a result of the increased rate of divorce and remarriage, and changes in the way men and women relate to each other have raised new questions relating to parenting, childrearing, sexuality, gender, and sex roles.

Yet the gradual growth of interest in family history involves something more than a faddish reaction to feminism, shifting family patterns, and current anxieties about whether the twentieth-century family is successfully performing its socializing and acculturating functions. The debate over the family epitomizes new concerns among historians with social history and the history of private life. The research on the family has provided new insight into the texture of everyday life of nonelite peoples; it has examined the meanings and sentiments attached to marriage, children, and domesticity. This work has also led to a growing understanding of the role of family and kinship structures in the division and transmission of property, the definition of social rank and status, and the allocation and division of labor.

Perhaps the major reason why family history has been an intellectual growth industry is that the family provides a bridge between two fundamental domains of human life and experience—between social processes and psychological processes. As a primary agent of socialization, the family provides a vehicle for studying the transmission and adaptation of cultural and psychological patterns from one generation to the next. As a social institution, the organization and structure of the family is closely connected with the organization of other realms of life, such as economics, politics, and religion. The family has become an important object of historical inquiry because it permits us to see relationships between changes in individual personality and larger social and cultural changes. In various ways, recent writings on the history of the family have served to illuminate the broad process of social and cultural change.

During the past ten years, the history of the family has been dominated by two approaches. The first embodies the characteristics and concerns of the "new" social history. Rooted in the conceptual and methodological concerns of sociology and social anthropology, the new social history has sought to use birth, marriage, and death records to discern demographic changes in residence patterns, household size, family organization, age relations within the family, and the developmental cycle of domestic groups (i.e., changes in family and household composition over time). Drawing upon census schedules, parish registers, and household lists, the work of the new social historians has emphasized a quantitative analysis of structural changes in the family. According to this viewpoint, the decisive shifts in the history of the family are demographic, involving decreasing family size, declining rates of mortality and fertility, prolonged residence of children in the parental home, heightened emphasis on the bond between spouses as opposed to other bonds of kinship, and more uniform timing of the life stages (such as the timing of attending school, entering work, leaving home, marrying, and bearing children within marriage).

The second approach has been conducted within the more traditional boundaries of cultural history and has sought to trace changes in sentiments and cultural conceptions surrounding the family, childrearing, gender roles, sexuality, and marriage. Building on the pioneering work of the influential French historian Philippe Ariès, scholars employing this cultural and psychological approach have contended that the critical shifts in the history of the family are not changes in demographic structure and form but in the values, expectations, roles, and functions assigned to the family. Focusing primarily on changes in public ideologies of the family, these historians have set out to trace the rise, beginning in the sixteenth century, of a new conception of marriage that emphasized the compatibility of husband and wife and viewed mutual affection and companionship as the ideal of married life. They have sought to describe a growing emphasis on the privacy and isolation of the immediate family group as well as a more intense concern with privacy within the home, manifest in the construction of discrete areas for sleeping, eating, and entertaining. Finally, the cultural work on the family has also sought to describe an increased concern of parents with children and child development and the use of less authoritarian methods of discipline in childrearing.

The demographic and cultural-psychological approaches to the history of the family have added greatly to our knowledge about family change. The most successful quantitative studies have served to illuminate the degree of diversity in patterns of family and kinship organization according to class, region, and ethnicity. Historical research on residence patterns; life expectancy; age relations; and mortality, fertility, and marriage rates has helped to clarify the chronology and nature of changes in family structure and composition over time. Research on marriage transactions and inheritance practices has shed light on domestic strategies for transmitting and accumulating wealth and property and on the relationship between household structure and such demographic and economic variables as the availability of land, labor needs, and rates of population growth. Cultural historians, drawing on literary, legal, and artistic sources as well as on surviving letters and diaries, have helped to illuminate changes in attitudes and beliefs associated with family behavior.

The study of families during the Victorian era shares many of the strengths and weaknesses characterizing the study of other periods of family history. Much is known about the demographic characteristics of Victorian families: their size and composition, their organizational structure, and their developmental cycle. We know a considerable amount about cultural conceptions of Victorian families, particularly involving attitudes toward privacy, child discipline, and sexual morality. Skeletons have been counted and speculations have been made about the consequences of their childhood experiences. Yet curiously little work has examined in detail the internal dynamics of Victorian homes. Much remains to be learned about the emotional and power relationships within Victorian families. Much remains to be known about the connections between public ideologies of the Victorian family, expressed in moral tracts, advice manuals, and imaginative literature, and family realities. And much remains to be understood about the relationship between the dynamics within Victorian homes and such variables as class, religion, and cultural orientation. By examining the lives of five figures who helped to shape, define, and disseminate an emerging ideology of the family, this book seeks to illuminate the tensions and internal conflicts of some Victorian homes that were "representative" in a very special sense that I shall soon spell out.

This book, then, is concerned with the intricate and subtle connections between the Victorian home and society, between the dynamics of the Victorian family and larger issues of authority, deference, and discipline in nineteenth-century Britain and America. By fusing various levels of analysis—showing how conflicts within specific Victorian households embodied and reflected broader historical tensions within Victorian culture—it seeks to show how problems of personal identity were linked to broader social and religious problems of authority and belief, and how the home became a focal point for many of the strains and conflicts of nineteenth-century culture.

The basic argument of this book is that Victorian family issues have two sides: they are private, individual, and psychological; yet these issues are also intensely public and are connected with fundamental shifts in society and in the roles and expectations attached to the family. It is my contention that the issues, preoccupations, and tensions of the families examined in this book have their roots in an emerging ideology that assigned new psychological and ideological responsibilities to the home; that the problems and stresses found in these families were intensified by special social, religious, economic, and cultural conditions specific to their backgrounds; and that these tensions and strains were colored by larger cultural and religious issues involving such central concepts as authority, deference, and legitimacy. Indeed, to anticipate a theme that runs through the book, I will argue that the special stresses and problems of the Victorian home reflect the broader historical problem of adapting the values of a deferential, hierarchical, patronage society to the values of an increasingly contractual, individualistic society. Far from being a "walled garden" or a "haven in a heartless world," the Victorian family both reflected the outside world and prepared people to participate in it.

The five individuals selected for this study—Robert Louis

Stevenson, George Eliot, Harriet Beecher Stowe, Catharine Sedgwick, and Samuel Butler—are obviously not representative of Victorian society in any statistical sense. One was a Scot; two were American; two English. Their years of birth range from 1789 to 1850. One was the daughter of an English estate agent; one was the daughter of an eminent Massachusetts jurist. Several held highly respectable views; others expressed distinctly unconventional opinions. All were exceptional in that they were extraordinarily popular and influential authors. And, as we shall see, the special problems and stresses of their family lives were related to distinctive religious, cultural, social, and economic factors specific to their personal backgrounds.

Nevertheless, I will argue that this group of talented and influential writers, in no way typical of the Victorian "man in the street," can illuminate basic tensions and underlying themes that lie at the heart of Victorian family life. From its inception, this study has been written with a specific methodological purpose in mind: to use the family as a bridge that will permit us to trace interrelationships among institutional developments, cultural shifts, and problems of individual personality. It is my conviction that the lines of social, cultural, and individual development intersect in the family and that, by studying in detail the private lives of a small number of men and women who are somewhat unrepresentative, we can see how cultural tensions, symbols, and conflicts are assimilated and dealt with by actual individuals. The figures described in the following pages are not representative in the sense that the term is usually used. Yet so long as we are careful to locate this cast of characters in a specific social milieu, we can view their lives as carriers of evocative, dramatic lines. Their artistic "intuitions" can sharpen our eyes to the pressures impinging on other Victorian lives. Rejecting social science illusions of totality, holistic mapping, or isomorphism, we can use a series of lives that interweave with others, in counterpoint—as in William Faulkner's *The Sound and the Fury*—to view and review the meaning of social and cultural change.

The group of authors chosen for this study is particularly well suited for illuminating the central problems and issues of nineteenth-century middle-class family life. These writers, in their personal letters and diaries, were able to articulate links between psychological and cultural patterns that remain unstated in the papers of more "typical" Victorians. Acutely aware of the intricate and complex character of the connections between family tensions and wider religious, moral, and intellectual issues of the age, they were able to give expression to feelings and perceptions that in other sources are often obscured by clichés.

There is another fundamental reason for using these figures' lives as a window into the Victorian world. The persons I have selected to study were tutors to an emerging Victorian culture that was transatlantic in character, and their writings reached enormous audiences in both Britain and America. Their public works were instrumental in helping to define and shape public attitudes regarding the family, gender roles, and domestic roles. By showing how personal family struggles within their natal homes embodied more general cultural tensions, I hope to point to some of the ways that later adulthood concerns were related to, and shaped by, family experiences. In this way, the book can suggest links between cultural expression and social experience.

Since this study is unconventional in its methods and purpose, a few words of explanation are necessary about its design and strategies of analysis. I approach the Victorian family through a series of highly selective case studies, developed in considerable depth against a backdrop of social history. Biographical case studies offer a specificity and a sense of chronological development often lacking in broader historical studies. Yet if case studies are to be historically significant, it is necessary to locate precisely the place of individuals within their societies. It is necessary to use explicit comparisons and contrasts to distinguish what is typical and what is idiosyncratic in their lives. And it is no less necessary to relate individual experiences to larger strains or controversies rooted in the special experiences of particular religious denominations or social groups.

In selecting subjects for this study, certain conventions of periodization and geographical division have been intentionally disregarded. A political historian might mark off time by political landmarks, shifts in voting patterns, or changes in administrative procedures, but for social historians no such precision is possible. Social historians cannot assume that changes in the demographic characteristics, emotional organization, or ideology of the family change in the same fashion, or at the same pace, as political events. Selections of subjects studied in this book have been made with an eye to representing the diversity of a particular strand of Victorianism over time.

The figures examined in this study were also chosen to demonstrate that there is a common constellation of values linking influential social groups in Britain and the United States—a complex of beliefs, standards, and cultural strivings here termed "literary culture." The concept of literary culture points to the defining characteristics of the strain of Victorianism with which this book is concerned—a transatlantic system of values that was highly sensitive to the significance of language, which held that education, entertainment, and individual and collective uplift were to be obtained through the written word. Literary culture was one of the ligaments tying together an Anglo-American world, and the authors examined in this book were central figures in this transatlantic network of ideas.

In addition to the case method, two other tools used in this study to understand the dynamics of Victorian family life are psychology and the analysis of shifts in language. The application of psychology to the study of history is still highly controversial, in part because psychology has often been used irresponsibly in historical works. Hence it is important to clarify how psychology is to be used here. Psychology can be used as a diagnostic tool to understand emotions, to interpret particular situations, or to develop insights into the dynamics of the psyche. Or psychology can be used in another way, as it is used here, sharpening our sensitivity to family interaction and suggesting fresh lines of inquiry, instead of providing rigid models or concepts to be applied.

Another tool for illuminating familial relationships is a close examination of the changing nuances of language—especially words pertaining to home, family, career, economic dependence, consent, and the nature of human bonding. A careful study of language can illuminate family interactions and be used to study affectivity in its social context. Language is useful to historians as an index both of emerging conceptions of thought and of patterns connecting distinct realms of life. By examining patterns of language taken from correspondence, it is possible to see how language was actually used within the home to impute blame, resolve conflict, and determine responsibility. In the late eighteenth and early nineteenth centuries, a large number of new words appeared in the language to deal with the nature of human bonding and the bases of social obligations. This set of words included a wide range of terms that antedated the nineteenth century but that only then were applied to social relations. An examination of these words can reveal how various spheres of life interpenetrated and how conceptions drawn from economics, law, and science carried over into everyday language and helped frame social relationships.

The organization of this book has been derived, as far as possible, from the dominant themes and preoccupations of the source material on the nineteenth-century middle-class family. Chapters 2–4 are designed to furnish the social and intellectual context of Victorian family life in Britain and America. After surveying, in Chapter 2, what social historians, demographers, and economists have taught us about the middle-class family in nineteenth-century Britain and America, we will move, in Chapter 3, to the moral, philosophic, and religious attitudes associated with the family and, in Chapter 4, to the social context in which the Victorian families examined in this book can be located.

In Chapters 5–7 we will turn to a detailed analysis of the dynamics of five particular Victorian homes. Chapter 5 deals with the conflicts between a father and a child or, rather, the way these conflicts were interpreted. In Chapter 6 we move from the personal family conflicts between a parent and child to the psychology of marriage and marital conflict. Chapter 7 illustrates some of the psychological and ideological responsibilities attached to sibling bonds; in particular, the way relations between brothers and sisters helped children to deviate from the expectations of their parents.

Victorians often regarded the family as a walled garden, yet the family walled in as much as it walled out. And while it is true that by entering the home individuals left the outside world behind them, in practice the values that governed people's behavior in the outside world entered into the family. The most important characteristic of Victorian home was supposedly its bond of sentiment; yet this same period saw the growth of legalistic conceptions of consent and contract. By tracing the lives of a number of the most prominent writers in nineteenth-century Britain and America, this book will show how legalistic and economic conceptions of value were brought into the home; how these values collided with the cult of sentiment; and how the conflicting messages of socialization, which stressed both the dictates of the heart and the supposed laws of economics, were or were not reconciled in actual family relationships.

CHAPTER 2

The Victorian
Middle-Class Family

F IVE scenes furnish us with an introduction to the Victorian
home and to the five families that will be our principal objects of concern. The first scene is of the birthplace of Robert
Louis Stevenson, a modest two-story terraced house in Edinburgh, Scotland. Set back from pedestrians and the street behind iron railings and a nine-foot-deep garden, the house epitomizes an emerging Victorian ideal of the home: this is not a
Georgian ideal of an attached townhouse located next to a square
but a new ideal, characterized by inwardness and privacy. Viewed
primarily as a place to be lived in, not as a visual object to be
gazed at from the outside, this home reflects a changing ideal
of the relation of homes to each other and to the outside world.[1]

Entering the Stevensons' house, the first sight to greet a visi-
tor would be a bas-relief with the terrifying image of the Massacre of the Innocents above the doorway of the inner hall. This
sculpture suggests the atmosphere of religious piety that is a
central element of the Stevenson household, an atmosphere that
is tied to a particular image of children. Idealized as representing innocent purity, children were also regarded as fragile and
easily corrupted creatures for whom adults carried a heavy burden of responsibility. This glimpse into the Stevenson household provides us with a first indication of the double-edged

character of the Victorian home, which was idealized as a "walled garden," a recuperative oasis from the materialistic corruptions of the outside world, but that was also regarded as the primary instrument for shaping children's character in order to prepare them for adulthood responsibilities.[2]

A second scene is of Harriet Beecher Stowe recalling the early days of her childhood. Her father seemed to her then "the image of the Heavenly Father," who had made her girlhood home "a kind of moral heaven, replete with moral oxygen, full charged with intellectual electricity." Her words indicate the enormous emotional and psychological importance of the father in the Victorian home, who stood as the embodiment of intellectual and moral authority. The father, whose role is so uncertain in the twentieth-century household, had much clearer responsibilities in the Victorian home, as a "moral force" and "governor."[3]

A third scene is a painting of domestic life by Samuel Butler, the author of *The Way of All Flesh,* completed in 1864. Butler depicted the daily prayer scene in his boyhood home in the small Nottingham village of Langbar where his father was rector. The painting shows the rector reciting from the Old Testament to the assembled family in the half light of the rectory sitting room. The family members are lined up along the walls, with the single exception of young Samuel, who sits behind his father, hidden in shadows. This painting, drawn by Butler when he was twenty-nine, illustrates the profoundly ambivalent attitude toward paternal authority that can be found in many Victorian homes. On the one hand, the family prayer scene or reading circle, presided over by the paterfamilias, exemplifies the symbolic importance attached to the home as a model of solidarity and as the moral custodian of society, responsible for transmitting the weight of culture across generations. On the other hand, Butler's painting suggests the torturous sense of guilt that could grow out of any questioning of this set of family arrangements.[4]

A fourth scene is of George Eliot, late in life, responding to the suggestion that she produce an autobiography. She dismisses the idea, claiming that she would have little to say. Of her girlhood, she writes, "the only thing I should care to dwell on would be the absolute despair I suffered from of ever being able to do anything." Even though the Victorian home is sometimes depicted as child centered and Victorian childhood is sometimes depicted as a carefree period before the acceptance of adulthood responsibilities, Eliot's words indicate that it was not a child's world in which her childhood took place. Her words suggest the enormous burden of expectations placed on children within certain Victorian homes, and a resulting sense of intense personal responsibility and potential weakness.[5]

A final scene is of the grave site of Catharine Sedgwick, a writer who is little remembered today but who, in the early nineteenth century, was the most popular American woman novelist before the appearance of Harriet Beecher Stowe. Her body is buried in the Sedgwick family plot in Stockbridge, Massachusetts. In the plot's center stands an obelisk, under which her father's body rests. Around this monument, forming a circle, lie the patriarch's children and their descendants, all buried with their feet pointing toward the body of the family's founder. The reason for this, according to historian Richard E. Welch, Jr., is that on the Day of Resurrection this will ensure that the Sedgwick family members will once again stand respectfully facing their father. For the Sedgwicks, as for many other families in Britain and America during the Victorian era, the family represented the most important symbol of stability and continuity, the only embodiment of a tangible past in a period of rampant change and self-seeking individualism.[6]

The last decade has witnessed exciting growth in our understanding of families during the Victorian era. Social historians, demographers, and economists have shown that the middle-class family patterns that we typically label Victorian were the product of complex demographic, economic, and ideological changes—particularly in the status and economic roles of women—that can be traced at least as far back as the mid-eighteenth century. These scholars have demonstrated that the Victorian idealization of the middle-class home as essentially a private place, a shelter against the turbulent seas of social change, was tied to broader historical developments, which we will survey here.[7]

Preeminent among these changes was a gradual alteration in the structure and membership of the middle-class household. Demographic historians have found that while in the seventeenth and early eighteenth centuries in England and colonial America the nuclear household (i.e., a husband and wife living in a private, independent household) was predominant, most people, at least in their youth, lived for a time in more complex household units, as a servant, an apprentice, a trade assistant, or a boarder. Thus, a survey of 100 pre-1821 communities in England found that 53 percent of the population lived in households that were large not only because of a large number of children but because of the presence of servants and apprentices. Definitions of the word "family" reflected the complexity of these large household units and generally encompassed all of the individuals living together in the same dwelling, including servants (who could be found in perhaps a third of all households).[8]

By the beginning of the nineteenth century, however, the middle-class family was thought of in a new way—as isolated from larger kinship structures and the world of work. Conceived of as an inward-turning, self-contained unit, the conjugal family was regarded as connected to the extended kin group and the outside society only on the basis of economic self-interest and voluntary consent. The increasing isolation of the conjugal unit was apparent in two sociological trends: in the increasing length of time adolescent children spent as residents of their parents' homes and in the declining proportion of middle-class households taking in apprentices, trade assistants, and clerks.[9]

Although there was a modest decrease in household size during the nineteenth century (in the United States, average household size declined from 5.8 people in 1790 to 4.9 people at the end of the century) the proportion of very large households remained high. Approximately a sixth of all households in mid-nineteenth-century England and America contained servants, and

a third of all households contained relatives and other boarders
or lodgers. Yet a subtle alteration in household composition had
taken place. One sign of change was in the living arrangements
of young people. During the first half of the nineteenth century,
it was still common for young men and, to a lesser extent young
women, to shift back and forth between their parents' home
and work experiences as members of other households. But by
the second half of the century, lengthening periods of formal
schooling, combined with later entry of middle-class sons into
the work force, led to a majority of children continuing to live
with their parents into their late teens and twenties. By the end
of the nineteenth century, the proportion of children remaining
in their parents' home into their twenties apparently exceeded
the proportion today.[10]

Change in household structure was also evident in a complex
reversal in the relationship between household size and complexity and social status. The homes of men engaged in the
professions, trade, and skilled crafts gradually became less likely
to contain nonfamily members or kin serving as apprentices,
trade assistants, or clerks. Those servants or lodgers who remained within these homes were apparently perceived in a new
way—not as quasi-kin, which was the way they were regarded
earlier, but as participants in an essentially economic relationship. The expulsion of apprentices and assistants from the middle-class household contributed to the prevailing image of the
home as isolated from the alienating world of work.[11]

For many laboring families, on the other hand, an important
way of responding to economic stress or the loss of a family
member was to take in a boarder, lodger, or relative. For these
families, the dislocations of the early industrial era encouraged
a return to earlier forms of mutual assistance based on extended
kinship and elastic residence patterns. The percentage of laboring households taking in kin and nonkin was quite high. Tamara Hareven and Maris Vinovskis found that 12 to 15 percent
of the mid-nineteenth-century American urban households they
studied contained nonimmediate kin, and 20 to 30 percent contained boarders or lodgers. The English findings are similar.

W. A. Armstrong found that in the mid-nineteenth-century areas he examined, 13 to 20 percent of the households contained non-immediate kin. In America, it was more likely for families to take in nonkin; in England, the proportion of resident kin was higher.[12]

Changes in the usage of language provide an index to the growing conception of the middle-class household as a private place, isolated from the broader kinship network and the world of work. The late eighteenth century saw the proliferation of terms distinguishing between the conjugal unit and broader notions of a household that included all the persons who lived under a single roof. New terms appeared to distinguish the immediate family from the broader kin network and earlier notions of family that had included servants, apprentices, and lodgers. A change in the use of the word "friend" also provides a barometer of change. Earlier, the word was used broadly to describe a network of kinsmen, friends, clients, and patrons to whom one owed obligations. By the nineteenth century, a more rigid distinction was drawn between one's immediate family, to whom one owed specific obligations, and friendship, which was supposedly free of any material obligations.[13]

The emergence of Victorian middle-class family patterns was also closely related to subtle changes in the economic roles and expectations of middle-class women. One indicator of change was a gradual limitation of the birthrate, a development that allowed parents to devote increased attention to children. By the second quarter of the nineteenth century in America, and by the 1850s in England, growing numbers of married women began consciously having fewer children and limiting the age at which childbearing ceased. A slowing of the birthrate was but one example of broader transformations in women's lives. During the last quarter of the eighteenth and the first years of the nineteenth centuries, there was a marked upsurge in the number of young unmarried women working for wages; there was a sharp upturn in female literacy rates as well as in the number of young women attending schools; there was a noticeable increase in the number of women delaying marriage or not marrying at all; and there was a gradual decline in rates of illegitimacy and premarital pregnancy, following a significant rise in the mid-eighteenth century. In England and New England alike, as a result of increased rates of male migration, the two societies had to confront the implications of a population in which women made up a growing majority.[14]

These demographic developments were closely related to a broader redefinition of women's roles and status. During the early nineteenth century, women received unprecedented opportunities, particularly among such religious denominations as the Baptists and Methodists, to assume leadership positions organizing religious revivals, establishing benevolent societies, and editing religious publications. Middle-class women also achieved a public voice in reform movements such as temperance and antislavery, and succeeded in winning employment opportunities in public schooling, journalism, and publishing.[15]

These changes in women's roles were intermeshed with a broader process of social change—a process social historians and economists associate with the expansion of a market-oriented economy, increased economic specialization, and rising living standards. For many middle-class families, these changes resulted in a decline in economic self-sufficiency and in customs in which many middle-class wives directly participated in their husbands' work. Earlier, for many farming families, the need for a money income involved many households in domestic industries, such as weaving and spinning, and putting-out systems of manufacturing, which employed all members of a household. The expansion of a market economy gradually extinguished many of these domestic industries, in which married women and older children had participated.[16]

For affluent urban households, economic change also brought striking changes. There was a gradual decline of earlier customs in which the wives of men engaged in business, the professions, and trade managed shops, kept accounts, and supervised apprentices. The effect of these changes was to increasingly isolate married women and their young children into what contemporaries called a "separate sphere of domesticity," which was dissociated from the masculine and supposedly more productive sphere of income-producing work.[17]

In strictly demographic terms, the patterns of middle-class family life in the nineteenth century differed dramatically from their twentieth-century counterparts. For example, throughout the nineteenth century the timing of life stages was far less rigid and uniform than it would be in the twentieth. The range of ages at which young people left home, graduated school, married, bore children within marriage, and entered work was much wider than it is now. One scholar has hypothesized that the relative indeterminacy of the transition to full adulthood was a potential source of tension in the nineteenth-century home. Much more than in the past, many young people over the ages of seventeen and eighteen were remaining at home with their parents. Thus, although a child might be anxious for the responsibilities of adulthood, he or she might remain at least partially subordinate to a parent. The essential point is that although lengthened residence within the parental home could lay the basis for increased emotional intimacy between parents and children, this factor could also be a source of potential strain.[18]

Other factors prevailing in entrepreneurial and professional households exacerbated such tensions. Social change in early-nineteenth-century Britain and America tended to bifurcate the experience of adolescents of different social classes. Affluent children saw their financial dependence upon their parents prolonged and intensified, in part because of an increase in the duration of formal schooling, and in part because of rapidly rising living standards, which greatly increased parental expenditures on children's upbringing. Particularly important among these expenditures was the growing cost of fitting a son for a future career. Children of laboring families, in contrast, were much more likely to enter the work force at an early age and to contribute significantly to their family's livelihood. The anomalous experience of affluent children, who remained both emotionally and financially dependent upon their parents far longer than their eighteenth-century counterparts and their poorer contemporaries, may have been a source of potential tension in the Victorian middle-class home. One indicator of this lengthened financial dependence upon parents is the relatively late age at which such children married, left home, and entered into professions, especially when compared with customs in the eighteenth century.[19]

The middle-class family patterns that gained prominence in the last years of the eighteenth century and the first years of the nineteenth deviated in important respects from their predecessors. By the early nineteenth century a marked decline had occurred in infant and child mortality. Adult mortality also declined, particularly after 1750, as a result of improved obstetrical care for mothers and a decline in the prevalence of epidemic diseases. One important implication of this trend was a gradual increase in the expected duration of marriages. The prolonged length of marriages contributed to a changing conception of the marital relationship: as a more permanent, less transient arrangement. Indeed, it has been suggested that given the low divorce rates of the nineteenth century the expected duration of marriages was longest during the Victorian era. Moreover, fewer children experienced the death of a parent during childhood. Furthermore, as a result of a decline in the proportion of remarriages (which accounted for as many as a quarter of marriages in early-seventeenth-century England), kinship patterns became less complex and less loosely structured than in the past.[20]

The family patterns described in this book need to be understood against a backdrop of profound social and economic change, extending from the mid-eighteenth century to the 1850s. Throughout Britain and America, these decades marked a rapid decline in household industries and in the economic self-sufficiency of households. The spread of a market economy, combined with increased economic specialization and rising living standards, had the effect of increasingly segregating middle-class women and their small children in what contemporaries regarded as a separate sphere of domesticity, psychologically divorced from the impersonal world of "productive" work. Middle-class children, who had directly participated in work as servants, apprentices, or participants in various putting-out systems of production, increasingly became the objects of parental expenditures—expenditures designed to prepare children for future adulthood roles and careers.

The middle-class family, having lost many of its traditional functions—to transmit a family craft or skill, to arrange marriages, or to offer care or patronage to dependent kin—acquired important new psychological and ideological responsibilities, which will be described in the next chapter. The paradox of the Victorian middle-class family is that whereas it was in certain respects, a more private institution than its predecessors—in that it was regarded as a bastion of private feelings and emotions—its functions were directed to a public end—to prepare children for adulthood roles by instilling self-discipline, an acute sense of personal responsibility, and sensitivity to the needs and expectations of other people. The middle-class family, having lost its main functions as a productive unit, received new burdens and expectations. In meeting these ends, however, the middle-class family had also lost important economic, social, and ideological supports.

CHAPTER 3

Literary Culture and
the Need to Shape Character

IN the previous chapter we surveyed changes in the middle-
class family's demographic characteristics and social functions in order to isolate the external traits that distinguished the
Victorian middle-class family from its predecessors. Such a picture of structural change is essential if we are to understand the
shaping social context of Victorian family life, the external backdrop against which specific family patterns can be located. As
will become clear, social factors directly contributed to the strains
and tensions of the Victorian home: the increasing isolation of
the middle-class family from broader structures of kinship and
work placed extraordinary psychological burdens on the home
while depriving the institution of economic and ideological autonomy.

A structural analysis by itself, however, tells us little about the
attitudes, sentiments, and expectations invested in the family.
To begin to understand the way Victorian family life was conceived, we must turn to the emotional, intellectual, and moral
attitudes that particular social groups in Britain and America
attached to the family, childrearing, and parenting. In this chapter we shall, first, demonstrate that the beliefs and expectations
assigned to the Victorian family need to be treated as part of a
single Anglo-American network of ideas that bound together

evangelicals, Congregationalists, Presbyterians, and Unitarians in provincial England, New England, and Scotland; and second, examine the expanding early-nineteenth-century literature on childrearing and family government, a literature that was closely related to broader controversies over the decline of deference, the immorality of physical coercion, and the need to combine authority and discipline with some kind of consent.

Today, the phrase "the English-speaking union" conjures up connotations of snobbery, arrogance, and cultural insularity. But during the mid- and late-nineteenth century, the idea of a broad literary culture uniting Britain and America gave expression to some of the deepest aspirations for self-improvement and respectability of many barely literate people in America, England, and Scotland. Robert Louis Stevenson and Harriet Beecher Stowe, more than any other writers, symbolized this literary culture. They could speak almost effortlessly to an American or British audience; they were cultural reference points: even marginally literate people had read "The Strange Career of Dr. Jekyll and Mr. Hyde" and *Uncle Tom's Cabin*. The amazing receptivity to their works gives tangible evidence of a common quest for culture shared by disparate groups in Britain and America. Literature was one of the ligaments that tied together an Anglo-American world; diverse groups in remote areas could feel a rapport through the imaginative world of literature.

During the early nineteenth century imaginative literature acquired new symbolic importance as "the key by which the feelings could be unlocked and the imagination given the freedom it demanded." Whether exhibited in a new passion for book-collecting; in a profusion of articles on "the blessedness of books"; or, in the 1870s, in the reorientation of school curricula around English literature, bibliolatry exemplified the Victorian belief that self-improvement, respectability, and even entertainment could be obtained at home through the written word. At a time when family traditions and local customs were losing their authority, literature absorbed a wide range of nonartistic functions: art provided models of speech, etiquette, taste, and fashion. Fiction shaped moral standards and furnished people of quite different backgrounds with a common frame of reference and a shared set of norms and aspirations.[1]

In order to appreciate the new psychological and ideological significance that was just beginning to be attached to reading and literature, we would do well to look at three specific households—Louisa May Alcott's, John Ruskin's, and Harriet Beecher Stowe's—that epitomize a broader shift in sensibility.

Louisa May Alcott's first childhood memory was of playing with books in her father's study, "building houses and bridges of the big dictionaries and diaries, looking at pictures, pretending to read, and scribbling on blank pages whenever pen or pencil could be found." It was in these infant scribblings that her first attempts at authorship were made, in such serious volumes as Francis Bacon's *Essays* and Plutarch's *Lives,* "my infant taste being for solid literature, apparently." Each morning, Louisa's father read aloud to his daughters for an hour, and these reading periods remained the "pleasantest" recollections of her youth. Years later, when a family friend described the Alcott girlhood home, she drew a picture of Louisa intently working in her room on a journal, which her father required her to keep, while other members sat in other rooms of the house, reading or writing in diaries, separate from each other within their own spatial boundaries, yet bound together in the world of literature and the imagination.[2]

Quite a similar scene would describe John Ruskin's boyhood home, even though his evangelical background was far removed from the Transcendental wild oats Louisa May Alcott was reared on. As Richard D. Altick has described the Ruskin household, each year Mrs. Ruskin read the Bible straight through with her son from Genesis to Revelation. Sundays were confined to reading such serious works as John Bunyan's *Pilgrim's Progress, Foxe's Book of Martyrs,* and Francis Quarles's *Emblems.* On other days, family life also revolved around reading, for after tea, Ruskin's father, a devotee of Walter Scott, read aloud to his wife and son from the works of William Shakespeare, Edmund Spenser, Alexander Pope, Oliver Goldsmith, Joseph Addison, and Samuel Johnson. Despite other differences in their background and upbringing, both Alcott and Ruskin were reared in households that assigned enormous value to books and words. Reading and writing, processes that are detached and inward-oriented and that place a high valuation upon words, helped shape relations between family members in these Victorian homes.[3]

The symbolism that Alcott or Ruskin would attach to reading is far different from that which we would assign to it today. We take for granted a division between popular culture and high culture. But during the nineteenth century the audience for serious literature was proportionately greater than it is today, and members of all social classes, excluding the very lowest, read novelists such as Charles Dickens who are now considered major literary figures, as well as writers such as Henry Wadsworth Longfellow, Stevenson, and Stowe, whose reputations have long since declined. Yet the reading of novels continued to be regarded ambiguously during the first half of the nineteenth century: the reading of imaginative fiction as opposed to more serious religious works still required justification as a worthwhile activity.

Lyman Beecher, Harriet's father, was one of the people who objected to novels on principle. An eminent Congregationalist preacher, the elder Beecher accepted the more rigid evangelical admonitions against imaginative literature: that it overexcites the sensibilities of the young; that it fosters an unrealistic outlook and ill prepares a reader for the harsh realities of life; and that the subjects of imaginative literature are generally morally degraded. Yet, after discovering the novels of Scott, Beecher urged his children to read these books on the grounds that such fiction refined the emotions, elevated the sensibilities, and improved the tastes. His ideas provide us with an indication of the justifications used to help legitimate art and literature during the early nineteenth century—that it served as an instrument of character formation and self-improvement.[4]

Victorianism has generally been treated as an exclusively English phenomenon. But during the nineteenth century, there was a constant flow of ideas among England, Scotland, and America, and the movement of ideas did not go in only one direction. To take an example, in the 1880s, a survey was conducted to determine the favorite authors of English schoolgirls. It is no surprise to discover that Scott and Dickens stood at the top of the list; but other findings are less expected. A popular American novelist named Susan Warner was ranked next to Shakespeare, while Louisa May Alcott and Longfellow surpassed Alfred Tennyson and Bunyan in popularity. Ahead of Lewis Carroll stood Harriet Beecher Stowe and Mark Twain. Another study, conducted in 1891, reached similar conclusions. It found that of the four books most commonly owned by "well-to-do" English laborers, two were written by Americans. In addition to owning *Pilgrim's Progress* and *Foxe's Book of Martyrs,* they also possessed *Uncle Tom's Cabin* and Warner's *The Wide, Wide World.* As these surveys suggest, there were important lines of connection between nineteenth-century British and American cultures, and the lines of influence did not extend outward solely from one side.[5]

Other pieces of evidence contribute to a picture of a transatlantic culture that is the joint creation of American and British authors. In the 1850s the most widely read novelist and poet in England were each American. It is significant that such artistic works as *Uncle Tom's Cabin, The Scarlet Letter, Hiawatha,* and Ralph Waldo Emerson's *Essays* had larger sales in Britain, in the first years after their publication, than in America. It would be a mistake to think that the Anglo-American connection was confined solely to the reprinting of books and essays. It is one of the curious ironies of American literary history that many of nineteenth-century America's foremost authors, and most outspoken cultural nationalists, spent long periods of their adult lives abroad, particularly in Britain. This was true of such quintessentially American figures as Washington Irving, who spent seventeen years abroad; of James Fenimore Cooper and Nathaniel Hawthorne, both of whom lived in Europe for seven years; and of Mark Twain, who lived overseas for eleven years.[6]

Nineteenth-century Anglo-American cultural relations pre-

sent a fundamental paradox. From the bitterness generated during the American Revolution and the War of 1812, through the
late-nineteenth-century diplomatic quarrels over Cuba and Ven-
ezuela, a recurrent theme in Anglo-American diplomatic relations is bitter hostility. Yet if one turns from diplomacy toward
religion, philanthropy, literature, and travel, one discovers un-
suspected lines of communication and cooperation binding together distinct groups in the two societies. The roots of this
transatlantic network of ideas were planted during the early
nineteenth century, in complex economic, philanthropic, and
religious connections that united British Dissenters with their co-
religionists, Presbyterian, Congregationalist, Methodist, Baptist,
and especially Unitarian and Quaker, in the United States.[7]

The pattern of connection tended to be highly selective, with
particular appeal to distinct groups on each side of the Atlantic.
In England, the transatlantic connection tended to have its
greatest impact among those groups most deeply touched by
the Evangelical Revival, especially among the commercial, manufacturing, and artisan classes in the new industrial towns, as
well as among other groups who saw themselves as residing
outside the "establishment," such as extreme liberals and people
of Scottish birth. Throughout the 1830s and 1840s, the great
British journals of opinion, such as the *Westminster Review,* the
Edinburgh Review, the *Poor Man's Guardian,'* the *Working Man's
Friend,* and the *Northern Star,* were acutely conscious of social
and political developments in America and repeatedly made reference to American conditions in constructing criticism of political arrangements in England.[8]

In America the groups that appropriated British models of
culture and reform were not the established national elites (as
William R. Taylor has shown, the American Revolution marked
an end to a long tradition of prominent southerners traveling
and studying in Britain). Rather, they were groups, particularly
in the Northeast, that were acutely concerned about the declining power and influence of the clergy, that looked to Britain for
models of economic and cultural progress and "practical Christianity," and that gloried in the advance of British imperialism

into India and the Near East as a step toward the Christianization of the world and the extension of Anglo-Saxon liberties. The increasing ease of transatlantic travel after the Napoleonic Wars encouraged a small but influential group of ministers, revivalists, reformers, artists, and student pilgrims (many of whom would become members of the group of intellectuals known as the Boston Brahmins) to travel to Britain to develop close personal ties with their British counterparts.[9]

To understand the popularity of such best-selling authors as Stowe and Stevenson, it is necessary to know that the first years of the nineteenth century witnessed the emergence of important cultural, religious, and philanthropic connections between influential social groups in Britain and America. One of the most interesting aspects of this burgeoning Anglo-American connection was a flood of moral tracts, periodicals, schoolbooks, and advice manuals published on both sides of the Atlantic. These books defined models of character, manners, sensibility, and respectability and helped to create a mass middle-class reading public, responsive to a common set of moral standards and cultural symbols.

An early example of this transatlantic literature addressed the problems of childrearing and family government. The remainder of this chapter takes us back to the first years of the nineteenth century, to the prescriptive literature on childrearing that flourished on both sides of the Atlantic Ocean. This background is necessary if we are to understand the intellectual, moral, and emotional attitudes that colored middle-class family life. As we shall see, when conflict erupted in a middle-class Victorian home, this personal family struggle drew deeper resonances from larger cultural issues of authority, legitimacy, and self-discipline. In order to understand the vocabulary, the associations, and the moral sensitivities that Victorians would attach to relations in the home, we must first turn to the cultural matrix framing Victorian family life. During the first decades of the nineteenth century, a small group of ministers, writers, and reformers on both sides of the Atlantic published innumerable guidebooks, tracts, and domestic novels dealing with "the art and responsibility of family government." This question had a growing urgency for people who aspired to improvement and release from the proscriptions of custom and tradition but who wanted to ensure that emancipation from the constraints of the past would not lead to a loss of social cohesion or coherence. Dissenters in England and their co-religionists in the United States rejected the Hobbesian notion that social order depended upon the fear of a patriarchal authority. But such people were concerned that the pursuit of individual self-interest would lead to social disruption unless such aspirations were counterbalanced by self-restraints internalized in the depths of individual personality. In their eyes, the main responsibility for instilling such restraints depended on the family and on the forms of government exercised by parents within the home.

The importance attached to the family rested on the perceived weakness of other social controls and authorities. By the first years of the nineteenth century, moralists were acutely conscious of the growing weakness of religious establishments, hallowed traditions, and such institutions as apprenticeship and the "fostering out" of older children that earlier in time had constrained individual behavior. An English writer typifies this concern about the diminishing influence of traditional institutional and communal controls. He lamented the declining "example and influence of an aristocracy" and of "collateral family influence, where the members of families scatter and migrate, as with us." Given the weakness of other religious and social authorities, social harmony depended on the moral culture of the family, which carried the burden of responsibility for reconciling the contradictory impulses toward expanding opportunity and social order and continuity.[10]

The importance attached to the family as society's chief formative agency, as the institution responsible for training the feelings and affections, derived intellectually from the ideas of John Locke and later Scottish moral philosophers of the eighteenth century. Their belief that children were almost infinitely malleable and plastic creatures, who could be shaped by their environment for good or ill, contributed to the sense of the family's preeminence. A diminishing belief in original sin, already evident in the heated debates on child depravity in the mid-eighteenth century, added to the concern over family government, for this meant that individual character was a product, not of sin or damnation, but of the influences of the domestic environment.[11]

Adding to the family's primacy were certain broad assumptions regarding "character formation," which originated in the writings of such Scottish moral philosophers as Francis Hutcheson and Thomas Reid. According to these figures, moral knowledge did not rest in the "understanding," which operated through the mechanical laws of association, rather, morality was rooted in such inner moral faculties as the conscience or sense of sympathy. These moral faculties were more effectively trained by parents' love and the influence of a beneficent environment than by rigorous religious or intellectual instruction. Parental neglect, improper emotional nurture, or a faulty domestic environment could impede the proper development of the moral faculties. By emphasizing the importance of the nonintellectual faculties in laying a foundation for morality and personal responsibility, the Scottish moral philosophy regarded the Christian home, even above the schoolhouse or the church, as the institution primarily responsible for shaping character.[12]

The significance assigned to the family was also a product of disruptive social changes that intensified interest in the problems of managing and discipling children. One of the underlying concerns of the early-nineteenth-century advice literature involves the decline of respect and deference to traditional authorities. Not even the family could be isolated from these democratizing pressures. By 1843, in the eyes of one commentator, "the great principles of liberty and equal rights . . . have penetrated even into the quiet havens of domestic life." Such pressures, according to another writer, had made it "infinitely more difficult to govern children than it used to be." No doubt, this authority exaggerated the obedience of earlier children; but this complaint does suggest an awareness that recent social changes had undermined traditional assumptions regarding authority, legitimacy, and discipline.[13]

During the early decades of the nineteenth century, moralists in America and Britain emphasized that obedience to authority required new justifications and explanations if parents were to be able to secure the "cheerful subordination" of their children. Parental authority, according to this emerging consensus, depended for its effectiveness on children recognizing its legitimacy. Put another way, the legitimacy of parental authority needed to be tested against some form of consent, against children's conscious perception of its legitimacy. This underlying concern with defining methods for securing the voluntary obedience of children to authority is one of the prevailing themes in the early-nineteenth-century literature on family government.[14]

The key to parental power lay in a concept the tracts on character formation called "influence," methods "silent and imperceptible" through which parents "invisibly" set limits to a child's expectations, instilled respect for the legitimacy of authority, and fostered sensitivity to social conventions and rules. This is a very different conception of "influence" and of socialization than had prevailed in the eighteenth century. Earlier, the notion of influence was associated with the power of political patronage and favor; but in the nineteenth century, the concept of influence was broadened to include not only political power but the moral and psychological influence one individual exercises over another. One of the dominant concerns of the tracts on family government involves the various meanings and forms of "influence"; the differences between male and female "influence"; and the ways "influence" is exerted, sanctioned, and internalized.[15]

The process of socialization also received new associations by the nineteenth century. Earlier, the process was thought of largely in terms of preparing children for public roles and responsibilities by instructing them in the inviolability of religious and social authority. The techniques prescribed for child discipline—breaking a child's will through intense psychological and

physical pressure or terrorizing a child with tales of abandonment, castration, and divine punishment—were intended to instill the values of citizenship by creating awe and fear of authority. By the nineteenth century the process of socialization was
increasingly conceived of in broader, more secular terms. Growing emphasis was placed on a nascent notion of internalization.
Here, the primary concern was not with the internalization of
moral prohibitions and rigid behavioral standards but with the
internalization of a capacity for self-government and self-restraint, precisely the values that could form the basis of a voluntary, noncoercive society. The object of childrearing, in the
eyes of a growing number of experts, was to develop a capacity
for self-control: by teaching children how to regulate and control their behavior, to suppress their aggressive impulses, and to
learn to do things for themselves without being dependent upon
their parents.

The aim of socialization was much broader than to instill a
sense of right and wrong. In an increasingly fluid, individualistic society, where the force of local social and religious values
was diminished, social stability appeared to depend on instilling
a capacity for self-government within individuals. Only by in-
ternalizing norms of duty and responsibility could society counteract the anarchic tendencies of democracy and individualism.
In an increasingly democratic era, children had to learn how to
resolve problems by themselves without appealing to external
authority. Children had to be trained in independence—to develop a capacity for self-reliance, self-assessment, and self-direction.

The development of a capacity for self-government depended,
according to the advice literature, on parents' ability to learn
the techniques for exercising moral and psychological influence.
It was not accidental that these popular writers were preoccupied with the theme of influence. The concept was well suited
to a period when questions of power, authority, and legitimacy
seemed increasingly problematic. It seemed increasingly clear that
in untraditional ways some people counted and others did not
and that new instruments were necessary to measure power and

status. It was apparent every day that some supposedly power-less groups, such as wives and mothers, exercised influence, and also that other groups, such as educated blacks who had overestimated the power and influence of rational moral argument, did not. In addition, the concept of influence complemented the growing revulsion against physical coercion. The essential point is that the key to authority and discipline was increasingly being viewed as lying in "invisible" forms of restraint.

The high responsibility assigned to moral and psychological influence rested on a number of assumptions. First, by the early nineteenth century it was a common assumption, even among traditionalists, that discipline was more effective when it was based on persuasion and moral influence than when it rested on coercion or fear. In a more democratic era, authority, when unaccompanied by some larger justification and legitimation, only provoked obstinance and resistance. Voluntary obedience depended not on fear but on the perception that authority is legitimate. Heman Humphrey, a president of Amherst College and an active participant in exchanges between American and English Congregationalists, provides a particularly conservative statement of this view. After describing the corrosive effects of egalitarian values upon parental authority, which Humphrey believed made children increasingly reluctant to submit to their parents, he argues that the primary challenge for parents is to instill in their children respect for the "righteousness" of authority, which would lay a basis for adulthood conceptions of legitimacy and authority. No man, Humphrey acknowledges, had less confidence in the power of moral influence to turn a soul to God; but in childrearing, he thought, it is critically important to demonstrate to children the reasonability of filial obedience and to combine discipline with associations of love. By fostering an intense emotional and psychological dependence of the child upon the parents, the child will become closely attuned to the parents' expressions of approval and disapproval. Humphrey attached particular stress to the advantages that accrued to parents by expressing wishes rather than positive commands to children and appealing to young people's incipient sense of right and wrong. These methods proved effective because they did not rely on rules that might be resented but on the invisible power of a parent's expectations and a child's instinctive desire for affection. As Humphrey bluntly put it, "there is no constraint like that of love."[16]

A second assumption gave added force to the notion that influence provided the key to domestic authority. In the early nineteenth century a growing number of social authorities could agree that social institutions, including the family, should rest on the voluntary cohesion of their members. Even theoretical defenses of the patriarchal family upheld an ideal of the family that rested, not on the subordination of family members into fixed, hierarchical roles, but on children developing a conscious recognition of the need, in an increasingly individualistic society, for subordination. Obedience remained a primary goal, but this was to be "cheerful" obedience, which was free and voluntary. Parents, by engineering "cheerful subordination in the home," could build the foundation of principles of duty and order that would carry over into public life.[17]

Female influence was believed to be particularly useful in mitigating domestic conflicts and enticing obedience from children. Discussions of female influence emphasized that character traits traditionally viewed as symbols of inferiority—such as submissiveness, plasticity, and a capacity for self-denial and sacrifice—in fact have enormous power to shape character, precisely because such "moral means" of influence are nearly invisible and do not provoke resentment. Moreover, the moral influence that grows out of self-abnegation, far from being degrading, is modeled on the example of Christ, who had demonstrated that submissiveness and selflessness are powerful tools of influence.

During the first decades of the nineteenth century, there were sharp disagreements over the techniques for influencing and disciplining children. But writers of quite different backgrounds agreed that parental restraints needed to be as subtle as possible. This assumption is vividly illustrated in an early English work on domestic education by Elizabeth Appleton that served as a prototype for later childbearing manuals on both sides of the

Atlantic. Appleton begins her account by drawing a picture of English children as restive under the curb of authority, disposed to violate laws, impatient with control, longing for self-indulgence, and hateful of opposition. Her point is that even English children had felt the leveling influence of democratic and egalitarian ideals. Under these circumstances, the author concludes that the most effective forms of discipline need to be as invisible as possible. There could be no greater mistake, she asserts, than to treat a child as if he were merely "a mechanical instrument"; for "turbulence, impetuosity, and disdain of controul" arise from rigorous physical discipline; and apathy, obduracy, and selfishness are the product of treating a child as if he had only an animal will. There are two reasons why child discipline should rely on moral influence rather than on physical punishment: first, physical coercion provokes resistance and hostility from children; second, breaking down a child's inherent willfulness or sinfulness damages his self-esteem and sense of personal responsibility, which are the foundations for a capacity for self-control.[18]

Several examples taken from the childrearing literature might illustrate what was meant by "moral means" of control. Lydia Maria Child, an American reformer, editor, and author, called on mothers to instill discipline within children, not by the establishment of rigid rules—which would inspire obstinance—but by anticipating children's needs and furnishing them with an example of "kindness and cheerfulness." Maternal example was an indispensable tool of influence, not only because it is "not possible to make rules enough to apply to all cases," but because a mother's "silent influence" appeals to a child's inherent desire for maternal approval and dislike of disapproval. Catharine Beecher, sister of Harriet Beecher Stowe and herself a promotor of higher education for women and an advocate of the idea that teaching was a profession for which women were particularly well suited, thought an even more effective technique for instilling self-discipline was to engineer a set of routines within a home. For example, if children learned to wait at the dinner table until other family members had been served, or were required to assist with household chores, they acquired habits of discipline that persisted into adulthood.[19]

Harriet Martineau, an English Unitarian and popularizer of laissez-faire economics, and Orson Fowler, an American phrenologist and writer, both viewed the provision of children with privacy as an instrument for instilling self-discipline. Fowler, for example, regarded private bedrooms for children as an extension of the principle of specialization of space that had been discovered by merchants. If two or three children occupied the same room, none felt any responsibility to keep it in order, and hence they grew up habituated to slatternly disorder. If children were liable to constant interruptions, they lost much time for study and self-improvement, and hence yielded their entire time to mental dissipation. For daughters, having a private room was doubly important, for it taught them how to keep house and how to receive and entertain company.[20]

The essential point made by these authors is that division of space within the home was necessary to locate and delimit responsibility. By giving individual family members their own separate spheres, domestic conflict was to be mitigated and self-discipline encouraged. An emphasis on personal privacy, therefore, was not in conflict with a stress on parental authority. Privacy was to be circumscribed for certain purposes and was to be utilized only for certain ends, such as self-improvement. Thus, privacy in the Victorian home had two sides: while in one sense it was designed to provide children with an inviolable space in which they were free from parental authority, the assertion of independence was to be confined to a particular place. By associating family roles with particular spaces within a house, hierarchy and status differentiation were to be symbolized subtly rather than stated outright.

The early-nineteenth-century childrearing literature raises difficult problems of interpretation and evaluation. Childrearing advice cannot be simply characterized as being in the direction of greater permissiveness or as a reversion to authoritarianism. The main aim of this literature was to find ways to instill self-discipline within children without physical coercion, by invisibly instilling habits of deference and respect. The emphasis in the childrearing literature on moral influence as the basis of authority was one expression of a much wider concern with establishing modes of social control that would not be regarded as authoritarian or illegitimate. Because moral influence supposedly derived its efficacy from children's recognition of its legitimacy, this childrearing technique could be upheld as intrinsically noncoercive. Yet the purpose was to make parental restraint as invisible as possible, and in this sense the concept of influence shares characteristics with modern behaviorism, in particular, a blindness to the dangers of psychological coercion when used for moral ends. Precisely because the early-nineteenth-century writers on child development felt a genuine concern about the dangers of physical coercion and were intent on removing arbitrariness and caprice from childrearing, they were in certain respects blind to the dangers of psychological manipulation. What differentiates the early-nineteenth-century advice manuals from the modern literature on manipulation is that the earlier behavior was not regarded as manipulative in any cynical way.

For all the concern with cultivating children's interior feelings and affections, the primary focus of the literature on family government was to define "moral means" of influence and control over behavior. The explanation for this almost obsessive concern with behavior in a literature ostensibly dealing with character formation lies, partly, in the early-nineteenth-century writers' conception of human psychology. The interior states that writers such as Humphrey and Child wrote about—conscience, character, feelings, and instincts—were not psychoanalysts' conceptions of psychological reality. Instead of focusing on "experiential" reality—perceptions, drives, needs, and desires—the early-nineteenth-century authors dwelt on what they called "emotions," predictably expressed and externally observable traits, in which inner motives and feelings were disclosed. The reality of these writers was highly behavioristic, a fact revealed in the highly mechanistic language they used to describe emotions and feelings.

The outpouring of advice books, manuals, and domestic novels dealing with "family government" emphasized a single theme: the need for self-government to counteract and compensate for the weakness of other religious and social authorities and as a means to self-improvement. Self-government, "the only effectual and lasting government—the only one that touches the springs of action, and in all instances controls them," as Catharine Sedgwick put it, was associated not only with initiative and self-reliance but with self-restraint, self-denial, and self-control—the qualities seen as needed to maintain domestic and social harmony without coercion.[21]

Self-government was to be instilled in children by cultivating emotional and psychological dependence upon parents. To achieve this goal, parents were advised to avoid the imposition of rules in governing children, to try to anticipate the needs and desires of their sons and daughters, to adapt methods of discipline to the character of each child, and to make discipline as subtle as possible. Rather than correcting each misdeed, parents were instructed to reserve physical punishment for cases of "willful disobedience." The object of punishment was not to suppress a single willful act but to instill self-discipline. The most effective punishments, accordingly, depended upon perception for their effect. More grievous than physical punishment were techniques designed to evoke guilt and to appeal to a child's sense of self-esteem, such as the withdrawal of love or expressions of parental disapproval. Thus, for Humphrey, the point of punishment was to instill an acute sense of personal responsibility. "Whatever the privation or other token of your displeasure may be, the delinquent must, if possible, be made to feel, that he has brought it upon himself, by 'hating instruction and despising reproof.' " He considered exclusion of a child from his parents' presence an excellent way to teach him to assess the consequences of his acts and to suppress instinctual desires, especially when accompanied by some such remark as, "Much as I love you, I cannot bear to see you, till you are sorry for what you have done, and will promise amendment."[22]

This characteristic technique of child discipline, which cultivates and exploits the child's emotional and psychological dependence upon the parents, is particularly well suited to generate a sensitivity to the opinions and feelings of other people. Emotional and psychological dependence on the parents is designed to provide a crucial spur for children to learn to control and regulate their own behavior, to desire to achieve, and to assert independence.

The issues raised in the early-nineteenth-century literature on family government are of more than abstract interest. This literature is useful in isolating themes that will recur in actual family lives. For example, one of the themes that will reappear in later chapters is the tension between an environmentalist goal of shaping character and an older patriarchal ideal of dutiful obedience to parental authority. There was a deep-seated tension in the Victorian middle-class home between a goal of cultivating self-government through the persuasive power of various kinds of influence and an opposing goal of deference to parental authority. We have earlier seen that the concept of influence depended on at least the appearance of voluntary consent. The tensions that result from this stress on voluntary consent will reappear throughout the case studies.

A second major theme is the emphasis upon internal as opposed to external enforcement of values. One of the primary concerns of the manuals on family government is that discipline not involve merely external conformity but that discipline be truly inward. Profound tensions were generated by this insistence on the primacy of interior states. For example, parents accorded a degree of independence and autonomy to children only insofar as they were able to provide symbols of internalized discipline and self-denial. For children, the preeminence of internal states of mind found a manifestation in an almost obsessive preoccupation with the "sincerity" of their inner feelings and beliefs. A third broad theme involves the discrepancy in childrearing between the cultivation of intense emotional and psychological dependence of children on their parents and an opposing demand for independence, self-direction, and self-government. As we examine relationships within particular Victorian households, we will see how the concepts of dependence and independence became self-conscious concerns pervading domestic interactions.

The emphasis in this chapter is on the new ideological burdens and responsibilities that were beginning to be attached to the middle-class home in the late eighteenth and early nineteenth centuries, particularly with regard to preparing children to be responsible members of an increasingly fluid, individualistic society. Not only was the family to instill a high degree of self-sufficiency, self-reliance, and self-direction, in young men particularly, but the institution was also responsible for counterbalancing these aspirations with a capacity for self-restraint and an internalized sense of duty and obligation. Given the weakness of other institutional and communal controls, the stability of society appeared to depend primarily on the ability of individual parents to instill a capacity for self-government within children. Social harmony and cohesion depended on the effectiveness of parents in engineering "cheerful subordination in the family" that would persist into adulthood.[23]

Yet by the early nineteenth century even social conservatives admitted that parental authority depended for its effectiveness on the willingness of children to tacitly consent to its legitimacy. Children hearing "how glorious it is to be 'born free and equal' " found it difficult to "understand for what good reason their liberties are abridged in the family." In other words, in an increasingly democratic age, parental authority and control had to rely, not on veneration and awe, but on the effectiveness of parents in winning their children's consent to discipline, which meant that authority and discipline had to depend on some form of moral or psychological influence.[24]

CHAPTER 4

Five Victorian Families

THE purpose of the preceding chapter was to provide a cultural context for understanding the dominant themes and concerns of Victorian family life. The premise was that the prevailing concerns of the Victorian family—particularly the emphasis on self-discipline as a substitute for other external forms of control—cannot be understood without reference to a transatlantic network of ideas known as "literary culture," which helps to explain the ideals, expectations, and beliefs that particular groups of people in Britain and America brought to the family. Without an understanding of literary culture, one cannot begin to appreciate the language or the emotional sensitivities that we commonly think of as Victorian. Only a certain kind of home would define "independence" or "proper discipline" in quite the same way that Robert Louis Stevenson's or Samuel Butler's would. Only in a certain cultural context would the personal family conflict between a child and a father stand for the broader issues it did in the Victorian middle-class home.

In this chapter we move from the broad set of cultural values and attitudes framing Victorian family life to the specific social and historical circumstances out of which the influential group of figures discussed in this book emerged. By closely examining the social settings in which they grew up, their family backgrounds, and their families' location within the social structure, we will be able to relate preoccupations and underlying concerns in their family lives to strains and stresses rooted in specific social environments.

At first glance, the subjects of this book might appear to hold little in common. As we proceed, however, we will discover certain consistencies, parallels, and recurrent themes in their personal histories and in the character of their family lives. We will learn that these people share certain common social factors in their backgrounds. These common facts will suggest that the central issues in their family lives are not simply idiosyncratic or intensely personal but are also a response to their families' social situations and to a specific intellectual milieu. But, before examining the underlying themes that link these figures together, it is necessary to briefly familiarize ourselves with the outlines of their biographies.

Few nineteenth-century writers could equal Robert Louis Stevenson in popularity or in the extravagant claims made for his reputation. A history of English literature published two years after his death called him "the most brilliant and interesting by far . . . of those English writers whose life was comprised in the last half century." The explanation for Stevenson's overvaluation as a critic, novelist, and poet lies in the undeniable romantic appeal of his life and character.[1]

Born in Edinburgh on November 13, 1850, Stevenson was plagued by chronic bronchial and gastric ailments that, in 1858, brought him close to death and that forced him to spend much of his boyhood indoors, unable to attend school regularly. He was descended on his father's side from a long line of engineers and on his mother's side from a parish minister and an Edinburgh professor of moral history. Though he was expected by his parents to enter the hereditary profession of engineering, he was averse to office work and was too weak physically for the demanding life of supervising construction, and at the age of twenty-one he agreed with his parents to prepare for the Scottish bar.

In the meantime, doubt began to assail Stevenson regarding the stern version of Scottish Calvinism in which he was raised. His father sought to restore his son's faith by argument, but this led only to painful personal disagreements. At the same time, Stevenson's health seriously deteriorated, and he felt forced to travel frequently abroad, to England, France, and Belgium. Although he was called to the Scottish bar in 1875, he did not practice. While preparing for the bar, he began to write essays on literature and travel as well as unpublished poems and tales. The publication of a series of essays in the *Cornhill Magazine* in 1876 brought him his first public attention.

In that same year, Stevenson met Fanny Van de Grift Osbourne, an American ten years his senior, who was separated from her husband, and fell deeply in love. Stevenson's involvement with a married woman filled his parents with consternation, which was exacerbated, in 1879, when he decided to follow her to California. Stevenson spent eight months in Monterey and San Francisco, suffering from pleurisy and malaria, and almost wholly penniless, before Fanny Osbourne agreed to marry him early in 1880. This was followed by a telegram to Stevenson from his father offering financial support, and in August 1880 the couple returned to Scotland to be reconciled with his parents.

Between 1881 and 1887, the year his father died, Stevenson published his best-known works, including *Treasure Island, A Child's Garden of Verses, Kidnapped,* and "The Strange Case of Dr. Jekyll and Mr. Hyde," all the while vainly seeking to restore his health in Davos, Switzerland; Hyeres in the south of France; and Bournemouth, England. His father's death marked an end to his visits to Scotland, and he, his mother, wife, and stepson set sail for New York. After briefly traveling across the American Northeast, he and his family embarked in 1888 on a yachting voyage to the South Seas, financed by a $2,000 guarantee from an American publisher for a series of letters describing the landscape and inhabitants of the Pacific islands. In 1890 Stevenson established his family's home in Samoa, which is where he died suddenly of a cerebral hemorrhage on December 3, 1894.

George Eliot, one of the supreme masters of psychological realism in the novel, was born Mary Ann Evans, on November 22, 1819, at Chilvers Coton in rural Warwickshire, the youngest of three children by her father's second wife (she also had a stepbrother and a stepsister). Her father was an estate agent, who had been bred to his father's trade of carpenter, and he reared his daughter in a conventional Anglicanism. She came under the influence of evangelicalism, however, from an aunt and the mistresses of two boarding schools she attended. At the age of sixteen, her mother died, and for the next thirteen years, until his death, she managed her father's household. In 1841, when her father turned his business over to a son, the father and daughter moved to Coventry.

In Coventry, George Eliot became acquainted with a small group of freethinkers and liberal Unitarians. Even before encountering these figures, however, she had begun to modify her religious beliefs. A youthful attempt to construct a pictorial guide to the history of the early church seemed to reveal only a pattern of ambiguity and schisms. Her reading of the works of Walter Scott also left her deeply troubled: he had shown that Papists might be truly virtuous while orthodox Calvinists might be bigoted. Finally, her reading of Charles Hennell's *Inquiry Concerning the Origin of Christianity* left her with acute doubts concerning the historical evidence for the Incarnation, the Resurrection, the Trinity, and the doctrine of atonement, doubts that led to her decision in 1842 to stop attending church. Her father threatened to settle with a married sister, but after several months father and daughter reconciled their differences, and she agreed to attend church.

The year 1843 saw the beginning of her literary career when she accepted the task of translating D. F. Strauss's volume of biblical criticism, *The Life of Jesus Critically Examined.* Her father's death in 1849, which left her with a pension of £100 a year, was followed by a visit to Geneva, where she labored over a translation of Baruch Spinoza's *Tractatus Theologico-Politicus;* a return to Coventry, then a move to London to serve as an assistant editor of the *Westminster Review.* In London she became acquainted with Herbert Spencer and, through him, with George Henry Lewes, editor of the radical journal *The Leader.* In July 1854 she decisively altered the course of her life by beginning to openly live with Lewes. At the time, Lewes was legally married but was precluded from suing his wife for divorce because he had earlier condoned her adultery. The union, which provoked bitter gossip, precipitated a painful split between Eliot and her family in Warwickshire.

Her literary productivity during the next twenty-five years is staggering. At the behest of Lewes, she undertook to write a story about an incident in her childhood parish. Published as "The Sad Fortunes of the Rev. Amos Barton" in 1856, the story enjoyed an immediate success. It was *Adam Bede* (1859), which sold 16,000 copies its first year, that brought her identity to public light. That novel was followed in rapid succession by *The Mill on the Floss* (1860), *Silas Marner* (1861), *Romola* (1863), *Felix Holt, The Radical* (1866), *Middlemarch* (1871–72), and *Daniel Deronda* (1876).

After Lewes's death in 1878, Eliot devoted herself to completing the last volume of his *Problems of Life and Mind* and saw no one but a son of Lewes's and a banker, John Walter Cross, who handled her investments. Sharing a deep-felt sense of grief (Cross's mother died a week after Lewes), a marriage was arranged between them. She was sixty-one; he was twenty-one years her junior. Seven months after their marriage, on December 22, 1880, she died at their new home in Chelsea.

One of America's first professional "women of letters," Catharine Sedgwick was the nation's most popular female novelist in the 1820s and 1830s. The daughter of a prominent Massachusetts attorney, a member of the Continental Congress, a Federalist senator, and a justice of the Massachusetts Supreme Judicial Court, she was born on December 28, 1789, in Stockbridge in western Massachusetts. Descended from seventeenth-century settlers of New England, she was related, through her mother, to the great conservative Dwight, Williams, and Stoddard families of "River Gods" of the Connecticut River Valley, who exerted profound influence on colonial American religious and political life. The sixth of seven surviving children from her father's second marriage, she was seventeen when her mother died, after suffering a protracted period of mental depression and invalidism. Her father's remarriage the following year, in 1808, occasioned a great deal of unhappiness among the Sedgwick children, and during the next six years Catharine spent her time in Albany or New York City with her siblings.

She shared the experience with such famous American writers as James Fenimore Cooper, Washington Irving, and the poet William Cullen Bryant of growing up in a family with strong Federalist and Calvinist traditions, and her religious and political views, like those of the others, underwent a gradual transformation. Having wrestled in her youth with the theological views of Samuel Hopkins, which had emphasized God's power and man's sinfulness (she blamed this stern version of Calvinism for "a hereditary tendency to insanity" in her family), her father's deathbed conversation by William Ellery Channing, later the leading exponent of American Unitarianism, freed her to modify her Calvinist heritage, culminating in 1821 with the conversion of her and two of her brothers to Unitarianism.[2]

A prison reformer, an advocate of property rights for married women, and a supporter of the abolition of dueling, Sedgwick turned to writing only in 1821, when she was thirty-two years old. Although her novels were set in her native Berkshire County and often dealt with historical themes, her works attracted a large following in England. Her last novel, *Married or Single?* (1857), was written to "lessen the stigma placed on the term, old maid"; Sedgwick herself never married. She died at the age of seventy-eight, on July 31, 1867, in West Roxbury, Massachusetts.

Harriet Beecher Stowe's most famous book sold an unprecedented number of copies for a novel—50,000 copies in eight weeks, 300,000 copies in a year, 1 million copies in sixteen months. She was born in Litchfield, Connecticut, on June 14, 1811, the seventh of nine children of Lyman Beecher, an eminent Congregational minister, and his first wife. Like Catharine Sedgwick, she was descended from seventeenth-century New

England settlers; the Beechers arrived in Boston in 1637. Her father, like Sedgwick's, had risen from modest circumstances (he was the son and grandson of blacksmiths) to study for the ministry at Yale. Both lost their mothers at an early age (Stowe was only four), had difficulty adjusting to new stepmothers, and grew up with the sainted memory of their lost mother held before them by their fathers. Each developed extremely close bonds of affection with a younger brother, and each encountered the imposing influence of a conservative father.

At the age of fourteen, after hearing her father preach a sermon on the text "I call you no longer servants but friends," Harriet announced that she had undergone an experience of Christ's saving love. Her father accepted her claims, but her eldest sister and a neighboring pastor questioned whether lambs were taken so easily into Christ's fold. They doubted whether she had experienced the conviction of sin that had to precede regeneration. Beset with doubts, she subjected her religious beliefs to close scrutiny and sought repeatedly to reconcile her vision of a stern, patriarchal God, "so silent, so unfeeling, so unsparing," with an opposing vision of Christ "as the Friend, Comforter and Guide." At the age of sixteen she began to teach at her eldest sister Catharine's female seminary in Hartford, Connecticut.[3]

The family moved to Cincinnati, Ohio, in 1832 when Lyman Beecher was named president of the newly founded Lane Theological Seminary and pastor of the Second Presbyterian Church. While teaching at her sister's new school, the Western Female Institute, she contributed sketches and essays to local periodicals, many of which were collected in *The Mayflower,* which appeared in 1843. At the age of twenty-four, she married a professor of biblical literature at Lane, Calvin Ellis Stowe, a widower nine years her senior who had previously been married to her closest friend. Though Stowe, a native New Englander, had been orphaned at age six and apprenticed in a papermill, he had graduated from Bowdoin College and the Andover Theological Seminary, and in 1850 he was offered a professorship at Bowdoin in Brunswick, Maine.

After moving to Maine, Harriet supplemented her husband's meager salary by running a small school in her home and by writing. She longed, as historian Barbara M. Cross has observed, for a calling more engrossing than that of a wife and mother (she had already gone through seven pregnancies), "closer to the 'sacred woman' of the Bible," and her reading of a 76-page autobiographical pamphlet by a former Maryland slave, Josiah Henson, inspired her to write *Uncle Tom's Cabin*. This novel interpreted the moral and psychological evils of slavery within the traditional terms of evangelical Protestantism. Employing such central concepts as mission, sacrifice, sin, rebirth, and regeneration, she spoke a language understood by millions of readers in America and Britain. Celebrated in England and Scotland during visits in 1853, and 1859, her popularity became clouded after the publication in 1869 of "The True Story of Lady Byron's Life," in which she claimed that Lady Byron had disclosed to her that Lord Byron was guilty of incest.[4]

Although she produced, on average, more than a book a year for thirty years, her life was plagued by penury, illness, and family tragedy. Her sixth child had died during infancy in a cholera epidemic in 1849. Her second eldest son was an alcoholic, and her youngest daughter suffered repeated attacks of nervous depression. Her last years were spent in Hartford, Connecticut, where her family moved in 1864, and in Mandarin, Florida, where she bought a house and an orange grove in 1868. Her husband died in 1886, and she died a decade later, on July 1, 1896, two weeks after her eighty-fifth birthday.

The epitome of the restless Victorian iconoclast, critical of all received opinion regarding morality, religion, and science, Samuel Butler was a painter, composer, and philosopher as well as a novelist. Born on December 4, 1835, in the rural Nottinghamshire village of Langbar, where his father was rector, Butler came from an illustrious family. His paternal grandfather had transformed Shrewsbury into one of England's more famous public schools and had subsequently become bishop of Lichfield and Coventry. His mother came from a prosperous Norwich family of Unitarians, which had gained its wealth from sugar refining.

After following his father's footsteps, graduating from Shrewsbury and entering St. John's College, Cambridge, Butler prepared for holy orders by becoming a lay reader to a London curate. His belief in Christian dogma was shaken, however, and he decided to return to Cambridge to study music and drawing. His efforts to become an artist were disparaged by his father, and it was agreed, as a compromise, that the family would help the son set up a sheep farm in New Zealand, where Butler remained from 1860 to 1864.

Butler's return to England at the age of twenty-nine found him still uncertain of his vocation. From 1868 to 1876 he exhibited paintings occasionally at the Royal Academy. His career as a writer developed slowly. A pamphlet entitled *The Evidence for the Resurrection of Jesus Christ as given by the Four Evangelists critically examined* appeared in 1865, a product of protracted researches into the history of the early church. In 1872 he published his utopian satire *Erewhon* anonymously. This book, which provided the basis for Butler's reputation during his own lifetime, earned the highest profits he received from any of his books, ∫69 3s. 10d. In 1873, he wrote *The Fair Haven,* an ironic defense of the miraculous nature of Christ's ministry. Between 1873 and 1885 he worked intermittently on *The Way of All Flesh,* his harsh examination of the rigidity and moral pretenses of the Victorian home.

In later years Butler turned his attention to Darwinism and the works of Homer and Shakespeare. First attracted to Charles Darwin's *The Origin of Species* while in New Zealand, in such works as *Life and Habit* (1877), *Evolution, Old and New* (1879), *Unconscious Memory* (1880), and *Luck and Cunning* (1886), Butler criticized orthodox Darwinism for overemphasizing the role of chance and environment in the process of evolution. Butler took the position that creatures respond consciously and unconsciously to changing circumstances by acquiring new traits and habits that they pass on to their offsprings. In this way, he sought to restore the importance of mind and purpose to the study of evolution. In his last works he took the view that the *Odyssey* was written by a Sicilian woman and that Shakespeare's sonnets were addressed to a man of humble birth. He died in London on June 18, 1902, at the age of sixty-six.

In reconstructing these figures' biographies, certain parallels, recurrent themes, and points of similarity have stood out. For example, one of the themes that recurs in their biographies involves the figure of the father, who emerges as the dominant adult influence upon these individuals during their childhood and young adulthood. Again and again, we will see the repeated image of the father as the embodiment of moral and intellectual authority. The childhood recollections of these subjects exhibit a striking pattern: of the father as the figure preeminently responsible for educating them, supervising the development of their moral character, and providing for their financial support. In each case, they would claim that it was the environment and atmosphere of the home more than the formalities of "didactic and perceptive" schooling that provided the basis for their education. For example, to the young Sedgwick, her most vivid childhood memories were of listening to her father read from "Hume, or Shakespeare, or Don Quixote, or Hudibras"; for Stevenson, of accompanying his father on his professional rounds to the Scottish coast and lighthouses; and for Stowe, of observing her father in his study, laboring over "some holy and mysterious work."[5]

In later life, Stowe would believe that the effect of such a household economy, dominated by the conservative and imposing father, was to tutor "each child in his personal 'insignificance' and 'in the virtue of non-resistance.' " Her point is that the primary task children faced in such intense, inward-turning, father-centered households was to learn how to accept and accommodate themselves to paternal authority. In contrast to our time, when the peer group has come to play a decisive role in socializing children and adolescents, in shaping tastes, and in defining social mores, in respectable middle-class Victorian homes the authority of the parents, and of the father in particular, was not in direct competition with other loyalties and attachments. Unrivaled by other social authorities such as the church, the school, or the peer group, the father did not perceive his role as involving pleasing children, but rather as training them, teaching them to respect authority, and fostering a capacity for self-government and self-control.[6]

In contrast to the description of the father as a moral and intellectual authority, the recurrent image of the mother is one of selflessness. For the women, in particular, each of whom lost a mother during childhood or adolescence, the sainted memory of a mother who had selflessly devoted her adult life to the family's good was a powerful image in their home—an image that contrasted sharply, in the case of Stowe and Sedgwick, with their stepmothers, who seemed to be little more than social butterflies, obsessed with the world of society and fashion. For these women, the contrast between their mothers and stepmothers served an important role in leading them to seek a serious and "useful" vocation in life. In addition, the absence of a mother who might have served as a concrete model of wifely submission may have led them to look to their father as a role model. Still, the association of the mother with selflessness and domestic loyalty and affection was strong even in the cases of Stevenson and Butler. Even when an angry exchange of correspondence shook the Butler household in connection with young Butler's religious beliefs, Samuel continued to write letters of deep affection to his mother. She might criticize his egotism and contrast his behavior with the unworldly selflessness of his father, and still Butler remained emotionally bound to her. Similarly, Stevenson, in the midst of painful disputes with his father over his religious doubts, intently sought to maintain intimacy with his mother, who clearly symbolized domestic feeling and affection.

A second broad theme linking the figures together is liminality and a sense of marginality. "Liminality" refers to these figures' sense of standing on the periphery of two cultures and of being incompletely assimilated into either. This sense of marginality was rooted deeply in their social background and the areas they were born into. They came from families with a clear sense of their place within an older social order but whose location in the emerging order was unclear. Their families were not directly threatened by the extensive social transformations of the period, such as the growing importance of the new industrial elite, yet there was a sense that values upheld by their households—of order, domesticity, and communal responsibility—were under siege.

Their fathers were men who had risen to positions of responsibility and influence within a social order based on family connections, marriage, personal patronage, and inheritance. They were men who tended to define themselves in terms of the vertical loyalties characteristic of the older social structure, a patronage society in which lines of kinship, connections, and interest had bound together social superiors and dependent, deferential inferiors. Given this background, it is not surprising to discover that deference and respect for authority were among the highest values upheld by their families.

The biographical evidence indicates certain similarities in the ways the fathers had achieved their social position. Stevenson's father, like his father before him, had become a partner in a family firm of civil engineers after serving an apprenticeship in his father's engineering office. Sedgwick's father, though the son of a Connecticut shopkeeper, had been able to study for the ministry at Yale because of the sacrifices of an elder brother. He was able to become an attorney because a second cousin consented to serve as his tutor. Lyman Beecher, though the son and grandson of Connecticut blacksmiths, was also able to study for the ministry at Yale because of the support of family. His rise to national prominence as a Congregational preacher followed the patronage of Tapping Reeve, a founder of America's first law school, who called Beecher from a pulpit on Long Island to a church in Litchfield, Connecticut.

Eliot's father, his daughter tells us, had raised himself from the status of an artisan to be one "whose extensive knowledge in varied practical departments made his services valued through several counties." Overseeing the surveying and building of roads, the mining and transportation of coal, the valuing of timber, and the draining of fields, as estate agent for a squire, Robert Evans felt a close part of a broad network of vertical bonds and loyalties. Butler's father, on the basis of family connections, had been ordained at the age of twenty-three, and spent much of his adult life waiting patiently for an inheritance from his father, the bishop of Lichfield and Coventry.[7]

One shaping experience that linked these men together was that each had had to learn how to accommodate his personal ambitions to paternal or other external authorities. In what we know about their lives, two themes stand out: a stress on the importance of filial submission and family loyalties and a stress that their children eschew all forms of passivity. The emphasis on the need for initiative is illustrated in a letter written by Theodore Sedgwick to his eldest son in 1801: "I remember how painful was my prospect when I was making my entry into life, without friends from whom I could expect anything, without any property, young, and with a most diffident opinion of my own talents. . . . To this I did not submit." The emphasis on deference and respect to social authority is illustrated in a childhood recollection recorded by Eliot: "I was accustomed," she writes, to hear her father "utter the word 'Government' in a tone that charged it with awe and made it part of my effective religion in contrast with the word 'rebel,' which seemed to carry the stamp of evil in its syllables, and, lit by the fact that Satan was the first rebel, made an argument dispensing with more detailed inquiry." Far from being contradictory, the value that was attached to deference and to personal initiative was deeply rooted in the personal experiences of the fathers.[8]

The sense of marginality experienced by our subjects was intensified by the fact that they sprang from areas that did not take part directly in the early industrial revolution. They were conscious of signposts of social transformation—for example, Eliot observed on the midland plains where she grew up "some sign of worldwide change, some new direction of human labour, has wrought itself," the ground blackened with coal pits, the air noisy with the shaking of looms—but such signposts served to reinforce a sense of living on the fringes of social change. Similarly, Stevenson had a sense of living between two worlds. He described Edinburgh, his boyhood home, as a "barbaric display of contrasts," divided between the "unwashed" in Old Town, looking down "from their smokey beehives, ten stories high," upon the open squares and gardens of New Town and its wealthy inhabitants. Stowe and Sedgwick shared the experience of growing up in Federalist strongholds in Connecticut and Massachusetts, respectively, that had maintained the old religious and social order, where the Edwardsian tradition in religion (dominated by stern Calvinist doctrines of predestination, the utter passivity of an individual in being saved, and election by God of those who would be saved) remained strong and where members of the older generation could still be seen wearing breeches, powdered wigs, and white-topped boots. Even when, in later life, these figures moved to the centers of publishing and culture and became part of a broader literary world, they continued to feel isolated and never fully a part of this new society.[9]

A third unifying theme is a loss of faith in dogmatic orthodoxy in religion—a loss brought on, as Humphrey House has noted, not by exposure to new thought—such as biblical criticism, extreme forms of continental rationalism, or unsettling scientific ideas, but by the influence of evangelicalism, with its insistence on sincerity, earnestness, and personal responsibility, the importance of service, and its belief in the moral imperatives of duty and inner struggle. The individuals who are the subject of this book all experienced protracted periods of spiritual despondency and doubt that were the legacy of the high expectations upheld by their religion. Less important than their specific religious denominations was the fact that each encountered a religion that defined ethical and moral issues largely in personal psychological terms; that is, in terms of inner struggles to overcome sinful inclinations and feelings of despair and to achieve holiness and inner peace. Each figure encountered a religion that upheld the possibility of achieving inner sanctity, personal holiness, and liberation from guilt; but this high sense of possibilities in turn contributed to an acute sense of personal responsibility and potential weakness.[10]

The impact of evangelicalism is strikingly apparent in Eliot's loss of faith in dogmatic Christianity. From an aunt and the mistresses of two boarding schools she early developed an abhorrence of worldly pleasures and a passionate concern with consistency, truth, and sincerity. Her reading of a life of William Wilberforce led her to resolve upon a life "sanctified wholly," while the writings of the American revivalist Charles Grandison Finney showed her the possibility of achieving "liberation" from the guilt of sin. She was attracted too by Isaac Taylor's *Ancient Christianity and the Oxford Tracts,* which argued that the early Christian church, far from representing the Tractarians' ideal of pure Christianity, was already characterized by corruption. At the same time, she planned a pictorial guide to the ecclesiastical history of the early church. The essential point is that the moral earnestness that can be traced to evangelicalism prompted intensive investigations of her religious feelings and beliefs.[11]

Stevenson's religious upbringing also made itself felt in his passage from faith to doubt. His father, Stevenson tells us, was a man of "a profound essential melancholy of disposition," filled with "a morbid sense of his own unworthiness," and Stevenson's religious doubts were in part a legacy of his father's intense moral earnestness. Stevenson's mounting sense of doubt concerning the stern creed in which he was reared was first brought on by repeated readings of the works of Herbert Spencer, which had been urged upon him by his father as a way of testing the depth of his religious beliefs. It is characteristic of these figures that they came to doubt religious orthodoxy not out of light-headed skepticism but out of passionate concern with truth and consistency. Sedgwick struggled through eight years of religious despondency before reaching the conviction that Unitarianism offered her the only salvation from hypocrisy. And Stowe, too, after having her conversion experience called into doubt, suffered a protracted period of spiritual despondency, in which she felt "set before and behind" by sin. Butler's break with orthodoxy was also rooted in an acute stress on truth, consistency, and the importance of personal feelings. In preparing for holy orders, Butler closely examined his reasons for being ordained. A close reading of the New Testament in Greek and of the commentators on the Scriptures provoked doubt, particularly in regard to the question of the effects of infant baptism on adulthood behavior and character.[12]

This pattern of religious doubt and spiritual despondency needs to be understood in terms of a wider shift in religious sensibility, a shift in emphasis from the Old to the New Testament. From the seventeenth century well into the eighteenth, the Old Testament provided the single most important source of thought for English Dissenters, Scottish Presbyterians, and American Congregationalists, providing explanations for the nature of society, morality, and human destiny. Surprisingly little attention was paid to the New Testament, to Christ and the Crucifixion, or to the Virgin Mary because of the association with Catholicism. For people who stood outside the Church of England, the tales of hardship, suffering, temptation, corruption, purification, and promise of the Old Testament provided a shared vocabulary and a common cultural heritage. In certain respects, these people were more Hebraic than Christian, emphasizing the Old Testament themes of family, law, and continuity over and above the New Testament themes of holiness and communion.

But increasingly this set of ideas was modified by the emotional religious revivals. By the end of the eighteenth century, Methodists, evangelicals, and revivalists were attaching new emphasis on the possibility of each individual undergoing a transforming religious experience. Eighteenth-century revivalism, which was a response to concerns with religious apathy and moral decay, stressed a sense of new possibilities, a need to move beyond outmoded creeds and traditions. The drift toward evangelicalism can be partly understood as a movement away from an older Hebraic religion toward the more otherworldly elements of the New Testament. One of the more radical implications of evangelical Protestantism was to define religion, not as a set of dogmas or laws, but as an inward experience in which each individual personally had to reexperience Christ's saving love. Evangelicalism did much to reinvigorate the notions of personal decision and choice. Salvation was not merely a matter of intellectual understanding or study; rather, it needed to be accompanied by a total change of heart and emotions.

For individuals who were touched by the influence of evangelicalism, there was a new sense of expectations: that each individual could experience the beatitude and liberation that accompanied union with Christ. Evangelicalism reaffirmed the meaning of Protestantism: that each individual could discover religion for herself or himself, apart from the testimony of the Bible. In its emphasis on personal experience, evangelicalism did much to foster earnestness in matters of belief and to make the quest for certainty, purity, and holiness a matter of central importance.

Whether Anglican, Congregationalist, or Presbyterian in background (and despite fundamental disagreements over such doctrinal questions as predestination and human perfectibility), the Victorian authors who are the subjects of this book were preoccupied during their young adulthoods with similar questions of religious belief. All felt wracked by doubt and weary of uncertainty and religious controversy. All regarded their families' religions as cold, stern, and lifeless and craved a religion that was more life-affirming. All craved sanctification that would free them from egotism and guilt. All sought a faith that would be consistent with the evidences of their own feelings. Yet later, in their adult lives, these writers would grapple with questions of identity and belief, not in the realm of religion, but in the realm of language and literature.

It is important for understanding these figures' choice of vocation to recognize that they were adapting older kinds of questions and concerns, previously dealt with in religion, to newer, more popular forms of expression. For these writers, fiction offered a secular mode of discourse in which certain traditional religious questions could be analyzed and in which they could express their personal psychological and religious experiences. Conceiving of their social role as that of "aesthetic teachers," they would agree with Eliot in regarding literature as "the highest of all teaching, because it deals with life in its highest complexity." Hostile toward dogmatism in religion and didacticism in literature—"if it ceases to be purely aesthetic—if it lapses anywhere from picture to the diagram—it becomes the most offensive of all teaching"—these writers continued to think of imaginative fiction in almost religious terms:—as an instrument for shaping character.[13]

In the remaining chapters, we turn to the major themes of this book, namely the personal family dynamics of a series of influential Victorian authors. Their family lives will be analyzed in terms of the specific roles that were most important in the middle-class Victorian home: father and child, daughter and wife, and sister and brother.

CHAPTER 5

Son and Father

THE theme of this chapter is the pattern of conflict and revolt between a father and a child in a middle-class Victorian home and the way this conflict was interpreted and understood. It is this chapter's basic argument that the personal family conflict between a father and a child embodied tensions and issues that stood at the core of Victorian culture and that no understanding of the pattern of emotional relationships within a Victorian home can be complete without a recognition of the way family experiences embodied larger cultural concerns involving such basic concepts as authority, duty, legitimacy, and personal responsibility.

In emphasizing the psychological importance of conflict with a father, this chapter does not seek to minimize the role of the mother. In the middle-class Victorian home, as in virtually all societies, primary responsibility for the care and rearing of children rested with women. Indeed, the pattern of relationships within the middle-class Victorian home was closely related to changes in the status and economic role of women. By the early nineteenth century, middle-class women, having lost many of their earlier "productive" functions, made motherhood a self-conscious vocation. Middle-class women were asserting increased responsibility over childrearing and control over domestic manners and morals. These women were becoming increasingly identified with the realm of affect and feeling. Nevertheless, it was the father, not the mother who created the atmosphere of rigid piety that prevailed in the homes we shall examine, and who became the symbolic antagonist for the children and a lightning rod for conflicts within the Victorian middle-class home.

The preeminence assigned to the father drew upon several sources. First, in the early nineteenth century it was an almost unquestioned premise that the family constituted a microcosm of the larger social and political world and that both natural and divine law endowed the father with patriarchal authority as "head" of a household. Political and religious theorists viewed the father's authority as part of a continuous chain of hierarchical and delegated authority descending from God. The close connections between conceptions of divine authority and paternal authority in the home are manifest in the use of language. From Jonathan Edwards, Jr., to Timothy Dwight and Samuel Hopkins down to Nathaniel Taylor and Lyman Beecher, New England Calvinist theologians spoke of God as a "moral governor," who, like a progressive parent, sought to win the "confidence" of his children through moral means of influence. The metaphor of God as a "governor" who earned his children's loyalty and affection without force of fear was a recurrent theme that united American divines with pietistic Low Church and Nonconformist Protestants in England and mirrors the contemporary conception of the father as a "governor" and "moral force."[1]

What linked these two conceptions of the government of God and the government of the family was a common emphasis on the idea that the object of authority was to develop a capacity for self-government. Much as a minister was to demonstrate to his congregation that true happiness lay in obedience to God's law, a father was to impress upon a child a recognition of the force of moral duty and obligation. Given the weakness of other religious and social authorities, the absence of strong communal traditions and other social controls, the "moral government" of the father was to create a foundation for wider social conceptions of authority, discipline, and duty.

A second factor giving added force to the father's authority lay in economic changes that had made the middle-class father the sole or main breadwinner in the family. A young man such as Robert Louis Stevenson remained financially dependent on his father well into his young adulthood, as he read for the bar, or, in the case of Samuel Butler, while he prepared for holy orders. For young women, whose occupational opportunities were minimal, financial dependence on the father may have been even greater. A shift in language provides an indication of a change in perception of the father's role. Where earlier "dependence" had suggested a wide range of relatives and associates with whom one was connected and for whom one was responsible, by the early nineteenth century the concept increasingly narrowed to denote financial dependence, particularly the dependence of a man's wife and children. This dependence was reflected, up until the mid-nineteenth century, in law—laws that prohibited married women from owning property, entering into business, contracting, and controlling their own earnings. Wives and children had long been considered dependents; but they were now dependent in a new way. Where in earlier times the authority of a father was reinforced by control of property, skills, or connections with a wider kin network, increasingly paternal authority was rooted in emotional bonds and money, particularly the money that supported his children's education and setting them up in a career.[2]

In the pages that follow, the figure of the father carries enormous symbolic significance. It is the father who stands as the symbol of public and external conceptions of authority and who serves as the chief authority figure within the home. It is the father who provides children with an example of instrumentality in contrast to the mother's affectivity. For middle-class families who aspired for improvement but who were anxious to conserve the values of the past, the figure of the father involved associations of continuity and legitimate authority. He was a "governor," not, in twentieth-century terms, a "pal." And yet, as we shall see, the father's authority could not be insulated from the corrosive effects of individualistic and egalitarian values. The authority of the father was increasingly cut off from the support of the broader culture. Market values and the values of political liberalism, which

rewarded self-reliance and independence and personal responsibility, penetrated into the home and threw into question traditional assumptions about paternal authority. As mothers exercised
increasing childrearing responsibility, the father's authority was
further undercut.

Symbolically, the conflict between a child and a father absorbed a wide range of other issues and gave tangible expression
to Victorian culture's concerns involving personal responsibility, internalized discipline, and preserving continuities with the
past. For fathers, who were losing their ability to transfer and
pass on their "status position" in society, the personal struggle
with a child was a way of testing the child's capacity for self-
discipline and denial. For children, who were dependent on their
fathers in new ways, there were two contradictory goals: to retain emotional bonds while overcoming economic dependence,
and to convert emotional bonds into acceptable adult forms.

The personal family struggle between father and child reflects
tensions deeply embedded within middle-class Victorian culture. It reflects dissatisfaction with older notions of authority
based on coercion, prescription, and hierarchy. Above all, it
mirrors a broader historical concern with setting up authority
on a new basis resting on individual responsibility and internalized self-discipline. What we will see in this chapter is that a
middle-class Victorian father's willingness to grant a child a degree of independence depended on certain symbols of internalized discipline and self-denial, symbols that set firm limits to the
child's assertion of autonomy. Far from fracturing the bonds of
family, a child's rebellion against a father was part of a larger
process in which acceptable limits to behavior were defined and
cultural patterns were transmitted from one generation to the
next.

The Hegemony of the Father

In 1894, at the age of forty-four, Robert Louis Stevenson died
of a cerebral hemorrhage after a lifelong struggle with tubercu-

losis. In eulogizing him after his death, mourners frequently referred to the "habitual gaiety" and fortitude Stevenson displayed throughout his life, though threatened by early death. To a culture that attached enormous value to achievement, competitiveness, and the strenuous life, Stevenson's success in triumphing over his infirmities was a potent symbol. His life provided a graphic demonstration that illness, weakness, and adversity could be overcome by force of will.[3]

During the nineteenth century the prevalence of recurrent and debilitating periods of invalidism elicited deep concern. The extent of physical debilities appeared to point to a fundamental antagonism between individual desires and instincts and the requirements of society and civilization—an antagonism that could be overcome only through self-denial and self-restraint, the qualities necessary to maintain social harmony and order without coercion. The Victorian fascination with invalidism and disease was a counterpoint to the interest in strength, independence, and self-assertion, and it betrayed a profound uneasiness about individualism. There was a deep-seated sense that individualism, unless contained and socialized, would result in a general process of society unraveling. For people who stood with one foot firmly planted in Calvinism and another foot rooted in romanticism, a mixture of hope and fear accentuated a need to counterbalance individualism with internalized self-restraints. This anxiety about individualism was manifest in the romantic association of tuberculosis with self-consumption, an association that raised dark questions about the ability of the unattached individual to stand alone without sapping the wellsprings of morality and obligation.

At the time of Stevenson's death, a few critics maintained that the writer who was celebrated in the public press was not the man they had known. Far from being a "Seraph in Chocolate," these critics charged, "this barley-sugar effigy of a real man" had been a hypocrite. His domestic life was marred by fierce and bitter conflicts with his parents that he dishonestly contrived to

The Birthplace of Robert Louis Stevenson: 8 Howard Place, Edinburgh. Courtesy of Lady Stair's House Museum, Edinburgh.

hide. That he exhibited cheerfulness when faced by death was only to do as any virtuous seamstress might. For this, he deserved no credit.[4]

The disparity between Stevenson's actual life and his public image, according to these dissenters, pointed to a more serious flaw. His art, like his life, was make-believe, rooted in the assumption that characters in a novel could all be mechanically arranged to produce a well-ordered composition. What marred his art was precisely what disfigured his self-manufactured image. The preciousness of his style enabled him to write of anything with an implacable lucidity, giving a quality of artifice and inauthenticity to his work. Incident was more important than character, action more than motive, phenomenon more than the underlying cause. If a note of propriety distinguished Stevenson's character from that of his contemporary Oscar Wilde, the two writers' works could be attended as part of a common chord: both wrote works marked by contrivance and artifice. To a younger generation, Stevenson's life and work were symbolic of all that was wrong with Victorianism: its preciousness, artificiality, and superficiality.[5]

After Stevenson's death, at the time of the publication of the novelist's personal correspondence, his estate's executors were deeply troubled by the thought that dissension between the novelist and his parents would be disclosed. The executors would have agreed that censoring Stevenson's correspondence to remove hints of family conflict was disingenuous, but they would also have denied that this was duplicitous. Their reasoning is revealing. Candor, in such matters, they were convinced, inflicted grave harm, not only upon Stevenson's family and his public reputation, but upon society itself. Certain veils were essential if social values were to persist. The conviction that the mere appearance of harmony was essential to preserve social values provided justification for the careful winnowing of Stevenson's unhappy past.[6]

The executors were not so blind as to think that family conflict did not exist. In fact, it was their knowledge that family contention was widespread and that it threatened to tear families apart that was a large part of their concern. Stevenson himself had publicly acknowledged that marriage and family life were fated to be checkered by disputes. Human beings, he believed, were not so virtuous as to escape caprice and moodiness, and therefore family life, which compelled individuals to interact on the most intimate of terms, was doomed to be depressing. But, he continued, much as friendships could withstand quarrels and separations and yet remain firm and vigorous, so the disputes interrupting family life ought to be dismissed as meaningless. It was this assumption that guided his estate's executors in deleting references to family conflict from the writer's personal papers. If family life was depressing, as Stevenson had intimated it was, then relentless efforts were required to make it less so. Toward the end of his life, Stevenson repeated this conclusion. His words were infused with the weight that comes from experience. A son's highest obligation, he wrote, was to fulfill the expectations of his parents. "He has to redeem the sins of man, and restore the world's confidence in children." What he seems to be suggesting is that one of a child's chief duties is to selflessly seek to diminish family discord.[7]

Each family member carried the heavy responsibility of quelling the selfish desires raging within himself. This, according to Sidney Colvin, professor of art at Cambridge, had been Stevenson's personal goal. Recalling how his friend had poured out his distress over the bitter disputes that had wracked his boyhood home, Colvin noted that Stevenson had never blamed his father for the troubles; he had dwelt simply on the tragedy of family contention. Because he strove intently to make things pleasant for his parents, Colvin added, Mr. and Mrs. Stevenson "assumed as a matter of course that everything was quite pleasant for him." They never knew what their son felt beneath the surface. As Colvin edited the Stevenson correspondence, Colvin disclosed the extent of the novelist's unhappiness to his mother, who claimed to be unaware of the extent of discord. Colvin attributed this ignorance to her husband's and son's ceaseless endeavors to conceal their disputes.[8]

Later, Colvin took pains to persuade Stevenson's mother that some reference to family conflicts in the Stevenson home could be allowed to surface, inasmuch as the relationship had not only weathered the storms but had emerged secure. Mrs. Stevenson would not yield to this argument. She voiced a ready objection: that family disputes were preeminently a private matter not open to public encroachments. Colvin ultimately insisted that he be permitted to publish the essential truth regarding family relations, but he promised to edit the letters according to the principle that family quarrels were only a case of two men "not understanding each other for a while." Despite his vivid memory of Stevenson confessing that he was "pestered almost to madness" by his father, Colvin agreed that propriety demanded that the details of family conflict remain hidden.[9]

It may be only a coincidence that the Victorian ideal of family order and harmony arose at the same time that carefully arranged still-life paintings assumed prominence in high art. Yet both of these developments seem to have been linked by a common concern with an appearance of tranquility and calm. Disorder, conflict, and contention were inconsistent with ideal sentiment. For people haunted by a nightmare vision of breakdown, splintering, and atomization, the exaltation of the harmony of the family seemed a necessary counterbalance to the divisive, disintegrating pressures of public life.[10]

At a time when society had seemingly lost the stabilizing influences of many institutional and communal controls, many Victorians looked to the home as a bulwark against disruptive social change, as a source of order and morality, a counterbalance to the individualistic and commercial pressures buffeting modern life. Viewed as sanctuary from the alienating and corrupting pressures of the outside world and for higher redeeming moral values, the family was invested with awesome psychological and ideological responsibilities. The family, having lost certain traditional economic, religious, and welfare functions, acquired new burdens as a place of security, order, and emotional fulfillment.[11]

This conscious perception of the home as a shelter of peace and harmony can be seen through the example of Robert Ste-

venson, a cousin of the novelist and his closest friend. Robert
was accused by his relatives of undermining Robert Louis's religious faith and his loyalty to the family. Yet Robert repeatedly
wrote his cousin that the family situation was "one of the most
important things to fetch right." In his letters to his cousin,
Robert sharply contrasted the tranquility of the home and the
sensuality and decadence lying outside. But even as he explained
the temptations of low life, he reasserted the attractions of domesticity and clung to the belief that "it is impossible to work
off happiness without it." Robert Louis Stevenson was considered by his relatives to be less debased than his cousin, and
his greater decency was evident in his stronger defense of home
life. He likened the home to a recuperative oasis where an individual received the sustenance necessary to stride out into life
and to act. He analogized the relationship between the home
and society to the relationship between a lover and the tender
heart of her beloved. With the sway of gentle cradling, the heart
was restored and enlarged. A base as well as a shelter, the home
was an island of stability and security in a world torn apart by
the critical spirit, rampant individualism, and bewildering social
change.[12]

Such a conscious association of the home with higher moral
and spiritual values, as a locus of affection and stability that
could be found nowhere else, gave a special poignancy and anguish to family strife. In a home that was conceived as a place
of peace and order amid the abrasive waves of social and intellectual change, a dispute between a child and a parent could be
regarded as a rebellion against the institution that stood at the
very basis of civilization, as a revolt against all larger conceptions
of authority and order, as a challenge to the very foundation of
morality and stability.

It is to the intense personal conflict that erupted between Stevenson and his father that our attention shifts. This family conflict at once illuminates the psychological and ideological burdens that were just beginning to be invested in the middle-class

Robert Louis Stevenson, at the age of four, with his mother, Margaret Isabella Balfour Stevenson, 1854. Courtesy of Lady Stair's House Museum, Edinburgh.

family and the deep personal conflicts that could result from the
new expectations and responsibilities attached to the home. It
is a case that suggests the way family conflicts within the middle-class Victorian home were defined and structured, and also
how the resolution of conflicts reflects a broader transformation
of Victorian values and attitudes.

The external details of conflict are easily summarized. Tension
first arose within the Stevenson household in 1867, when Stevenson was seventeen, about to enter Edinburgh University to
prepare himself to become an engineer. But the future novelist
expressed an aversion to the profession and in 1871 decided to
abandon engineering for the law. Conflict openly erupted between father and son in 1874 when Stevenson began to express
doubts about the Scottish Calvinism in which he had been raised.
Family differences were compounded when, after being called
to the bar in 1875, Stevenson decided not to practice but to write
instead. Conflict temporarily was abated in 1875 when Stevenson
wrote an *Appeal to the Church of Scotland* to placate his father
about his religious views, but strife was revived in 1879 when
Stevenson became romantically involved with his future wife,
an American divorcée, Frances Osbourne. Father and son
reached a reconciliation only in 1880 after Stevenson married
Frances Osbourne.

When the publication of Stevenson's personal correspondence
brought family dissension to public light, the novelist's mother
attempted to quiet gossip by claiming that arguments between
father and son were confined to a single topic, religion. Sidney
Colvin, editor of the correspondence, thought Mrs. Stevenson
doubtless right as to the main cause of the quarrels. But when
he suggested that Stevenson's choice of occupation had also
sparked arguments, Mrs. Stevenson castigated the professor for
his audacity. There was no evidence to support this claim, she
insisted, so "why do you say that Louis' change of profession
led to a painful misunderstanding between him and his father."
Although her child's decision not to become an engineer, like
her husband, was a disappointment—"a very great disappointment"—Mrs. Stevenson asserted that her husband never con-

sidered quarreling over the matter. In her eyes, the mere suggestion that an argument might center on the selfish desire to perpetuate her husband's career was an insult.[13]

Colvin had touched on a source of concern to Mrs. Stevenson, however, and during succeeding months she attempted to gather evidence to refute suspicions that religion was not the main cause of family disputes. While Mrs. Stevenson admitted that decisions surrounding the choice of a vocation created some strain in the family, her son and husband had in fact conspired to keep the mother ignorant of this dispute. Indirect evidence uncovered by Colvin attests that husband and son intentionally tried to narrow the signs of conflict entirely to a debate over religious dogma, and this evidence supports Mrs. Stevenson's claim to have knowledge only of religious discord. But even if there are intimations that conflict over religion was part of a larger dispute, we still must ask why religion became the point at which father and son ostensibly clashed.[14]

Superficially, religion appeared to be one point safe from conflict. Had not Stevenson only recently thanked God that he was never tempted to disbelieve? And had he not informed his mother that he found Herbert Spencer's works "awfully twaddley in parts," an opinion he knew would gladden his father's heart? Nor was it obvious that Stevenson's father would respond harshly to religious heterodoxy. Although he considered himself a strong conservative, he supported the extension of legal rights to women, a sentiment that found another expression in his establishment of a Magdalen mission, a house of refuge for reformed prostitutes. By tolerating his nephew Robert, who was believed to be an atheist, the engineer indicated that he could consider blood more important than religion. Earlier, he had even argued in public in behalf of tolerance for Catholics. When Stevenson and his father clashed over religion, they had consciously chosen the battleground.[15]

Their battle was waged over one great issue: what limits were to be placed on man's self-assertions. Thomas Stevenson considered himself a scientist, but as his son observed, his role as a scientific witness cost him many qualms, since the scientific method raised the specter of all authority being susceptible to reason. In a brief volume on the evidences of Christianity, written during the contention with his son, Stevenson looked to non-Christian sources of evidence for proof of his religion. The testimony of the physical sciences, of Judaism, and of pagans all confirmed, in his opinion, the central tenets of Christian faith: the supernatural origin of life, the existence of a messiah, and the reality of Christ's miracles. By turning to non-Christian testimony, he believed he had found a source of indisputable facts. But to look to alien thinkers for support for Christianity was to make religion susceptible to external criticism. And it was this susceptibility that the elder Stevenson denied.[16]

To Thomas Stevenson, the dilemma was clear-cut. If people were freed from divine revelation, there was no other basis for human morality except individual self-interest. Concepts of duty or utility, in his view, were simply the arbitrary creations of "moral cucumbers": such notions were either a rationalization for pure selfishness (if the natural harmony of interests was assumed) or else an arbitrary restraint upon the freedom of the individual. The important question was simply whether an individual accepted the inviolability of divine law or not. If one accepted revelation, then one lived according to the laws of love and friendship. If one did not, and Thomas Stevenson directed this point to his son, then all love and friendship were dissolved. Individual motives were what mattered, and if one rejected Christianity, then any arbitrary action was conceivable.[17]

Bentham, not Darwin, was the villain in Thomas Stevenson's morality play, for Bentham had interwoven a doctrine of selfishness with a tone of moral self-righteousness. As strongly as he opposed atheism, he said he could respect disbelief as an honest mistake; but he positively rebelled against notions of "moral duty." Duty, when dissociated from Christian revelation, provided no firm basis for morality or social obligations. He was convinced that there must be a contradiction when freethinkers foreclosed their minds to anything that could not be explained by purely physical laws. Dogmatism, in his view, was the central flaw of Benthamism: a conviction that they knew what was best for the greatest number. But if dogmatism was the greatest mistake of freethinkers, then the elder Stevenson realized that he would have to be satisfied if his son simply suspended judgment on matters of religion. In his book he admitted that no evidence could directly prove, for example, that miracles had taken place. What he hoped is that a sufficiency of evidence supporting some points of Christianity would enable his son, and others, to accept all the religion on faith.[18]

Ultimately, Thomas Stevenson rested his argument on an appeal to his son's emotions. He told his son about the anguish a mother felt when she lost her child (he played upon the parallel of the Stevensons' feeling that they had lost their own son). Each sight of the empty and silent nursery bled the mother's heart anew in a way that was unknowable. "Tell me," he demanded of his son and other "philosophising sceptics," "if there be nothing dark and mysterious here." The emotions of love and death, he believed, were inexplicable in purely utilitarian terms, and to remove the consolation of religion was to defraud a mother of her dearest hope. The phrasing of Stevenson's argument is revealing. Religion was identified with a conception of family harmony and order; for the strength of a household rested on an almost religious basis; not upon arbitrary conceptions of moral duty, criteria of utility, or patriarchal authority. Unlike Utilitarianism, which reduced all human qualities to measurable factors, and which omitted the emotions from its calculations, religion existed on a higher plane. Yet the tragedy of Thomas Stevenson is that he could conceive of no higher criticism of Benthamism than that it defrauded people.[19]

The fact is that Thomas Stevenson and his antagonists shared many values and preconceptions: a belief in the existence of absolute and unchanging standards of morality, a belief in the need for transcendent moral principles to guide and elevate human behavior, and a belief that moral laws were susceptible to proof by reason. That Thomas Stevenson had adopted many of the values he claimed to reject is manifest in his arguments defending the value of the home and family life. His justification was that the institution was necessary to reconcile the demands of individuals for emotional gratification and society's need for stability. But his tacit premises—that the family was a vital institution because it promoted societal happiness and fit the exigencies of human nature—were precisely the same assumptions held by the philosophic radicals, and suggest how far Utilitarianism had been incorporated into the intellectual establishment. As proof of his contention of the value of the family, the elder Stevenson felt compelled to use the Benthamite criterion of value.

At issue in the conflict between Robert Louis Stevenson and his father was God's authority. But religion, in this case, proved to be an arena for other conflicts between a child and a father. Mirroring an intense personal struggle over religious authority was another struggle to transform childhood forms of dependency into acceptable adult, and characteristically Victorian, forms. The relationship between Stevenson and his father illustrates a broader process of accommodation within the middle-class Victorian home—a process through which "influence" was exerted, sanctioned, accepted, and internalized. The personal family conflict over religion illuminates another process—the process through which a father sought to legitimately influence a son's choice of vocation and spouse and to symbolically test his child's capacity for self-government. The religious conflict also provided the child with a vehicle through which to assert a degree of autonomy and independence while struggling to maintain family bonds. Dissension in the Stevenson household helps to illustrate how problems of individual development intersect with broader religious controversies.

Whereas conflict between Stevenson and his father was limited prior to adolescence, according to the novelist's recollections, a change in their relationship occurred as the future novelist reached his early twenties. Stevenson's earliest letters record an image of his father as protector and playmate. When Stevenson suffered his first serious adversities upon entering school and falling ill, he turned to his father, not his mother, for succor. Giving substance to his image of his father as his personal protector was the knowledge that his father responded on re-

Robert Louis Stevenson, at the age of seven, with his father, Thomas Stevenson, 1857. Courtesy of Lady Stair's House Museum, Edinburgh.

peated occasions by taking his son along with him on rounds
inspecting the lighthouses along the Scottish coast. Later in life,
Stevenson's portrait of an ideal father—as childish and playful,
anxious but eager to encourage a spirit of experiment and adventure in his children—strongly resembled his idealized picture
of his own father.[20]

Yet Stevenson's childhood recollections suggest that his boyhood was not wholly happy. In a letter to his cousin Robert,
Stevenson mentioned that, with the single exception of his father, he had no friends with whom he could pour out his "wa-
tery and flaccid sentiments" (a reference that is suggestive of
prunes and bowels, and of issues of constipation that will recur). But Stevenson's comment was reflected in a series of disclosures of his sense of loneliness and isolation. In her diary, his
mother frequently commented on her child's loneliness. Her reaction is expressive of a reliance upon family ties: when her son
was lonely, she took him to visit, not other children, but his
grandparents. Adding to Stevenson's loneliness were his father's
frequent absences from home, which were required by his occupation. If Stevenson was to find companionship, he had to
locate it within his family. If this situation heightened his emotional dependence on his father, it also helped set the stage for
later battles to assert independence. In his picture of his father
as a playmate for the small son, Stevenson suggests a late or
even post-Victorian pattern of the father as a big "pal." Given
the emotional and ideological burdens of the Victorian family,
these intense father-son bonds in lieu of the "normal" Oedipal
struggle would create added difficulties for the child in breaking
away from his family.[21]

Tension between father and son first emerged at a time when
young Stevenson was selecting a vocation. Thomas Stevenson
long desired his son to succeed him as an engineer. Having
encouraged this ambition by assisting his son in the study of
mechanics, he initially felt betrayed when he discovered young
Stevenson's disenchantment with engineering. Yet the elder Stevenson expressed not acquiescence but joy upon his son's choice
to become a legal advocate. But when his son chose to become

a writer, the father felt free to intervene. His objection was simple: an artist would be unable to support his parents in their old age. This objection may seem curious given the fact that Thomas Stevenson financially supported his son until the father's death, but it gave expression to a traditional conception of the family as a welfare institution. That the elder Stevenson enunciated his objection in economic terms illustrates how tightly economics was interwoven with the conception of the family; not only conceptually but legally the family was an economic unit. At a time when old notions of welfare for the aged had collapsed, the family was the only remaining source of financial security. Unlike engineering or law, literature offered little hope of financial reward. In Stevenson's native Scotland, penury was common for even the best-known writers. How much less might be expected from an invalid? [22]

The controversy between Stevenson and his father over the necessity of Christianity as a basis for social values began at a time when the relationship between the two was undergoing certain larger changes. In respect for the wishes of a dying relative, who charged that there were atheists within the family connection, young Stevenson's cousin Robert was barred from his home. This incident might not have been significant except that it led the future novelist to inquire into the unchristian behavior being directed toward his cousin. What he discovered was that his opinions did not matter, that he might speak the words of Christ but be unheard. And Stevenson took this as evidence that he had allowed himself to be regarded as a dependent child within his family. This incident magnified his sense of personal dependency, a sense of dependence that was compounded by his feeling that he was too well suppered and well clothed. All this seemed to indicate that he had failed to prove his fitness for an independent life. [23]

Yet, Stevenson would not openly quarrel with his father for another year. Between 1872 and 1873 Stevenson formed his first firm emotional ties outside his immediate family. During the summer of 1873, when he was twenty-two, Stevenson became acquainted with two persons who would become his closest friends. One, Sidney Colvin, praised his unpublished literary work and confirmed Stevenson's intention to become a writer. His other acquaintance, Frances Sitwell, became, apart from his parents, his first serious emotional attachment. Thomas Stevenson watched apprehensively as his son established strong personal ties outside the home, but young Stevenson's return home brought only discord.

The roots of religious turmoil were planted long before the first open quarrels. As has been stated, tensions had already arisen over the treatment accorded Stevenson's cousin Robert, which had magnified his sense of dependence on his parents, and over the future novelist's apparently irresolute pursuit of a career. But it was only after a reordering of emotional relationships gave Stevenson a firm emotional base outside the home that he clashed with his father over religion. This is not to imply that the bitter family dispute over religion was in some sense an externalization of other personal psychological conflicts. Rather, religion provided the Stevensons with a common language and a common set of symbols by which they could give tangible expression to their central concerns with authority, self-discipline, independence, dependence, and self-denial. The entire family dispute embodied larger cultural tensions and contradictions that found their clearest expression in religion.

Looking back upon the causes of family conflict, Thomas Stevenson came to believe that Herbert Spencer was somehow responsible for undermining his child's faith in religious orthodoxy. As an engineer, Thomas Stevenson was well aware of the connections between science and skepticism, and he repeatedly urged his son to test his religious convictions against rationalistic principles; one of his tests was to have his son read the works of Spencer. Robert Louis had himself feared that his religious faith might be shaken and was profoundly relieved to find that Spencer's work had not converted him. Yet, having tested his religious views, much to his father's pleasure, by reading Spencer, the younger Stevenson persisted in scrutinizing his religious affections. But his inner searching only served to intensify an anxiety that his religious faith was dishonest. In his father's view, religious faith required constant vigilance, and young Stevenson's continued doubt was a legacy of his father's expectations.

Although his initial reading of Spencer did not shake Stevenson's religious convictions, the books did have an important psychological effect on him. The works of Spencer intensified Stevenson's concern with personal responsibility and gave the question of the "fitness" of his beliefs a new dimension. In letters to his cousin, Stevenson expressed deep qualms regarding the "fitness" of his views. He said he was concerned "not so much for a proof of their fitness (in the sense of propriety), as for a suggestion of some dishonesty to myself in the means I took to find them." What troubled Stevenson was not whether his views were socially respectable or not but whether his views had been honestly arrived at. He described the cheerful acceptance that greeted his religious views at home, but this easy acceptance seemed to provide an insufficient test of whether his convictions were truly sincere. He expressed a fear that in religion he was simply truckling to his parents' wishes. He informed his cousin that he needed a calling that would provide a test of his character and his beliefs. He wrote, "I want an object, a mission, a belief, a hope to be my wife," and one suspects that his use of the word "wife" was a way of expressing his belief that his calling would have to take him outside his parents' home.[24]

During the course of their conflict, the family members were driven to extreme positions. Where Thomas Stevenson initially blamed his nephew Robert for family dissension, he quickly came to brand his own son an atheist. The son, in turn, called his father a hypocrite who was unwilling to grant the right of freedom of conscience and of private judgment. Where originally young Stevenson limited his religious uncertainties to questions about the evidence for certain Christian doctrines, he came to adopt the language of Herbert Spencer. When he wrote his parents, he observed that the family was "incapable of motion" and called this a sign of "infirmity of purpose."[25]

Such arguments as Stevenson directed against his family could be made only at the cost of great personal anguish. Although there is no doubt that he in fact hoped to create distance between himself and his parents, the young writer expressed great pain and guilt regarding his behavior. By assigning responsibility for his behavior to divine necessity, however, he was able to partially reduce his intense sense of guilt. In a letter to Frances Sitwell, for instance, Stevenson asked why God had made him such a curse to his parents. And as deeply as he hoped for concord, he feared that he had permanently destroyed his father's happiness. "O if he would only *whistle* when he comes in again!" But Stevenson feared that he had "forever stopped that pipe." He lambasted himself for having proven himself so little help to his father in his old age. In much the same terms Stevenson's father was deeply troubled by the thought that he had permanently lost his son. He observed that it was a heavy burden for a man to reach the end of his life and see nothing but disintegration facing himself and his family. The sense of futility in his words was colored by the message of Herbert Spencer. While antagonistic to the thrust of Spencer's argument, he was much affected by it—believing that Spencer offered a highly accurate description of life—and spoke of his own unhappy condition when he wrote that "undercutting a man's faith is a *very* serious matter."[26]

In reconstructing the religious dispute within the Stevenson household, we are able to see the symbols and sanctions that a child could invoke in order to obtain a degree of moral autonomy from a father. In order to assert a measure of self-determination, Stevenson invoked a variety of symbols of internalized discipline and self-denial to demonstrate his capacity for self-government. At a time when traditional conceptions of authority and deference were being questioned and transformed—when submission to worldly authority was as repellent as the notion of enslaving another human being—both Stevenson and his father agreed that the son's independence depended on his ability to demonstrate an internalized sense of duty. Emphasis on duty and self-denial, in turn, were closely related to the critical symbol of Jesus Christ, who exemplified, to both son and father, a model of selflessness, sacrifice, and an ability to bear pain for the sake of a larger good. That obedience was symbolized in religious terms again demonstrates the way religious concepts interpenetrated with personal family issues, and provided models for behavior.

To the suspicion that he was guilty of placing personal interests above those of the family, Stevenson responded by admitting that he was far from pleased with himself. Everything that his father charged was true: religion, resignation, and peace in believing could only follow self-control. But could self-control be imposed from without? Could his father expect him to sincerely believe if he was being pressured? To a friend Stevenson confided that he was not a lighthearted scoffer, much less an infidel. But his fear of self-deception and dishonesty could be overcome only as he looked into his own soul. To do otherwise, he added, was to live his life as a falsehood.[27]

To the fear that his impiety was a sign of disloyalty and disrespect to his parents, Stevenson replied that he remained steadfast in his love. He told his mother and father that they should never fear the loss of their son's love, although he was certain to lose them because of their deaths. Reversing the positions of the family members, he charged that his parents did not understand his love for them, for he would gladly give up anything worldly for their sake. To the impression that he was unwilling to make sacrifices, Stevenson countered by demonstrating his selflessness. He cheerfully requested a Bible from his mother. And as he earlier had taken the bar examination to please his father, so now he competed for an Edinburgh professorship, even though he knew the Scottish climate was harmful to his health. When he explained the reasons for his application, he stated: "What should I care for my dignity when my father is concerned?" The question stood as a witness to the son's resolve to look into his own soul and yet remain true to his father.[28]

How could Stevenson prove his firmness of character? One

answer was to show that he remained faithful to the ways of his forefathers. In a family history, he contrasted the first flowering of the Stevenson family during his grandfather's generation with its present condition, and the present suffered in comparison. The Stevensons were already a family of engineers during the eighteenth century, but the profession was far different from its modern counterpart. "It was not a science then," Stevenson wrote, "—it was a living art." Instead of being guided by a transcendent sense of nature, the modern engineer had stooped to using formulas and diagrams. He was no longer engaged in adventures that resulted in the transformation of nature. Stevenson's grandfather was depicted as a potent rebuke to the present. His grandfather had founded a family line and led his people like a patriarch. Like Stevenson himself, his grandfather was religious but had acquired worldly traits.[29]

Stevenson's family agreed that the portrait was overdrawn. But to the novelist, this family history offered proof of the disparity between his father's generation and his grandfather's. In a letter written shortly before his death, the author of *Treasure Island* insisted that civilization had become grimly mechanical, "a reflex with us." The ills that Stevenson depicted were twofold. To the tension-ridden Victorian family, Stevenson pointed to the Scottish clan as an alternative. As a counter to the restraints of civilization that had leashed man's instincts, Stevenson looked fondly on the ruggedly masculine world of his grandfather. His grandfather's age, marked by creativity, instinct, and strong family bonds, stood as a counter to his present life and an oblique way of downgrading his own father.[30]

Ultimately, the only way Stevenson could prove his strength of character was to put himself through a series of self-administered tests. The ultimate test, for Stevenson, was to be able to achieve financial independence from his parents. In a letter written immediately prior to his death, Stevenson identified the ills of civilization with the economic pressures that coerced individuals to conform to social conventions. "The key to the business is of course the belly," was the way he put it. These words reflect earlier fears that his parents would use their economic leverage to force him to conform to their wishes. And this anxiety drove Stevenson repeatedly to seek financial independence. In his letters, the goal of economic independence became dissociated from any single aim, such as establishing his own household. Instead, financial independence acquired symbolic significance as proof of his strength of character and willpower.[31]

Similarly, his ability to bear illness was held up as proof of his fortitude. He had suffered deeply, he told his friend Colvin, "but I am built for misfortunes; they digest in me like prunes . . . and you behold me still smiling." Stevenson's reference to prunes is perhaps psychologically significant. Prunes make one run, and Stevenson is being digested like prunes; hence, his misfortunes tear him apart, and yet he remains smiling—further indication of his firmness in enduring hardships and suffering. To his father, Stevenson admitted that an engineer's life was checkered; but far worse, he claimed, was the incapacity to do a day's work. Illness was a way of demonstrating his courage and tenacity in coping with adversity. "Never was a man further rèmoved from literature than I; yet I go on daily." As this quotation suggests, invalidism was a way to prove strength of character and at the same time rebuke selfish economic activity. For Stevenson, self-denial provided evidence of character and inner motives that could be exhibited in no other way.[32]

Stevenson's marriage in 1880 to Fanny Osbourne brought a sudden halt to the family's religious turmoil. Despite the bitterness that had marked the dispute between father and son, the turmoil ended almost as abruptly as it had begun. Reconciliation between the family members was rapid and surprisingly complete. Writing in the wake of the reconciliation, Stevenson minimized the religious differences that had divided father and son. He informed his father that they had but a single disagreement, involving the degree to which religion should be a public matter. As a token of their reconciliation, he gave his parent the right to criticize the religious content of his literary work. In later years, outsiders commented on the degree to which Stevenson resembled his father in religion. A family friend wished wistfully that Thomas Stevenson might have lived to see his son lead his household in prayer. And another observer testified that Stevenson's prayers seemed heartfelt. Taken together, these facts suggest that conflict between father and son involved issues in addition to religion.[33]

The dispute between Stevenson and his father over religion embodied another, equally fundamental issue—the repeated efforts of a child to find sanctioned ways of asserting independence. To understand the intensity and poignancy of the family conflict that wracked the Stevenson household, we must recognize that what was going on between father and son was not regarded as purely a personal dispute or a struggle for dominance but as a moral conflict involving the very meaning of such central cultural concepts as authority, independence, and self-government. In the context of the dependency-encouraging environment of the middle-class Victorian home, a central challenge for a child was to discover symbolic ways of testing and proving his capacity for independence.

From a very early age Stevenson's parents had sought to instill in the child a high degree of self-sufficiency, self-direction, and independence. One of Stevenson's earliest memories was of being advised by his father of the importance of learning to think on his own, and this message was repeated again and again. In 1883, when Stevenson was thirty-three, his mother consoled him on the premature death of a friend. She explained that this friend "was taken out of this world because he had not the strength to buffet with it." Fearing that her own child had but a short life expectancy, she sought to remind him that life was a struggle in which only the strong and self-reliant survived. Yet such calls for independence were balanced by efforts to maintain the child's dependence on the parents' approval and disapproval. There was no necessary contradiction between the goal of independence and the cultivation of intense psychological and emotional dependence within the home: for according to the Scottish moralists, Christian morality was rooted in the home and in respect for "the natural bonds and legitimate pleasures" of the family. One example might serve to illustrate the connection Stevenson's parents drew between Christian morality and the bonds of family. When Stevenson was twenty-seven years old, his mother chastised him for failing to keep his parents informed of his whereabouts. Even though he was an adult, she looked upon his behavior disparagingly and asked him whether "the 'clog called conscience' [has] fallen from you altogether?" For Mrs. Stevenson and her husband, independence, to be secure, needed to be balanced by continued dependence on the parents' opinions and sanctions.[34]

What we see throughout Stevenson's brief life is the repeated effort to prove to his parents his capacity for self-government and his inner, spiritual progress. From the time when he was twelve, and wrote a letter brimming with enthusiasm, exclaiming "I have done something! I have taken a great step!" he sought desperately to assert his independence. In letters written from the age of thirteen until well after his marriage, he reassured his parents that he was struggling to help support the family. Shortly after his father's death, he sent a brief note to his mother informing her that finally he could send her money. He expressed regret that his father had not lived to see the day when his son supported his wife. Young Stevenson's love was proven, his vocation vindicated, his loyalty confirmed.[35]

Stevenson's note can be read in two different ways. Although nominally the letter tells of a child who has proven his loyalty to the family, it also implicitly reveals a child who is claiming to have supplanted his father. In Stevenson's mind, adulthood and the role of breadwinner are equated, and in his letter the novelist celebrates the fact that he has finally assumed the role of the family's provider. To become a man, in his opinion, required a son to be financially independent, for no one had proved his manhood until he had demonstrated the capacity to support himself.

In defining adulthood in economic terms, the novelist's views were highly conventional, but with a crucial difference. Circumstances seemed to have conspired to make Stevenson incapable of achieving economic independence. Because of his physical frailty, he long feared that he would never be able to support himself, and he repeatedly called on God and Satan, the Unknowable and the Universum, to give him strength. "If I can only get my health back, by God!" he characteristically exclaimed to a friend, "I shall not be useless as I have been." Yet this goal of achieving economic success also led to enormous tensions and inner conflicts. It was a major paradox of Stevenson's life that he hungrily sought wealth and success and at the same time, felt that the climb for wealth and independence corrupts the self and corrodes domestic bonds.[36]

Toward the end of his life, Stevenson expressed deep misgivings about having become a writer. Certainly he had more than overcome his father's objection to art, that it was not a profitable activity. And his pursuit of art and literature had probably prolonged his life, since this permitted him the luxury of idleness, a remedy to illness "cheaper in the long run" than drugs. Yet he still wondered if his decision to write had not been too costly to his relationship with his parents.[37]

Stevenson's ambivalence about art reflects a more fundamental ambivalence toward wealth and success. After "Dr. Jekyll and Mr. Hyde" was published in 1886, Stevenson shared in a great financial boom for writers. He was offered $10,000 for a newspaper column in the *New York World,* while Scribner's paid $15,000 for a minor dramatic collaboration. Stevenson calculated that his royalties alone would return £1,000 a year. Yet despite frequent resolutions to banish all thought about money from his mind, Stevenson's correspondence reveals an almost obsessive preoccupation with finance and suggests how much he needed his income psychologically. As Stevenson's wife noted, the writer had a limited capacity to cope with financial dependency and desperately sought to achieve wealth and success—the symbols of professionalism and freedom from his father—at great risk to his health. Yet because of deep misgivings over the moral dangers of materialism, Stevenson felt great uneasiness over his quest for wealth. In his view, money bought freedom, but at the expense of higher moral values and the virtues of domesticity. "We are whores," was the way he described writers, ". . . whores of the mind, selling to the public the amusements of our fireside as the whore sells the pleasures of her bed."[38]

Stevenson's misgivings were not merely idiosyncratic; they were cultural. The commercialization of literature during the nineteenth century resulted in the accumulation of immense incomes from a supposedly nonproductive career, in contrast to a "productive" vocation such as engineering. Yet this affluence raised great tension for artists, who presumably wrote for their own pleasure, but who became responsible to a staggeringly large reading public. Many nineteenth-century authors had to face the fact that supposedly effete art paid.

In his uneasiness over the effects of success and wealth, Stevenson revealed one of the underlying sources of his religious conflict with his father. For Stevenson, the quest for moral independence and self-determination became intertwined with a quest for financial independence. His letters to his father are filled with metaphoric references to his financial dependence on his parents—the "sacrifices" his parents had made, the "obligations" he owes, the "debts" he has "accumulated." That Stevenson made conscious use of metaphors based on concepts of contract, implied obligations, and debt is a tangible expression of his conscious guilt and concern over his financial dependence on his parents. This use of language raises important questions of how economic life was accepted and integrated into, or denied and repressed from, conscious structures of meaning. In an emotional variant of laissez-faire, terms taken from the "productive" realm of business were increasingly applied, in the nineteenth century, to social relations. The use of terms such as "manipulation" or "debt," which originally had an economic connotation, may express a recognition of a relationship between financial dependence and social subordination that was otherwise evaded or negated because of guilt.

Stevenson in Perspective

From Charles Dickens's *Dombey and Son* through Samuel Butler's *The Way of All Flesh* and Edmund Gosse' *Father and Son,* one of the central concerns of Victorian fiction and autobiog-

raphy is with the problem of generational continuity and discontinuity. Confronted by the bewildering scientific and religious upheavals of the mid-nineteenth century, such writers as
Anthony Trollope, William Makepeace Thackeray, Dickens,
Eliot, Butler, and Gosse took as a central theme the way that
one generation adapted and reacted against the intellectual and
moral inheritance it received from its predecessors. It was in the
torturous relations between family members that the process of
moral and cultural change received its most poignant and an-
guished manifestation. In the feverish attempts of a son or
daughter to define a distinctive personal identity while maintaining continuities with the past, the process of social and cultural change was played out in microcosm.

One of the most striking characteristics of the pattern of conflict and revolt in Victorian fiction and autobiography is that
only rarely does filial rebellion result in a total break between
the generations. Family arguments were structured in such a
way as not to directly challenge paternal authority. Instead of
youthful rebellion breaking the bonds of family, filial revolt provided a ritualistic way for a child to demonstrate a capacity for
self-government while reaffirming loyalty to certain fundamental family values. At the same time, a parent could afford a child
a degree of moral independence while obtaining symbolic evidence of the child's internalized sense of duty. In this light, filial
rebellion can be understood as one of the patterns through which
cultural values were transmitted from one generation to the next.
The pattern of family conflict can be viewed as an instrument
for maintaining cultural continuity, while permitting important
modifications and adaptations.

In fiction, a major source of family strife was rooted in the
ambition of parents to ensure that children maintain certain
continuities with the past. Whether this took the form of a demand, sometimes unconscious, that a child pursue a hereditary
family vocation or retain certain traditional religious beliefs, even
the parents felt forced, in the end, to concede that the child's
decision had to be voluntary. In an increasingly democratic,
evangelical age, decision making had to rest on at least the ap-

pearance of voluntary consent. One of the processes we witness in Victorian fiction is the technique through which parents sought to obtain consent through the persuasive power of various forms of influence.

In the following pages, we will see that the pattern of filial revolt we witnessed in the Stevenson household was not simply individual or idiosyncratic. Although Stevenson's conflicts with his parents grew out of the personal needs of individual family members for loyalty and autonomy, these issues were not simply personal. In his conflict with his father, Stevenson debated on a religious plane the sanctioned limits of self-assertion. To people who held to a religious frame of reference, religion could become a testing ground on which a child could strive for independence without denying love for parents or belief in the sanctity of the home. Torn between an ideal of independence and self-government and an ideal of deference and dutiful obedience, individuals like Stevenson found that evangelical religion offered a set of ideals and symbols that helped to reconcile basic tensions surrounding the central cultural concerns of deference, self-discipline, and individual responsibility. In their debate over the limits of divine authority, the Stevensons were able to address other, related questions, such as how a parent might legitimately "influence" a child and how a child could transform childhood forms of dependency into adult relationships. That son and father selected religion as the key battleground was both because religion represented an arena free of base and selfish motives and because the father-child conflict embodied issues that were not merely personal or psychological but ultimately moral.

By comparing events in the Stevenson household with the experiences of three other Victorians who shared a Scottish and evangelical heritage, we can place the Stevensons' behavior into clearer perspective. In examining the domestic lives of Catharine Beecher, the sister of Harriet Beecher Stowe; Thomas Babington Macaulay, the eminent English historian; and Edmund Gosse, the noted English literary critic, we will see a series of variations on the father-child relationship first manifest in the

Stevenson family. Underlying the similarities in these house-holds is the Evangelical Revival of the late eighteenth and early nineteenth centuries, which represented a reaction against the eighteenth-century religion of decorum, gentility, optimism, and reassurance, and which defined moral life as a struggle to shape the character in the image of Christ. Stevenson, Beecher, Ma-caulay, and Gosse can serve as representations and expressions of Victorian middle-class culture at various points in time.

Like Stevenson, Beecher, Macaulay, and Gosse looked to their families as the focal points of their lives. Although they differed in their regard for their parents, all identified their fathers, not their mothers, as the central moral and disciplinary figures in their household, despite evidence of the mothers' influence. All but Macaulay remembered their fathers as playmates during their early childhoods, and in the historian's case, the father's behav-ior can be understood as a counterweight to the adulation of other adults. Yet all of the figures experienced emotionally in-tense domestic lives, isolated from neighboring households, in which their closest ties were with parents and siblings. All the children insisted that they were encouraged by their fathers to assume positions of family responsibility. And at the point of leaving home each child clashed with the father; and each, rather than simply breaking away from the family patriarch, made a series of accommodations with paternal authority.[39]

For Catharine Beecher, who would become an important American educator, lecturer, and writer on domestic economy, the central problem of her young adulthood was to establish a degree of autonomy within her family while under enormous pressure to marry. For her, the impulse to assert her indepen-dence and not marry was strong, especially when leaving home seemed to entail submission to another person's will. At this time in her life, she and her father came into conflict over an issue that did not directly challenge paternal authority—the question of whether she would undergo a conversion experi-ence—but that raised important issues involving deference, de-pendence, and discipline.[40]

When Catharine was twenty-one, in 1821, her father still treated her as a financially dependent minor, but he also urged her to assume the duties of her deceased mother and to go through a conversion experience. The elder Beecher's wish that his daughter undergo a religious conversion, as Kathryn Sklar has brilliantly shown, gave expression to another wish—that she would marry. If, for an earlier generation of reformers, benevolence offered a way of externalizing religious tensions, for the Beechers religion offered a stage on which to act out family conflicts. At issue in the religious controversy were the amount of guilt Lyman Beecher's daughter felt for her sins and the degree of commitment she felt to God. By emphasizing obedience and loyalty, instead of faith, Beecher betrayed his foremost desire, that his daughter obey his will. Ultimately, the only way he could test his daughter's subjective feelings was to examine her character for its loyalty, devotion, and piety.[41]

In her response to her father's arguments, Beecher revealed the actual issues at stake. Like Stevenson, she drew upon a conception of the home as the chief source of her happiness and of her father as a vital part of her home life. But unlike Stevenson, she could admit sinful self-regard and argue that selfishness had been implanted within her involuntarily. When social interactions were framed in terms of self-sacrifice and self-denial, then her father might be obligated to give in to her wishes.[42]

It is important for understanding the meaning of Beecher's personal struggle with her father over religious conversion to recognize that this conflict absorbed a whole range of related issues. Beecher's girlhood struggle over whether she was capable of undergoing a religious conversion was closely tied to another, equally fundamental problem: working out her relationship to the moral and intellectual heritage that was symbolized and transmitted by her father. The tragic death of her fiancé in a shipwreck months after she had refused to undergo religious conversion crystallized her objections to her father's Calvinist religious doctrines. She felt unable to believe that individuals were inherently depraved, and she came more and more to believe that their fate depended on their childhood environment. An equally important issue for Beecher was to find a female vocation that was the equivalent to the role of minister assumed by her father and seven brothers. Her father, responding to the declining status and prestige of the New England clergy, had warned that unless America's western frontier was rapidly Christianized, its population would become a "poor, uneducated reckless mass of infuriated animalism." Beecher seized on this message and argued that women, in their roles as mothers, teachers, and writers, were responsible for ensuring the stability of democratic institutions by shaping the moral character of the American people.[43]

When Thomas Macaulay, the future historian, returned home from Cambridge in 1822 at the age of twenty-two, having failed a graduation examination, his father expressed the family's disappointment. Giving added weight to the family's unhappiness was the assumption that the child was responsibile for carrying on the family's evangelical traditions. The son of a transplanted Scot, the grandson and great-grandson of Scottish Presbyterian ministers, Macaulay was taught to see himself as the bearer of his family's religious values. From his early years, the family had looked to Macaulay to continue the abolitionist crusade. Thus, when Macaulay had earlier begged to be allowed to return home from school, his father reminded him that Christ had left his Father for thirty years but faced his troubles cheerfully. If the child was to help bring the family's reform efforts to a successful conclusion, he had to learn self-reliance and independence.[44]

From his mother and sisters, however, Macaulay learned a slightly different ideal. As his father confided to a close family friend, the son's real passion was his love of domesticity. The extent of Macaulay's reliance upon the affections of his family gave added pain to his academic failure. Macaulay was driven almost to breakdown by his father's criticism of his failure on the examination. As Macaulay's biographer John Clive has shown, the son's reaction was largely repressed but was apparent in his slovenly habits and appearance. Only once was there a political altercation between son and father. Religious tensions were apparent in the son's refusal to participate in a Bible Society and in his avoidance of church services. Ultimately, it was Macaulay's connection with a Cambridge periodical that his father deemed immoral that proved to be a testing ground. Macaulay eventually submitted to his father's will but explained that his dissociation from the magazine was due entirely to his father's religious scruples. Clive has shown how, in later years, Macaulay sought to diminish the significance of political and economic controversies by reducing them to matters of impersonal moral and social circumstances. In much the same way, he reduced familial discord to an impersonal question of religion.[45]

Like Stevenson, Macaulay sought to prove his loyalty to his father through self-administered tests of character. It was the issue of antislavery that allowed Macaulay to symbolically illustrate his strength of character and his capacity for self-sacrifice. As a member of Parliament he spoke out against his own party partly as a way of pleasing his father on the issue of antislavery. Antislavery provided the young man with a way of proving his filial loyalty and his allegiance to the family's ideals.

Despite tension between father and son, the family strove to maintain a sense of intimacy. Much as Stevenson's mother tried to dissuade her husband from pursuing the religious dispute with their son, Macaulay's mother tried to convince her husband to reestablish close ties with their child. At the same time, Macaulary formed extremely close ties with two younger sisters, which apparently allowed him to feel that he had partially assumed the role of father in his own family. In his eyes, Clive writes, the attachment to the sisters was a counterbalance to life's competitiveness and a justification for Macaulay's strides toward fame. When the two sisters married, he wrote before their weddings, that he would have nothing left but ambition. Family ties offered both an antidote for, and justification of, public ambitions.[46]

As Clive has pointed out, other nineteenth-century figures, including Thomas De Quincy, Benjamin Disraeli, Charles Lamb, Harriet Martineau, Samuel Rogers, and William Wordsworth developed extremely close attachments to brothers and sisters. As Clive explains, when moral factors militated against sexual

experience and economic considerations discouraged early marriage, intense emotions might be directed into the home. And
yet, it should be observed, the ideal of marriage was also strong,
and for Macaulay's two sisters it offered the only way to achieve
independence from their parents and brother. Macaulay may
have described his relationship with his sisters in terms of mutual affection, but it seems clear in retrospect that he strove desperately to create the sense that he was the focal point of their
emotional lives. His struggle for his sisters' affection can be
properly appreciated only when it is seen as part of a broader
family conflict: of a son attempting to assert a degree of self-
determination while remaining faithful to the family's traditions.[47]

In 1907, Henry Adams completed his great biography, *The
Education,* the most profound retrospective summary of what
happened to Catharine Beecher's "educator" world. The same
year, Edmund Gosse, an eminent English literary critic, anonymously published his own autobiography entitled *Father and
Son.* Like Adams, Gosse looked at his life as a metaphor of the
experience of his generation, and in the relationship between a
son and a father he saw embodied the major religious and ethical conflicts of the age. Both Adams and Gosse were left with
a sense of shattered expectations; both were left with a sense of
tragedy regarding what the Englishman called the departure of
a dying Puritanism. Both men had a sense of standing between
two epochs and of being unable to believe the creative fictions
that might give their lives meaning.

To Adams, this sense of uprootedness was symbolized by the
declining status of his family: the strong grandfather succeeded
by the ineffectual father. To Gosse, this sense of upheaval was
symbolized by the conflict between a father and a child. For
Gosse, as for William James, the roots of the personal family
conflict lay in the child's need to preserve his "inward will." For
his father, a geologist who feverishly sought to defend the
teachings of Genesis against Darwin, the child's opposition to a
parent represented an attack upon all authority. By dwelling
upon the anger of the Lord, and not his pity and love, the son

thought that his father had identified himself with the Almighty. And giving added pain to the religious arguments between Gosse and his father was the knowledge that he, like Macaulay, had been dedicated by his parents to the service of the family.[48]

Although Gosse was largely unaffected by the Scottish common sense philosophy, his family situation differed little from that of the other persons we have discussed. The son of a minister of the Plymouth Brotherhood, Gosse shared the others' experience with a religion that stressed the ideals of piety, individual responsibility, and filial loyalty. Even more important was the high burden of family expectation that was placed upon these people, for this sense of high expectancy gave an awesome significance to their actions. Finally, Gosse shared an acute sense of being cut off from the outside world, a sense of marginality that increased his desire to prove himself on a larger social stage. For people such as these, the most important question was whether adulthood independence could be obtained without breaking the bonds of family. In each case, a personal struggle with the father became a testing ground for the child's capacity for independence.

Dimly, Gosse perceived that behind his father stood his mother's will, even after her death. When the dissension occurred, he acknowledged that it was not from one but from both parents that he was separated. What his observations suggest is that in a household where the child's closest tie was with the mother—the same situation facing Robert Louis Stevenson, who was also an only child—identification of the father as the major antagonist might serve as a way to maintain intimacy with the parent who symbolized the home. Gosse' only regret was that as a child his parents had not wrapped him in the folds of supernatural fancy, so that his mind might have been longer content to follow their traditions in an unquestioning spirit. Like Stevenson and Macaulay he remembered that his childhood play had been mixed with the practice of religion. And he also recalled that this had led his first act of disobedience to be directed against religion.[49]

Of his parents and their beliefs, Gosse wrote that "they were quite unfitted to struggle with the world," and his words bore the mark of Spencer. But Gosse later insisted that the only liberation he sought was not from religion but from his father. Precisely what he objected to in his father, he was not sure. Yet the dilemma seemed clear; if he was to preserve his inner will against the pressure of his father, he had to rebel against his father's religious faith. "Either he must cease to think for himself," Gosse wrote, "or his individualism must be instantly confirmed, and the necessity of religious independence must be emphasized." In the end, he admitted that his spirits were divided "between the wish to stay on, a guarded child, and to proceed into the world, a budding man," but his religious faith had been irretrivably lost. His only satisfaction was that father and son were able to obey the higher law that says that family loyalties must be honored and sustained.[50]

Generational Continuity

In this section we will see that the pattern of generational conflict between a father and a child was not incompatible with a high degree of generational continuity. A child might rebel against a father over fundamental issues of religious authority and yet subsequently be preoccupied with the same concerns: authority, self-discipline, and continuity. The explanation for this pattern is that in the middle-class Victorian home filial rebellion provided a crucial instrument for transmitting cultural values from one generation to the next. For it was during the intense personal conflict between a child and parent that social roles and values were defined, struggled with, assimilated, and invested with larger associations of religious duty and obligation. Revolt against a father, which was in certain respects a substitute for earlier patterns of religious conversion, was an important vehicle of cultural continuity, symbolizing acceptance of Christian morality and a capacity for self-control.[51]

The paradox that has been suggested—that filial rebellion was a mechanism of generational continuity—is vividly illustrated in

Stevenson's life. Despite heated arguments with his father, Stevenson developed a conception of the father's role that was virtually identical to his parents'. Like his own father, Stevenson regarded the father's responsibilities in almost religious terms: to teach a child that the Christian life is a life of struggle, to overcome sinful desires, and to develop a capacity for responsible self-government. Because the younger Stevenson also shared his father's contradictory concern with the cultivation of deference and respect for authority and the encouragement of self-reliance and initiative, he also tended to vacillate between the ideals of dutiful submission and independence in the rearing of his own son.

In the spring of 1880, when he was twenty-nine, Stevenson married Fanny Osbourne, an American divorcée ten years his senior. Because his bride had two children from her previous marriage—a daughter who was twenty-one and a son who was twelve—Stevenson was suddenly thrust into the role of father. For Stevenson, the prospect of becoming a father had long been a source of great anxiety. Although he admitted a deep longing for children, he had informed a friend that he did not think he could bear the "pain" entailed in having them. Stevenson acknowledged that his fears were those of a woman, not a man's. At the same time, he confessed a "shuddering revulsion of the necessary responsibilities of life," and his uneasiness suggests the heavy ideological responsibilities with which the role of father was invested.[52]

Yet in the same breath that Stevenson articulated his fears of becoming a father, he also gave voice to a strong impulse to financially support his parents and to found his own family. When he finally succeeded in financially assisting his mother, he wished that his father could have lived to see this moment. He admitted that his regret sprang from a "mean reason": to vindicate his choice of profession. That his motive might have been even "meaner," to make his father financially dependent upon him, he did not acknowledge. But as this example suggests, family loyalties served as an important psychological justification for the emotional investment Stevenson placed in his literary work. In a letter to his mother, he proposed supplementing

his fiction and poetry with writing for the theater, which he
declared was a gold mine. His motive, he insisted, was not
wealth; rather, he simply intended to rescue the family from the
one thing his father could not bear, scrimped money. In Stevenson's view, the paternal role was largely a role of economic
provider, and this association helps to account for his shouts of
triumph when he finally succeeded in supporting his own family.[53]

In retrospect, we can see the ways that Stevenson's marriage
to a divorcée eased his exit from his parents' home and his transition into a paternal identity. His departure from his parents'
home was justified as a means of aiding people even more dependent than himself. When Stevenson decided to follow Fanny
Osbourne to California in August 1879, to his parents' shock
and dismay, he responded by emphasizing his self-discipline and
capacity for self-sacrifice. Such restraint appeared in the most
compromising circumstances. After leaving family and friends in
pursuit of his future wife, he and Fanny Osbourne lived on
opposite sides of San Francisco Bay. From his relatives in Scotland he received words of criticism concerning his trip to America, but in response he noted his self-discipline.[54]

Neither love nor sex was responsible for his exertions. He
sought no favor for his endeavors, he insisted, only the satisfaction that came from being able "to protect" a dear one. He
prayed that God might keep him "brave and singleminded" in
his efforts to assist his friend. When he first met his future wife
in France, he wrote of having two invalids to care for instead
of one, and he used the same argument in California to demonstrate his selflessness. A friend commented that Stevenson "has
acted and gushed and excited himself . . . into the heroic spirit,"
and there can be no doubt that by appealing to the ideal to
chivalry the young novelist sought to win approval for his endeavors. With his parents he used another argument. He told
his mother and father that if they could love his future wife, he
could love them better.[55]

Even after his marriage, Stevenson sought to display his selflessness. William Dean Howells, the novelist, had attacked the

propriety of men who not only had mistresses but stooped to marry them, and Stevenson chose this occasion as an opportunity to justify his own behavior. In a letter to Howells, Stevenson attacked the editor of the *Atlantic Monthly* for casting aspersions on the motives for a man's marriage. Personally, he was honored that his wife had chosen to divorce her husband in order to marry him. But, he added, "according as your heart is," each would decide this matter. In his argument that emotional relationships were matters strictly of the heart and his assertion that his marriage was a product entirely of his wife's needs and desires, Stevenson was able to deny personal responsibility for his marriage.[56]

In rearing Fanny Osbourne's twelve-year-old son, Stevenson exhibited virtually the same concerns that his father had shown. Having become a father, he stressed the same contradictory themes his own father had emphasized: the importance of filial deference and respect for parental authority and strength of character and independence. This ambivalence was not merely idiosyncratic. According to an emerging consensus, social order and harmony depended on the voluntary acceptance of internalized self-restraints and limits, which would compensate for the weakness of other social and religious authorities. And the main burden of responsibility for ensuring such voluntary acceptance fell upon the father.

Immediately after his marriage, Stevenson wrote a letter to his parents asking for the name of a respectable Swiss boarding school. The novelist explained his request this way: to illustrate his disapproval of laziness and passive dependency on his stepson's part, he threatened to use the boarding school as punishment. Ten years later when the child, Lloyd Osbourne, declined to enter college, Stevenson vocally objected to his stepson's hesitations. In his words, his primary responsibility as a father was to equip his child "for his own battle after I am gone." If he were to ensure that his child would have the moral and physical character to be able to stand on his own two feet after his parents' deaths, then a father had to force a son to develop these qualities.[57]

Yet at the same time that Stevenson sought to instill a capacity for independence and self-control in his son, he also sought desperately to cultivate a high degree of emotional loyalty and dependency. When, in 1885, the stepson proposed to visit his real father, the Stevensons' reaction was immediate and harsh: if the child made the visit, they "shall be done with him forever." All claims upon education and future assistance would be lost. Even though Stevenson had once objected to his own father's attempt to employ financial coercions on him, now he and his wife pointed to the facts that they had educated young Lloyd, had given him a home and provided for his future as reasons why the boy needed to demonstrate his loyalty. Later, Stevenson's wife noted that her son now depended on the novelist for all his wants and then characterized this as the truest sign of affection. Her words revealed how financial dependency had become a critical symbol of family loyalty.[58]

We have already seen the way that certain symbolic modes of behavior helped to conceal and accommodate fundamental conflicts in Victorian values. By identifying certain forms of behavior as examples of self-denial and self-sacrifice, middle-class Victorians were able to reconcile inconsistencies in values, between an insistence on deference and submission to authority, on the one hand, and a stress on individual responsibility and voluntarism, on the other. Lloyd Osbourne, like Stevenson before him, made skillful use of such symbols. When the Stevenson correspondence was being collected, Osbourne demanded that reference be made to the fact that his stepfather had demanded that he sacrifice personal ambitions for a career and remain at his side. Although the stepson had been offered positions as an official on a government commission and in a publishing house, he remained faithful to his stepfather's wish. With this act of self-denial, Osbourne continued, he had sacrificed his immediate desires for the sake of his stepfather and family.[59]

What we have witnessed is a peculiarly Victorian conception of social relations, in which contradictory values and impulses are concealed or reconciled by various symbols of self-denial and internalized discipline. Torn between an ideal of dutiful obedience and a goal of voluntarism, an insistence on self-denial provided a way to ensure authority and obedience while preserving individual responsibility. That the language of social relations emphasized such terms as "sacrifice," "duty," "debt," and "obligation"—terms that carried associations with the realm of economics—was not accidental. Such terms at once revealed a desire to place social relations on a more moral basis than hierarchy and prescription and an awareness of the complex and convoluted relationship between social relations and economic obligations.

The problems confronted by the Stevenson family were not merely idiosyncratic; they were historical problems, the problems of a particular era, culture, and class. The family's experiences were not simply the way that one talented and troubled young man and his parents attempted to get along with one another. The fundamental dynamics of the Stevenson family manifest themselves in similar but not identical forms in other families that were also concerned about the decline of deference, the social consequences of individualism, and the weakness of religious and social authorities that could reinforce social order. It is only within this context that we can understand the paternal concern with self-discipline and self-denial. Fearing both the anarchistic tendencies of individualism and older forms of authority, Victorians of diverse backgrounds looked to individual self-control and self-discipline as the only secure basis for social harmony and advancement. Only by realizing that family conflicts within the middle-class Victorian home involved not only personal or psychological issues but fundamental social and moral issues—involving the struggle to instill self-restraints, to compensate for the weakness of religious establishments and hallowed traditions—can we fully appreciate the awesome symbolic significance attached to the personal struggle between father and child. For when a child's future seemed to depend not on his parents or family but on his capacity to support himself, then it was the father's highest responsibility to ensure that he had developed a capacity for self-government.

CHAPTER 6

Love and Marriage

I N 1882, when he was thirty-two and newly married, Robert Louis Stevenson was asked by a young admirer to define the essential characteristics of love. In reply, Stevenson described love as the very antithesis of man's workaday relationships. Stevenson glorified love as life's highest experience, through which a man's spirit was strengthened, his faith sustained, and his aspirations directed away from that which is base, false, and superficial toward a higher ideal. Love, he said, is what gives meaning to life, eradicates feelings of loneliness and isolation, and provides people with a model of selflessness. In a civilization made mechanical by positivistic science and the relentless impact of manufacturing, love was an almost mystical experience, a form of intuition that could be understood only subjectively, apart from the rules of logic. In a world characterized by selfish greed and mean self-seeking, the love of a woman was a source of altruistic emotions and consolation that could be found nowhere else.[1]

Stevenson proceeded to warn his young friend that in actuality love, too, often failed to achieve this high ideal. In a world in which the highest goal of life was respectability or monetary success, love itself was tainted by the commercial spirit. As mean acquisitiveness and narrow selfishness dominated the public sphere, the quest for power and possession intruded into the intimacies of love. Under these circumstances, Stevenson de-

clared that the whore was less selfish than the lover. In a world
in which men had lowered their aims to a merely material level,
"the brothel is a more ennobling spot" than the *"amourette"* or
marriage.[2]

No one can read Stevenson's words without being struck by
the way love is symbolically connected with a wide range of
seemingly unrelated issues. Love is glorified here as an answer
to mechanistic conceptions of science that conceived of man as
being in the grip of natural and social forces that "predestined"
his actions, to religious doubts and fears of meaninglessness, to
the competitive and commercial spirit that threatened to reduce
life to "rank conformity." What is interesting about this conception of love is the way it addressed, and attempted to answer,
some of the deepest problems and needs of the time: the desire
to find concrete analogues to abstract religious beliefs; the longing for inspiration and symbols of ideal fulfillment; the quest
for moral certainty, which could be found in the heart but not
in the head. One result of the evangelical revivals of the late
eighteenth and early nineteenth centuries was to reinvigorate
the search for symbols and values that could dramatize religious
beliefs and aspirations. And no idea was more central to evangelicalism than love: it was through an experience of Christ's
saving love that the soul was instantaneously transformed, that
men achieved release from their guilt and sins, and that men's
souls found consolation and ultimately redemption.[3]

To examine Victorian feelings about love and marriage is to
see how abstract ideals and values taken from evangelical religion were used as a symbolic language to articulate broader
hopes and fears—personal and cultural—and how love helped
to give concreteness and confirmation to religious needs and
aspirations. The experience of three figures—Robert Louis Stevenson, George Eliot, and Harriet Beecher Stowe—will illuminate the needs and problems to which love was an answer. From
Stevenson we will learn about the anxieties that the ideal of
romantic love was designed to counteract. From Eliot we will
gain insight into the deeply ambivalent way a middle-class Victorian woman might anticipate marriage. From Stowe we will

gain an understanding of the symbols and sanctions that a woman might invoke to increase her independence and authority within marriage. A theme that emerges from examination of all three figures is the contradictory nature of marriage, being both contractual and sacramental. Throughout this chapter, a special effort will be made to place these cultural themes in the context of the new understanding that is emerging from social history. As we proceed, emphasis will be placed on the similarities in the influences shaping these figures' ideas about love and marriage: anxieties about independence, dependency needs, spiritual qualms, and acute feelings of weakness and personal isolation. To stress the similarities and not the differences in how men and women perceive marriage is, of course, not to suggest that there might not be some differences in perception; however, exploration of this topic is left for another time.[4]

Our inquiry begins by examining love letters written by Stevenson in 1873, when he was twenty-three, to his first serious romantic attachment, Frances Sitwell. Before turning to a detailed analysis of these letters, it is necessary to consider the circumstances in which they were written. Sent at the time that Stevenson had first begun to quarrel with his father about religion, these letters reveal how the Victorian cult of love furnished a vocabulary to address critical moral and intellectual problems—problems of religious doubt, concerns about the consequences of individualism, and fears of impotence and weakness. At the time of the correspondence, Frances Sitwell was married but estranged from her husband. Stevenson lived at home during the course of most of his relationship with Mrs. Sitwell, and his behavior was almost embarrassingly proper. Her letters were discreetly addressed to him at his men's club, where they were collected from a porter. If letters were to be shown to others, he was informed beforehand. Throughout the affair, Stevenson maintained the posture of a young man immune to such frivolous attractions.[5]

That the Victorian exaltation of love was designed to answer some of the deepest moral and intellectual problems of the era is graphically evident in Stevenson's love letters. There are two

major themes in Stevenson's references to love. Abnegation of
self represented one pole of his definition of the emotion. In
Stevenson's references to love there is a recurrent theme that
while jealousy, hate, selfish greed, and acquisitiveness are the
dominant characteristics of daily life, these vices are incompatible with true love, as devotion to an object of esteem dissolves
man's essential egotism and as reverence to a loved one disciplines the masculine drive for self-gratification. In Stevenson's
view, a man's soul can be drowned by immersion in egotism
and self-seeking, or it can achieve transcendence, depending on
whether he finds a true love object. In his own life, he knew
that his character was in constant danger of descending to the
depths of pride and conceit and that without love's saving power
his higher aspirations would be crushed. Thus, he felt impelled
to repeat constantly "how necessary" Frances Sitwell's "friendship is to me and how very vain a show I should be without
it." The conclusion was immediately evident: without love and
the guardianship of a woman, Stevenson lacked the strength
and willpower to resist the forces of temptation that wrestled
for control of his soul.[6]

The other pole of Stevenson's conception of love was a longing for intimacy and intensity of feeling. In his love letters Stevenson describes the great problem of the age to be the need to
maintain a sense of vitality and optimism in a world in which
science has divided man into elemental clay and a lifeless soul.
In response to the contention that man was but a mechanism,
dull and cold, only half-awakened to the impulses of the soul,
Stevenson responded by exalting in the flesh: "it is this matter
that thinks and thrills and is shaken all through with delicate
sympathies," he declared. In a world in which the human soul
seemed to be lost amid impersonal social and physical forces,
vivid sensuous experience provided a way of reaffirming the primacy of individual feelings.[7]

Burdened with an intense sense of personal weakness, Stevenson looked to love as a source of strength, certainty, and security. Through love, according to Stevenson, a man could escape
from a heartless, disapprobatory world. It is significant that when

Stevenson explained his need for love he said what he needed "was something to fall back on a little," and he beseeched Frances Sitwell not to "join all the world in thinking me an unfeeling and hard hearted dog." In a reaction against the cold, impersonal, competitiveness of public life, Stevenson expressed deep longing for a strong feminine will he could submerge himself under. In short, he wrote, "what I want is a mother." Even though his desire was to hug and kiss and be caressed, he did not find the comparison inappropriate. For, he added, "I think it must be what ought to be felt for a mother."[8]

That Stevenson defined his need for love in terms of his longing for a mother was partially a result of personal circumstances. He wrote his letters to Frances Sitwell at a time when his relations with his parents were deeply strained, a situation that magnified his sense of personal loneliness and isolation and left him, in his words, "crying out in want of a mother." The fact that he longed for a mother, the figure representing the warmth and security of his boyhood home, was in part an expression of a deep personal fear that his father would engross his own mother, a fear he conveyed to Mrs. Sitwell. In the dependency-encouraging context of the middle-class Victorian home, the loss of the affection of the mother was equated with abandonment by the family, and Stevenson expressed acute anxieties about being "deserted" by his parents. In response, he asked Mrs. Sitwell to replace his mother, and he promised to be her son.[9]

Although Stevenson's definition of love in terms of a child's dependence on a mother was partly a product of individual circumstances, this conception of love also reflected a broader Victorian context. As Victorian culture developed during the nineteenth century, it established competition, achievement, strength, and self-reliance as its highest forms of masculine goals. Problems of dependency became more intense for men who were denied acceptable public outlets for emotional dependency. Forced to deny any needs for love, solace, or consolation in public, such needs were directed inward, in love relationships, in which a man became dependent on a woman's care, help, and support. Yet rather than expressing these dependency needs directly, Stevenson expressed his emotional needs indirectly through a vocabulary that owed a heavy debt to evangelical religion. The love of a woman, for Stevenson, was in important respects analogous to love of God. Here his vocabulary is instructive: after emphasizing his personal weakness and his profound personal needs, he proceeds to explain his total dependence on Mrs. Sitwell for support and his willingness to put his fate into her hands. His attitude toward her is an attitude of "devotion," "reverence," and "worship"; his desire was for fusion, for total love and "communion." Stevenson at times appears to be quite conscious of the connection between his feelings for Mrs. Sitwell, man's adoration of God, and the experience of Christ's saving love. In his words, he was a drowning man who clung desperately to Mrs. Sitwell for support. Only her selfless sacrifice could rescue him. In repayment, he pledged his love and ceaseless devotion. "You must help me," he implored, "and I must live to do honour to your help." In return, he would be her "son," her "faithful friend," her "priest." [10]

If we look closely at Stevenson's love letters, we are soon struck by the way Mrs. Sitwell's virtues are exalted as compensation for his personal defects. Her moral idealism counteracts his ravenous ambition; her capacity for self-sacrifice corrects for his vulgar egotism; her moral purity compensates for his weakness. Idealizing her virtues was a way of indicating that his vices and flaws were inconsequential. This attitude, which glorifies women as the moral supports and guides of men, recurs again and again in Stevenson's love letters and contributes to an image of men as not wholly responsible for their actions. Stevenson expressed this attiude precisely when he wrote that "all that you feel for me . . . is so much better than I feel myself to be that I begin to loathe myself as an imposture." Nor was Mrs. Sitwell's love important only as a source of moral strength. Stevenson proceeded to explain that her love was important for yet another reason; it gave him the strength to resist dependency upon other people, in particular, from his parents. Her love showed that only a "fictitious and imprisoning thread" bound him to his parents, and that "ours are the nations that can shut our eyes to the tatters of slavery."[11]

As we look closely at Stevenson's conception of love, we can see the ways in which it gave expression to central religious attitudes of the time. In his emphasis on self-renunciation as the defining characteristic of love, Stevenson accented the same aspect of love that was stressed in evangelical religion. In his love letters he laid special emphasis on the notion that his love was voluntary and unconditional and that he freely placed his fate in her hands. Even as he and Mrs. Sitwell were parting, he reaffirmed his willingness to accept rejection: "I will still be your son, dear," he wrote, "if you will be my mother, or rather whether you will or not." Stevenson gladly welcomed the sufferings he would have to undergo as a result of his passion, for they promised to inspire and ennoble him. When the standard of love is placed so high, then anything less would be useless in laying the foundation for self-control and teaching him to resist temptation: "I am afraid," he observed, "had I been more fortunate, you would have been less useful, and so, on the whole, the sum of help would have been diminished."[12]

This attitude, with its idealization of the role of a woman in the spiritual elevation of the man who adores her, is obviously indebted to the tradition of courtly love. Nevertheless, Stevenson's conception of love is not simply chivalric, nor is it platonic; it is Victorian. Stevenson's conception of love was closely related to Victorian concerns with self-discipline, willpower, and moral idealism, concerns that are sharply delineated in his references to sex.

Since the 1920s it has often been said that Stevenson was a "Victorian rebel" who violated Victorian mores about sex. What gave substance to this label were the facts that twice Stevenson was romantically involved with married women and that he openly criticized Christianity for failing to recognize and hallow sex. Yet this characterization has made it difficult to account for the lack of public outrage over Stevenson's affairs or his reluctance to deal with romantic conflict, indeed with women at all, in the bulk of his fiction. It should be stressed that Stevenson's behavior can be interpreted innocuously. His two romances were with women estranged from their husbands. During a period preceding his marriage, when he and his wife were living in the same city, Stevenson persuaded his father to visit him in order to assure him that the couple's living arrangements were acceptable. And he prefaced his remarks about Christianity and sex by asserting that he should have been more restrained during his youth and shown more respect toward women. The fact is that for all his conviction that sex ought to be portrayed as a natural part of life, Stevenson was curiously unable, even in letters, to describe sexual attraction convincingly.[13]

Only when one recognizes that sex carried disconcerting associations with exclusiveness and jealousy, aggressiveness and appetite, can we understand Stevenson's reluctance to deal explicitly with sex, even in his love letters. While glorifying the beauty of romantic love, Stevenson struggled at length to distinguish love from lust. Love is explicitly identified with the realm of the spirit; it is free from any moral blemishes. The impulses associated with the flesh and with sex, on the other hand, are among the basest and most degrading. The emotions aroused by lust were the most degrading in the evangelical catalogue: temptation, an inability to check the desires of the will, and a loss of self-control. Because of these associations, Stevenson was reluctant to deal with sex.

But obliquely, he did touch on sexual matters. After viewing the Elgin Marbles, the statues of the Greek Fates located in the British Museum, Stevenson related his feelings about sex by contrasting the Greek ideal, which he thought lay in physical passion, with its "modern" counterpart, spirituality. By placing the two ideals of sex in opposition, he was able to increase the distance between himself and the subject matter; yet he wavered precariously between the two ideals. He admitted the attraction of the Greek ideal of purely physical love: "Think dear," he wrote to Mrs. Sitwell, "if one could love a woman like that once, see her grow pale with passion and once wring your lips out upon

hers would it not be a small thing to die." But Stevenson betrayed his uneasiness by immediately qualifying this admission
by juxtaposing the Victorian ideal of ideal sentiments: "Not that
there is not a passion of quite another sort, much less epic, far
more dramatic and intimate, that comes out of the very frailty
of perishable women. . . . This is another thing, and perhaps
it is a higher." By shifting the meaning of words, Stevenson was
able to create a degree of distance between the two ideals of
love. Whereas his first reference to "passion" is to intense physical emotion (though the subject grows pale and is turned into
a statue), his second reference is to passion of a religious character, of the love that arises "out of the lines of suffering . . .
out of the thin hands wrought and tempered in [the] agony" of
Victorian women. By juxtaposing images that are usually bonded
together—in this case, physical passion and intimacy—Stevenson created psychological distance between the two ideals. But
Stevenson's feeling toward the two types of love was ambiguous; the fact that the Victorian ideal is only "perhaps a higher"
one is a token of his ambivalence. In each case, curiously, the
outcome of love is death; either the death that arises out of
passion and lust or the death that arises out of frailty and weakness. Where the man is obliterated in a torrent of ungovernable
emotions, the woman dies a slower death, which is more poignant because her sensitivity is "tempered in agony to a fineness
of perception." [14]

In his next letter Stevenson took some pains to establish his
distance from the Greek ideal. The Greek women offer no
temptation, he said, because "they are of another race, immor-
tal, separate." To read Stevenson's letter is to sense his discom-
fort with the feelings aroused by sex. "We do not desire to see
their great eyes troubled with our passions," he wrote, explaining that conscience had to restrain masculine emotions. Stevenson was torn between two conceptions of love. Attracted to
both ideals, he rejected the love characterized by passion and
lust for the supposedly higher love of selflessness, reverence, and
veneration. Sex did not flaw the higher love; passion was trans-

muted into a religious sense of suffering and sacrifice. Love is here exalted as a spiritual experience, a form of uplift, through which a man overcame shame, guilt, and temptation.[15]

Elevating love onto a religious plane offered a way of dissociating the emotion from man's baser impulses. Yet the exaltation of love as something essentially spiritual echoes the centrality of religion as the defined area of conflict within a family. In both cases, religion provided a symbolic language and a testing ground for central cultural tensions involving individuality, dependence, independence, and self-discipline. In his love letters, Stevenson refers to Mrs. Sitwell as his mother, his Madonna, and his Consuelo, and asks that he be her priest. With these words, he seeks to attach a religious aura to their relationship and therefore to avoid associations with lust and sensuality. This was also a way of heightening the sense of intimacy; to speak of love in religious terms was "a statement of sympathy, a sense that some one else knows and thinks with one in their sorrows." But, in addition to intensifying a sense of emotional intimacy, religious imagery also conveyed a sense of sexual intimacy, something Stevenson felt incapable of expressing directly. In broaching his need for consolation, Stevenson came perilously close to sexual explicitness: "I cling to you Madonna, my mother; think of how you must be to me throughout life the mother's breasts to suckle me." But Stevenson never pressed the imagery further. Thus, religion appears to be used as a sanction to legitimate demands that can be justified in no other ways. Because Stevenson's relationship with Mrs. Sitwell was framed in religious terms of duty and obligation, it validated Stevenson's demands for love and consolation. When Stevenson asked for Mrs. Sitwell's affection, he was able to attach a note of piety to his request that made refusal inconceivable: "I am yours and you have a duty to me," was the way he made the point. "And I will demand from you sympathy & comprehension & forgiveness."[16]

As Stevenson's letters illustrate, love is not only a psychological subject; it is also an historical topic. During the nineteenth century, ideas about romantic love were deeply colored by evangelical notions of divine love, and the vocabulary used to describe the emotion of love gives some sense of the way the emotion was likened to religious sentiment. To study Victorian conceptions of love is to see how the grave religious, moral, and intellectual problems of an era can be absorbed by the most private and intimate of feelings. In an age that felt great apprehension about the baser manifestations of individualism—such as sensuality, jealousy, and acquisitiveness—to sacramentalize love and view it as pure and holy was to demonstrate the capacity of men for higher moral feeling. In an age haunted by materialistic scientific doctrines that regarded man as nothing but an engine of egotism, love proved his capacity for subjective feeling. In an era seeking desperately to avoid doubt and fears of meaninglessness, love showed that man was not solely a slave of the passions but had a capacity for a higher moral life.

When George Eliot was twenty, she felt an intense sense of despair. Her brother was considering marriage, and she stared gloomily at the prospect of "being an unoccupied damsel, of . . . being severed from all the ties that have hitherto given my existence the semblance of usefulness beyond that of making up the requisite quantum of animal matter in the universe." What made her sense of despair so acute was her troubling suspicion that she would never have her hand taken in marriage. "Every day's experience," she recorded, "seems to deepen the voice of foreboding that has long been telling me, 'The bliss of reciprocated affection is not allotted to you under any form.'" In her words we hear her conscious efforts to achieve that state of resignation that had been held up before her as an ideal by an evangelical schoolteacher. For unless her heart was "widowed in this manner from the world," she would "never seek a better portion; a consciousness of possessing the fervent love of any human being would soon become" her "heaven," and therefore would be her "curse." [17]

No one can read Eliot's girlhood letters without being struck by the mixture of hopes and fears that were all part of her vision of marriage. Although a daughter of a member of the Church of England, Eliot was profoundly influenced by the evangelical ideals of holiness and asceticism and was deeply troubled by the temptations to worldliness and personal gratification that she associated with marriage. When she heard of weddings, she tells us, she could "only sigh," for marriage partners were simply "multiplying earthly ties which are powerful enough to detach . . . heart and thoughts from heaven." Another source of concern about marriage lay in a fear that most personal bonds between people "are so brittle as to be liable to be snapped asunder at every breeze." Only a person who had overcome the forces of worldliness in his or her own soul could safely marry, and she could not consider herself one of the elect. Feeling that her own inner nature was "not pure, not chastened," she was firmly convinced that it could "not be indulged," lest she lower her moral aims.[18]

To understand Eliot's deeply ambivalent attitude toward marriage, it is necessary to recognize that her responses to marriage were colored by basic tensions and associations within evangelical Protestantism. If we look closely at her early letters, we are struck by her desire to find objective correlates to religious values. Her early letters provide a graphic record of a soul torn alternately between a high impulse roward self-sacrifice—"to spread sackcloth 'above, below, around' "—and an intense craving for ideal fulfillment—for "excellence and beauty in beings and things of only 'working day' price." This attitude, with its emphasis on commitment, purity, and holiness, is exactly what we call evangelical, and without understanding this set of values it is impossible to understand the set of aspirations and anxieties that she brings to the subject of marriage. On the one hand, she longed for a calling, a mission, "some possibility of devoting myself where I may see a daily result of pure calm blessedness in the life of another." Her "only ardent hope" for her future life was "to have given to me some woman's duty" by which she could dedicate her life to the service of another soul. This cry for a mission was closely associated in her mind with marriage, which would provide a channel for her altruistic emo-

Marian Evans. From the painting by Francois D'Albert Durade, 1849 (when the future novelist George Eliot was 30). Courtesy of the National Portrait Gallery, London.

tions and high moral feelings, and which would also provide immediate and direct confirmation of her efforts. Yet at the same time Eliot viewed marriage as an instrument through which she could express her moral aspirations, she coupled these high hopes with intense fears. Christian self-sacrifice was her highest ideal, but she feared that cravings for self-gratification could be found even in the highest actions of life, even in "the martyr at the stake." Deeply depressed by her inability to discipline and control her will, which was manifest in the fitfulness and instability of emotions, she felt that she had no right to aspire for anything more than "peace" and "uniformity of character." "A single word," she observed, "is sometimes enough to give an entirely new mould to our thoughts"; and therefore she concluded that "to me it is pre-eminently important to be enclosed within the veil, so outward things may only act as winds to agitating sails, and be unable to send me adrift." [19]

It was her weakness of will that fated her to a life "within the veil," but this prospect raised the terrifying specter of total isolation and uselessness. Even a few years later she would be haunted by a nightmare vision of solipsistic isolation, "a sort of madness . . . just the opposite of the delirium which makes people fancy that their bodies are filling the room." Two decades before the publication of *Alice's Adventures in Wonderland* she experienced a haunting sense of being wholly alone, without anyone to sympathize with her feelings or someone to whom she could dedicate herself: "It seems to me as if I were shrinking into that mathematical abstraction, a point," she observed sadly, "—so entirely am I destitute of contact." [20]

True, she had "friends most undeservedly kind and tender and disposed to form a far too favourable estimate" of her, but she could not help longing for something more, aspiring for a "woman's duties." For a woman like Eliot, standing at a midway point between evangelicalism and romantic idealism, the search for an object of dedication and duty, the quest for a calling in which she could abnegate self, became a central object of longing. She looked with anguish at "the prevalence of misery and want" around her, but this only served to intensify her apprehensions that she was "supine and stupid, overfed with favours." Like so many individuals brought up in an atmosphere of evangelicalism, she longed for a calling that would teach her the discipline required to suppress her immediate desires, the strength to gain control over her will and affections, and the power to repress her sensual appetites. Here, she is particularly concerned with marriage as a key symbol of self-restraint and virtue through which she could renounce herself and devote herself to a higher service. Uneasy over her one "besetting sin, which is an ever struggling ambition," she desired "to be so intent on the improvement of present time and present blessings as to allow myself no leisure for dreaming about my worldly future." Yet no matter how hard she tried to transcend all selfish concern, the impression kept intruding itself of the need for someone to sympathize with her. She spoke of having "no one who enters into my pleasures or my griefs, no one with whom I can pour out my soul, no one with the same yearnings the same temptations the same delights as myself." But this longing for sympathy, she insisted, could not be met simply by her female friends; she needed a different calling.[21]

Torn between an aspiration for total self-sacrifice and self-renunciation and a continuing fear of egotism, impurity, and isolation, Eliot resolved this tension by seeing in marriage an objective correlative to evangelical religious ideals—the dedication to duty, the attitude of devotion, the identification of holiness with self-denial. What for earlier Dissenting Protestants and Low Churchmen was an essentially civil arrangement is here exalted as a sacrament through which one can free oneself from egotism and selfish greed. Thus, marriage ties in with the growth of neo-Catholicism in nineteenth-century England. In Eliot's view, marriage is not only a means through which a woman could perform her female duties; marriage is analogized with that union with Christ through which the soul is saved.

We cannot begin to understand the combination of hopes and fears and insecurities that George Eliot invested in marriage unless we first realize that these concerns were related to more general social and economic trends. Recent social-historical studies have suggested that, for many young women in Britain and America in the early nineteenth century, marriage and adulthood marked in a new way a closing off of freedoms enjoyed in girlhood—freedoms, as Tocqueville noted, that had a

real novelty. During the half century following 1780, women
between the ages of fourteen and twenty-seven received unprecedented opportunities to work outside the home and sell their
labor in the marketplace, or to sit home and decorate an affluent
household. This development meant that many young women
received kinds of freedom previously inconceivable. A profound
change in girlhood experience, including new opportunities for
education and work, raised women's expectations for self-
fulfillment. Marriage, therefore, might be regarded as representing a more difficult transition point than previously. This portrait of marriage as requiring a radical shift in women's identities was the subject of some comment by nineteenth-century
social commentators, such as Tocqueville, who was struck by
the extent to which the girlhood "independence of woman is
irrecoverably lost in the bonds of matrimony." [22]

Social history impinged upon Victorian marriage in other
ways. Recent scholarship has charted two somewhat contradictory social developments that can help illuminate the shifting
expectations attached to marriage. A shift in the kinship system,
related to increased rates of geographical mobility, placed
heightened emphasis on conjugal bonds at the expense of ties
to the natal family, meaning that a woman's identity became
increasingly linked to her future husband. At the same time, a
growing number of educators, ministers, and moralists argued
that only mothers, through their uplifting influence over the
home and children, could counteract the effects of commercial-
ism and individual self-interest. The effect of this ideology of
"domesticity" was to enhance the psychological and emotional
responsibilities of marriage, burdens that weighed particularly
heavily upon women. [23]

In the final analysis, while changes in the social role of women
might tell us why marriage became a more difficult transition
point for young women, such changes do little to help us understand the way a young woman might perceive marriage. To
understand the values and associations that Eliot invested in
marriage, we must look elsewhere, to the realm of religion. For
what we will see is that the vocabulary she used to express her

George Eliot's Girlhood Home at Griff, on the Arbury estate, Warwickshire. From J. W. Cross, George Eliot's Life As Related in Her Letters and Journals.

ambivalence regarding marriage is precisely the same vocabulary she invoked to express her ambiguities regarding her father's religion. Precisely the same concerns with selflessness, renunciation of self, and devotion to a high object of duty are evident in her ruminations on marriage and a bitter clash, in 1842, with her father over the subject of religion, when she refused to attend church for four months.

In Eliot's letters, she explains to her father that her chief objection to his religion is its selfishness. "Calvinism," she is recorded as saying, "is Christianity, and that granted, it is a religion based on pure selfishness." "Selfishness" here refers not only to criticism of the notion that Anglicanism is the wellspring of all virtue but to a broader picture of man that regarded all human actions as self-interested and that asserted that private vices could be public goods. Weary of complacency, tired of "platitude," of "*ennui,*" she proclaimed that her "only desire is to know the truth," her "only fear to cling to error." She hastened to reassure her father that she was no light-minded skeptic. He could entirely remove from his "mind the false notion that I am inclined visibly to unite myself with any Christian community, or that I have any affinity in opinion with Unitarians more than any other classes of believers in Divine authority." She hoped to reassure her father that she continued to admire and cherish "much of what I believe to have been the moral teachings of Jesus himself." Yet if she was to be morally honest, she could not simply parrot her father's beliefs but had to struggle for truth on her own. Again she affirmed that it was selfishness she felt called upon to struggle against with all her power—selfishness that had been embodied in "the system of doctrines built upon the facts of his [Jesus Christ's] life and drawn as to its materials from Jewish notions." [24]

It is significant that in these passages Eliot identifies the selfishness of Calvinism with the Hebraic emphasis on prescribed law and authority. Traditionally, law and authority had been upheld as necessary to contain individual self-will. But evangelical religion, with its emphasis on sincerity, earnestness, and perfect holiness, defined sin as selfishness and made the quest to transcend selfishness a constant concern. What Eliot is saying, in her critique of marriage and her arguments against her father's religion, is in essence that no matter how pure a person's ultimate goals, if an action provides self-gratification, then it is selfish. This was what she meant when she spoke of the egotism of the martyr at the stake, and it was this impulse to self-gratification that she believed detracted from the purity of marriage and the wholeness of her father's faith.

If we take a close look at Eliot's words, we might hypothesize that her evangelical vocabulary provided a language and a set of sanctions through which she could assert a degree of moral and intellectual independence while sparing her father's authority any direct attack. Residing in a halfway house between Calvinism and a new order in which traditional hierarchies and authorities were directly called into doubt, Eliot found in evangelical religion's stress on personal responsibility, purity, and perfect holiness a way to express certain ambivalences about marriage and religious authority without having to admit that she was attacking socially established morality. To a Victorian who was anxious to assert a degree of moral autonomy but who felt a need to demonstrate that this was not a challenge to the broader network of authorities essential to society's stability, an emphasis on self-denial and the pursuit of virtue provided a way to reconcile personal independence and external authority.

This conscious concern with balancing personal moral independence and deference to authority is manifest in the way Eliot phrased her religious disagreements with her father. When she speaks of their dispute, she emphasizes that she has no desire that this quarrel over religion detract from her familial duties. She wrote that her worst fear was that their arguments would force her into "involuntarily leaving" her father and that her deepest wish was to be able to "minister in the least" to his comfort. She had no desire to prolong the contention, but her uncompromising duty was "to walk in that path of rectitude which however rugged is the only path to peace." A true Christian must have the moral strength to resist the pressures of conformity, and therefore she vowed that "the prospect of contempt and rejection shall not make me swerve from my determination so much as a hair's breadth until I feel I *ought* to do so." To a friend she admitted her distress that her actions had rendered her "an adjunct to a family instead of an integral part," but this stood as proof positive that her struggle against hypocrisy was not simply a disguised form of selfishness, but stemmed from a dedication to truth. Behind these intricate references to suffering, renunciation of self, and dedication to duty—so remote from our time when most people embrace the pleasurable and the self-indulgent—lay a variety of conflicting impulses and values: a longing for a degree of self-determination, a desire to test and strengthen her moral character, a wish to repudiate the pleasurable and accept the painful as a way to master the will. What is important to recognize is the way that conflicting desires and commitments were reconciled and accommodated by evangelical language; in this case, contradictory impulses toward asserting a degree of intellectual independence in the realm of religion and maintaining deference to paternal authority.[25]

In her attempt to affirm her moral autonomy while maintaining ties to her father, Eliot's behavior closely resembles the patterns of family relations previously observed in the Stevenson, Beecher, Gosse, and Macaulay households, and she showed similar sensitivity to the need for maintaining paternal authority and family continuity. The need for her father's authority is the central concern she expresses while ministering at her parent's deathbed. She felt strangely, we are told, "that these will ever be the happiest days of life to me." She explained that "the one deep love I have ever known has now its highest and fullest reward." She could not help but think that "the worship of sorrow is *the* worship for mortals." Her heart was purified by her sorrow and her ardent devotion to the service of her father; her character was disciplined. All her selfish concern was transcended and her sight lifted from the commonplace and private to the higher purposes of the soul.[26]

When so great a significance is invested in the deathbed vigil, which becomes an archetype of self-sacrifice and dedication to moral duty, then death itself can bring only uncertainty and confusion. This can be seen in Eliot's tormented reaction to her father's death. "What shall I be without my Father?" she asked plaintively. Without the discipline furnished by her parent's authority, she feared "it will seem as if part of my moral nature were gone." It is only with an appreciation of the depth of these concerns about her moral character that we can understand the form that her grief took upon her father's death—which seems to indicate an element of wish, and of guilt, in his passing. Writing a few days after his departure, she says that she has "had a horrid vision of myself becoming earthly sensual and devilish for want of that purifying influence." Her feelings were deeply divided. On the one hand, she felt an intense sense of liberation from the constant demand that all her actions had to be directed to a high and serious purpose. What she felt was a sense of release "from the apprehension of what [Charles Grandison] Finney well describes, that at each moment I tread on chords that will vibrate for weal or woe to all eternity." On the other hand, this sudden sense of freedom only seemed to make it more important that she find new objects to which she could devote herself in the pursuit of duty. More than ever, she was convinced that "perfect love and purity" had to be her "goal."[27]

As religious belief became more difficult for Eliot, more and more she came to see in love, commitment, and self-sacrifice analogues and concrete examples of sin and redemption. The passionate and selfless devotion to a loved one helped to overcome the growing shadow of doubt and to discharge anxieties over her sudden independence from her father. When many traditional beliefs had given way to doubt, Eliot looked to love to compensate for the weakness of religion and other moral authorities. The need for love to correct the weaknesses of religion is evident in a passage of a letter she wrote shortly after her clash with her father over religion. She drew upon the example of "non-conformity in a family" to illustrate a far wider social problem, the disintegration of the traditional basis of moral order "on a larger scale in the world." A family member felt doubt in traditional Christianity, and "could not make his reasons intelligible, and so his conduct is regarded as a relaxation of the hold that moral ties had on him previously." Soon, the other family members "are infected with the disease they imagined in him; all the screws by which order are maintained are loosened." Initially, liberation of their souls from a "wretched giant's bed of dogmas" led to a euphoric "feeling of exultation." But within a year or two, "the experience of our own miserable weakness which will ill afford to part even with the crutches of superstition" brings about a realization that when "agreement between intellects seems unattainable," *"truth of feeling"* is "the only universal bond of union." In the end, the only secure basis for "a person's happiness" lay, not in abstract dogmas, but in feelings of love, sympathy, and resignation.[28]

In her belief that love and sympathy were necessary to compensate for personal deficiencies and intellectual perplexities, Eliot, like Stevenson, was not alone. At almost precisely the same moments in their lives, at the point of first contemplating their transition away from their natal families, Charlotte Brontë and Harriet Beecher Stowe gave voice to similar concerns. In 1827, when she was seventeen, Stowe was wracked with anguish and doubt. She thought, "I could wish to die young," "so useless, so weak, so destitute of all energy" she felt. Her mind was often so perplexed that she felt incapable of praying, and it seemed as if she was incapable of resisting temptation. She longed to feel "perfectly indifferent to the opinions of others" but feared that "there was never a person more dependent on the good or evil opinions of those around than I am." It was the "the desire to be loved," she feared, that was "the great motive for all my actions." At her brother's urging, she read the Book of Job seeking consolation but was deeply perturbed by what she found. She was haunted by the picture of a God who would strip "a dependent creature of all that renders life desirable," who, "instead of showing mercy and pity," sought to overawe humanity "by a display of power and justice." She longed for a different sort of God, not one who governed through fear and dread, but "a being who sympathizes with his guilty afflicted creatures." Reading the New Testament, she envisaged a God of another kind, of love and not of wrath, a God "as merciful and compassionate," and declared that "just such a God as I need." For a person like Stowe, brought up on evangelicalism, with its ideals of holiness and perfect love, and filled with a romantic longing for feeling and passionate dedication to a cause, the ethos of sympathy, consolation, and love came to dominate her thoughts.[29]

Charlotte Brontë expressed virtually identical sentiments. In 1837, when she was twenty-one, she confessed to dread about making the slightest religious profession, lest she "sink at once into Phariseeism, merge wholly into the rank of the self-righteous." No friend could "imagine how hard rebellious and intractable all" her feelings were, and she declared that if the doctrines of Calvin were true she was sure she was already an outcast. The thought of her "secret vanities, and uncontrolled passions and propensities" ate deeply into her conscience, and she longed for the strength to master the worldly desires that battled for control of her soul. She felt bewildered by doubt and isolated from the supports that might give her moral strength; and she expressed an acute fear of abandonment. Fervently she spoke of a haunting fear of being deserted, and she deeply longed for someone to sympathize with her thinking.[30]

It would be a mistake to press the parallels between George Eliot, Harriet Beecher Stowe, and Charlotte Brontë too far. But what linked these three figures together was that all were troubled by religious doubts; all were anxious about their capacity to lead a Christian life of self-denial, devotion to duty, and moral earnestness; and all looked to love as an answer to problems of moral weakness, religious perplexities, and an intense sense of personal isolation and despair. That each one turned to love as a way to resolve feelings of doubt and psychological depression calls attention to a significant point: love here is not something solely physical or emotional but something higher, modeled on Christ's saving love, through which the soul is purified, strengthened, and redeemed. At the moment when these women were first impelled to grapple seriously with the question of marriage and their future relationship with their natal families, each expressed acute concern about her capacity for a life of independence and voiced a poignant fear over the support held out by her religion. Each, in turn, expressed a strong desire for a source of love that would compensate for the weakness of her moral character. Although each would in time become a model of female achievement, each betrayed a deep anxiety regarding independence that took the form of an acute ambivalence about religion.

Little documentation exists with regard to George Eliot's union with George Henry Lewes or her subsequent marriage to J. W. Cross. But the sources that have survived underscore the way marriage was regarded as an answer to fundamental personal and intellectual dilemmas: anxieties about independence, the psychological consequences of individualism, and the longing for a marital union as an anchorage in a sea of doubts and a shelter from selfishness and despair. Marriage is exalted as a deliverance from narrow selfishness into a union of souls, strikingly similar to a religious union with Christ. When Eliot described her relationship with Lewes, she pictured their union as "a sort of Siamese-twin condition," which she held up as an ideal. In such "supreme self-merging love," there was no loss of independence on the part of the partners, for such an essentially spiritual union was free of such base emotions as jealousy. The irrefutable proof that she and Lewes had achieved perfect union, she thought, was "that difference of opinion rouses no egotistic irritation in" the other. True marriage was to be found in mutual dependence and transcendence of self, which, Lewes said, brought a "new birth." And as in evangelical religion, this "new birth" brought sanctity and a transformation of the soul.[31]

When George Eliot set out late in life to inform her family and friends of her decision to marry J. W. Cross, she explained that she needed to marry in order to exorcise the impulses toward "self-absorption" and "laziness" that had reemerged since Lewes's death. Marriage, she thought, would give "me a more strenuous position" from which to resist the temptations to selfishness "I was in danger of before." The worst of her privations following Lewes's death had been "not the privation of joy but of ardent sympathy." Severed from Lewes's devoted sympathy, she felt herself growing "hard" and "very selfish" and explained that her sorest need was for a love that would enable her to surmount the debilitating effects of her grief. Only by recognizing the psychological and social functions assigned to marriage—as an object of duty, a protection against egotism and selfishness, a school for strengthening and purifying the character—can we fully appreciate the beliefs that Eliot invested in the institution.[32]

The example of George Eliot is significant because it indicates the awesome expectations, fears, and needs that a Victorian strongly influenced by evangelicalism might bring to marriage. Analogized to that union with Christ that brings about a new birth of the soul, marriage was assigned a wide range of quasi-religious functions. Marriage was "not a mere indulgence of taste and provision for enjoyment, but a powerful instrument of discipline and self-subjugation." Craving for spiritual peace, writhing in despair over her capacity for an independent life,

George Henry Lewes (1817–1878). From a drawing by Rudolf Lehmann, 1867. Courtesy of the Trustees of the British Museum.

longing for a source of spiritual and emotional support, a Victorian such as Eliot looked to marriage as a place to dispose of her doubts and anxieties, as a high object to which she could passionately dedicate her moral energies, and as a source of strength. We turn next to how another writer, Harriet Beecher Stowe, viewed marriage in actuality.[33]

The current fashion in historical research on marriage is to apply analytical tools and conceptions drawn from the social sciences to historical materials. Borrowing from anthropology, social historians have shown that like marriage in other hierarchically arranged societies, Victorian marriage served important strategic functions: it helped define levels of society, maintain class positions, and locate an individual's place in the social structure. Drawing upon psychology, social historians have viewed marriage as an arena of conflict, accomodation, and adjustment. In the midst of such efforts to interpret Victorian marriage in contemporary terms, we might do well to examine Victorian marriage from another perspective, to try to understand the terms in which a particular Victorian couple—Harriet Beecher Stowe and her husband, Calvin Stowe—perceived and interpreted relations within marriage. To those who are still interested in what people in the past felt, this example vividly reveals the ways that domestic roles are apportioned, that arguments are made and structured, that influence is exerted and sanctioned.

To an age such as ours, which views marriage as an essentially secular and private arrangement, a social custom and not a divine ordinance, warranted by its role in rearing children, understanding Victorian marriage can be a difficult task. Viewed by contemporaries as an instrument of sanctification and as a means to holiness, Victorian marriage was described as a vehicle for inculcating a capacity for self-discipline and self-restraint. William Gladstone's famous definition of marriage, widely read in America as well as in Britain, gave pointed expression to premises shared by Victorians of quite different persuasions. "Marriage," he wrote, "derives its essential and specific character from restraint." By restricting the choice of a spouse to a single person, it concentrates the affections. By forbidding the carnal use of women in any relation inferior to marriage, it guards the dignity of both sexes. The object of marriage was not simply the happiness of the married parties or the welfare of children but was to strengthen and discipline the will and to master the desires. It is, as Gladstone said, a "school for heaven." As religious turmoil grew and difficulties of religious belief increased—and many continental countries adopted civil marriage—the notion of marriage as sanctified, as "holy matrimony," persisted in Britain and America, the twin archetypes of the emerging market economy. In a time of profound and bewildering change, to able to portray marriage as a sacrament, as an instrument for transforming human emotions into things pure and spiritual, was a way to resist the intense pressures of modern life.[34]

To a person like Harriet Beecher Stowe, whose life was spent in an agonizing struggle to come to terms with her Calvinist heritage, marriage provided an answer to religious perplexity and to the states of despondency that her bewilderment brought. Dispossessed of any secure religious faith, tormented by deep internal conflicts that frequently left her in despair, what she sought in marriage is explicitly identified as an "exemplification of religion." In her letters, marriage is held up as an instrument through which she and her husband could achieve that transcendence of self that her religion defined as "true virtue." As traditional religious beliefs seemed abstract and lifeless, she turned the more closely to marriage as a tangible embodiment of her religion's ideals of holiness and piety and stressed marriage's daily duties and sacrifices as a means to sanctification.[35]

The needs and aspirations that Stowe would project on to marriage were rooted in earlier worries and anxieties involving religion. Brought up in the Edwardsian tradition of Calvinism as modified by her father, Lyman Beecher, yet heavily influenced by the Episcopalianism of her mother's family, through

Harriet Beecher Stowe. From a crayon portrait by George Richmond, 1853 (when the novelist was 42). Courtesy of the Stowe-Day Foundation, Hartford.

her life Stowe felt a deep ambivalence toward her father's religious legacy. Like her father, she found the essence of sin in an individual's discontent and ambition, and she longed for the beatitude that came with the experience of divine grace. Torn between a desire to achieve a life of purity and self-denial, yet haunted by a daily sense of vanity and imperfection, she, like George Eliot, wholeheartedly sought in marriage an object of duty to which she could dedicate herself passionately and selflessly.

The anxieties and worries Stowe would bring to marriage can be studied in her girlhood letters. To her brother Edward and sister Catharine, she confessed the evanescence of her deepest feelings and her sense that she was not fit for anything useful, and said that she would remain a useless sinner unless she found that divine love that "could supply the loss of all earthly love." What we see in her letters is the severe strain and anxiety that wracked the evangelical conscience. A sensitive mind, striving to achieve the standard of Christian virtue that is defined as absolute purity and selflessness, might experience life as a series of spasms between feelings of impotence and despair and of optimism and hope. What one sees in her letters is a longing for an experience, analogized to marriage, in which she could overcome her self-love and achieve that mystical altruistic love that she conceived of as true virtue. She spoke of her need for a source of strength that she might cling to for support, then allowed that "anything but the most distant reverential affection seems almost sacrilegious." What she yearned for was a love that would help to "purify and reform" her flaws, that "will never be irritated or impatient," and that "will never show me my faults in such a manner as to irritate without helping me." Deeply dismayed by her dependence "on the good and evil opinions of those around" her, she pined for the assistance of one who would be aware of "the utmost of my sinfulness, my waywardness, my folly" and who would yet "still have patience." In passages such as these, Stowe is expressing her anguish over the sternness of the austere God of Calvinism and looking for the support of the spirit of Jesus, and his gospel of forgiveness and love. Yet one can hardly read her words without

The Beecher Family, 1859. Standing, left to right: Thomas K. Beecher, William Beecher, Edward Beecher, Charles Beecher, Henry Ward Beecher. Seated, left to right: Isabella Beecher Hooker, Catharine Esther Beecher, Lyman Beecher, Mary Beecher Perkins, Harriet Beecher Stowe. Absent: Charles Beecher who died in 1843. Courtesy of the Stowe-Day Foundation, Hartford.

growing conscious of the anxieties and needs that lay behind these sentiments. Her major worries are fears of guilt, isolation, and moral weakness. Acutely conscious of the growing fragmentation of the Beecher family and of the loss of familial support and companionship, she declared that her deepest need was for "peace" and "love." [36]

It was in the nature of evangelical religion to portray Christianity, not in terms of metaphysical abstractions, but in more concrete terms, and Stowe would seek in marriage a tangible model of virtue and sanctification. For a woman oppressed by a sense of intense personal weakness and spiritual depression, seeking desperately on an intellectual level to emphasize the role of Christ above that of the Calvinist Father, marriage acquired profound symbolic significance. Marriage is portrayed here as an antidote to the sufferings of conscience, a remedy to weakness and want of faith, a corrective to feelings of dejection. These aspirations and needs no doubt had their roots in her personal relations with her family, but her religious longings—to substitute a God of love for the austere authority of the Calvinist Father—shaped her ideals of marriage.

Stowe's conception of marriage—as a means to grace, as a buttress for her soul, and as a school for sanctification—had enormous appeal to people who were troubled by rampant social change and who looked to the family as a stabilizing and regenerating force. As we examine Victorian conceptions of marriage, it quickly becomes apparent that two distinct themes are intertwined: a contractual and a sacramental view of the marriage relationship. According to the contractual notion, marriage was a relationship founded on the basis of free choice, voluntary consent, and reciprocal duties and obligations. It was a model relationship in which no person would "subjugate, and tyrannize over, and do violence to" another individual. Repeatedly, Victorian moralists proclaimed that marriage did not involve the merging of a wife's "individuality in that of her husband." Rather, marriage was a vehicle of self-discipline and restraint. Interwoven with this contractual conception of marriage was another ideal that emphasized the sacramental basis of the partners' commitment. In this view, the marriage relationship was modeled on the union of Christ and his body as his church, and was upheld as an instrument for shaping the character in the image of Christ. Marriage is represented here as involving attractions that "are mental, not animal. Each loves the other's *soul* mainly, instead of body." Marriage is exalted as a model of "perfect identity," "the union of two souls in one," and is characterized by "self-oblivion" and absorption into another's identity.[37]

Any tensions between the contractual and sacramental ideas about marriage was reconciled by evangelical imagery. Two complexes of images and ideals shaped the Victorian mythos of marriage, an ideal of Christian love and an ideal of Christian freedom. Historically, these two sets of ideas had been used to describe the relationship between God and man, but in the nineteenth century these concepts were increasingly used to depict the relationship between wife and husband. Here again we see the way the love of God serves as an analogue for love between spouses. In evangelical thought, the ideal of Christian freedom involved an immediate recognition of personal insufficiency; an acute awareness of dependence on love to wash away doubt and shame; and a conscious acknowledgment of the need for self-renunciation as the only way to achieve a higher, more holy life. The evangelical conception of Christian love identified love with an attitude of reverence and selflessness; love was portrayed as a source of redemption. Christian love involved a conscious recognition that the achievement of selfhood was dependent on union with a source outside one's life.

To spiritualize love was a way to psychologically distance the institution of marriage from associations with sensuality, lust, and passion, emotions that were identified with religious impurity, moral weakness, and guilt. To be able to identify marriage with Christian love and Christian freedom was a psychological means of exorcising worries and insecurities that Victorians brought to marriage. In emphasizing the nineteenth-century cult of romantic love, scholars have tended to ignore the huge nineteenth-century psychological literature, written in Britain and America, that describes the fears and dangers to which the stress on spiritual love was a response. As we look over this literature, we see the way the glorification of marriage represented a reaction against the ugly emotions and impulses that could be let loose in married love. Undercutting the romantic mythos of marriage, Herbert Spencer, writing in 1855, saw the basis of love in the human impulses for physical gratification, love of approbation, and practical proof of power. Similarly, the philosopher Alexander Bain argued that "egotistic and selfish emotion diffuses itself over all matters related to love," and he was joined by J. D. Morell in locating the essence of love in man's "intense desire for the sole and perfect possession of" another person. Given the association of love with lust for power and possession, it comes as little surprise that Victorians would try to sentimentalize the relationship. To identify marriage as a sacrament dissociated love from lust and sensuality and transformed marriage into an instrument of self-discipline.[38]

We must be wary of deriding this vision of marriage as simply an example of Victorian sentimentality. We might better recognize it as an intellectual construct, a fiction, which served to counteract the most troubling aspects of the marital relationship and to redirect human emotions in a pure and moral direction. To be able to think of marriage as a spiritual contract and an instrument of sanctification was a way to portray a relationship free from associations with carnality and lust, dominion and subservience. To think of the Victorian pattern of beliefs about marriage as an intellectual fiction is not to mistake it for fact, nor is it to dismiss it as irrelevant. We might best understand this fiction as a set of symbols that helped shape and influence perceptions and behavior within marriage. Like a legal fiction, to which it bears a resemblance, it furnished a vocabulary and a set of sanctions invoked in actual marriages.

It is important to bear vividly in mind that Victorians approached marriage with very different values and concerns than do people of our age. Convinced that certain traditional institutions and hierarchies were essential if society were not to collapse, Victorian moralists desperately believed in the importance of preserving marital unions. Like us, they recognized "that love often *does* decline instead of increasing with years." But unlike modern writers on marriage, this truism was not taken to mean that individuals should be free to move on to another relationship. If a certain kind of passion fades over time, we are told, the marriage relationship must be founded on another basis. Sympathy, not lust or passion, was to provide the adhesive for marriage. A person dominated by carnal love was buffeted by the winds of circumstance. Love could be a secure basis for marriage only when it was transmuted into something purer and more selfless. This viewpoint, which regarded sympathy as the basis of morality and personal responsibility, originated in the writings of the Scottish moralists of the eighteenth century; and it provided a way to conceptualize a relationship in which dependence was mutual and reciprocal, in which the parties were motivated by selfless emotions, in which the spouses provided each other with guidance and moral support.[39]

Those who exalted this ideal of sympathy were acutely aware of the conflicts and contention that marred individual marriages. But such moralists believed that sympathy alone had the power "to mold out the bone of contention." Drawing a pointed analogy with the evangelical ideas of love of God, it was argued that the assertion of rights and claims within marriage was inappropriate. As in their relationship with God, men and women were without rights and had no just claim to special consideration. Much as God's mercy was exercised through acts of grace, kindness in marriage depended on acts of sympathy, not on rights that one might claim as one's due. This rejection of "emotional legalism" and emphasis on the transforming power of sympathy was a way to exclude notions of power from the marriage relationship and to place marriage on a higher moral basis. The foundation of enduring love originates in sympathy, a compassionate understanding of another person's needs and weaknesses together with an ardent desire to alleviate these. Sympathy here is the capacity of entering into the feelings of another and aiding him, not simply with pity, but with patience and consideration. To rely on rights instead of on sympathy raised profound dangers, for "victory at the expense of affection is defeat, and capitulation conquest."[40]

Such concerns with sympathy and mutual dependence should not be regarded as of only abstract interest. Notions of sympathy provided a symbolic language and a frame of reference that parties to a marriage used to influence behavior. That this was the case will become clear as we closely examine the marriage of Harriet Beecher Stowe. For such a woman, the language of sympathy enabled her to think of marriage as an object of duty and furnished a vocabulary through which she could legitimately voice claims within marriage and exercise influence over her husband's conduct.

Stowe's conception of marriage as an instrument for strengthening and purifying the moral will is graphically manifest in a letter written on the eve of her eleventh wedding anniversary.

As we examine her words, we see her purposeful effort to make marriage a means for resolving problems of the severest kind: problems of religious doubt, of discovering an ideal object of duty, of finding a moral anchor that would keep her from slipping into spiritual despair. In January 1847 she reflected on her feelings about marriage. God, she wrote, had led her and her husband into married life "to humble us & grieve us & show us what was in our hearts." Only by gradually realizing what an overpowering struggle the Christian life entailed, to learn to discipline the will and to overcome selfishness, could she and her husband become true Christians. When she had first married, she "was a very different being from what I am now." Her whole desire, initially, was to live in "absorbing passionate devotion to one person." This had made her first separation from her husband an almost intolerable trial. Then she had invested her happiness in the hope of being a mother, and again time had only brought trial, pain, perplexity, and constant disappointment. As bitter as the lesson had been, she now praised God for teaching her that she "should make no family be my chief good & portion." What she had learned through bitter experience was that the purpose of marriage was not to be an instrument of personal gratification but a medium of spiritual "improvement" and "mutual watchfulness" in which spouses "might exercise correcting power over each other."[41]

Only by recognizing that the purpose of marriage was to help people achieve a life of Christian discipline could she and her husband remove "the past obstacles to our happiness." To think of marriage as simply a contrivance to bring personal happiness led a husband and wife to focus on each other's flaws, not on the sympathy and patient support they could offer each other in self-improvement. Certainly, this had been true in her marriage. At the time of her wedding, "one might naturally have inferred" that "two persons both morbidly sensitive & acute . . . one hasty & impulsive—the other sensitive & brooding" would have much painful friction. But she now was convinced that this friction would not be there except that it was Providence' intention to "throw the heaviest external pressure," to confront us with "the very things calculated to irritate and try" us most, in order to teach individuals to resist selfish desires and to strengthen their wills. It was only when she had come to see marriage as a foundry in which the soul was chastened and purified in the daily fires of affliction that she believed she viewed marriage in its proper light—as an instrument of mutual improvement and moral uplift. Even the drudgery and routine of family life acquired symbolic significance when regarded as tests and trials. For a woman like Stowe, seeking to soften the merciless and terrifying elements of Edwardsian Calvinism, marriage became the single place where she could actualize her religious aspirations.[42]

For her husband, too, marriage provided a place where he sought desperately to resolve the central anxieties of his life: his strength to handle the ordeals and obligations that God had placed on him and his concerns about his sensual inclinations. Led by certain "skeptical doubts" to wonder if he was losing his faith, and frightened by reports of ministers who had become "addicted to intoxication" and abandoned themselves to "licentiousness," Stowe was convinced that it was only his wife that kept him from sinking into the slough of despond.

When the mind suffers "a great deal of mental agony" wondering "whether the whole Bible is not after all a humbug," the only solution lay in the consolations of love. One cannot read Calvin Stowe's letters without sensing the profound feeling of moral weakness that lay behind his love for his wife. He said he tried intently "to be spiritually minded," and yet he found himself lapsing repeatedly into "a deadly longing for all kinds of sensual gratification." To a man staggering painfully under the weight of severe spiritual doubts and fears about his ability to support his family financially, a wife might become a source of strength and consolation available nowhere else, a moral custodian for his soul. Burdened with a troubling sense of religious doubt, he called upon his wife to support his "feeble and tottering steps," and he believed that the only way he "could have some hold on Christ" was through her. In a deep state of spiritual apprehension, Stowe sought to resolve his doubts and per-

Calvin Ellis Stowe (1802–1886). From an 1850 engraving. Courtesy of the Bowdoin College Library.

plexity by seeking in married love total fulfillment, a state where "every desire I have, mental and physical, is completely satisfied and filled up, and leaves me nothing more to ask for."[43]

We have been concerned in this chapter with different ways in which religious needs and aspirations were objectified in love and marriage, and both Calvin and Harriet Beecher Stowe sought to transform their marriage into a vehicle for mutual improvement. It is difficult to read their letters without being struck by the amount of attention devoted to explaining each other's faults and to seeking to construct a plan "to improve & be improved by each other." In these exchanges we have a rare glimpse of the ways that "influence" was exerted in a middle-class Victorian home. Here we see how the fiction that marriage was an essentially spiritual relationship between moral equals was used by a wife to exercise influence over her husband's behavior. In evangelical homes, where a premium was placed on duty and self-sacrifice, such values were constantly appealed to in order to influence and shape behavior. An age like ours can find such harping on duty and self-denial only morally pretentious. Yet this emphasis on duty and moral improvement needs to be seen in another light—as a peculiarly Victorian mode of discourse, through which one party to a marriage might legitimately make demands of another.

This style of argument is clearly illustrated in the letter Stowe wrote to her husband on the occasion of their eleventh wedding anniversary. She begins her letter by explaining that for all her husband's faults, they are the faults "of one beloved," and therefore it was clearly her moral duty as a wife to methodically examine his moral flaws and to help "burn away" the "traces of the earthly." In reviewing the obstacles to his moral improvement, it seemed to her that they were of two kinds. First, there was her husband's hypochondria, his extreme depression that often centered on imaginary physical ailments. More serious was one grievance that had particularly weakened the "foundation for mutual respect & affection": that was her husband's tendency to hastily censure her for her mistakes and demand that she confess her failings and weaknesses to him. In Stowe's letter we see how an emphasis on sympathy and moral uplift can be subtly transformed into a covert way of exercising control over her husband's behavior. What we are witnessing is a radical redefinition of a wife's role. By identifying the home as an instrument of salvation, a wife assumed a new responsibility: to assert an uplifting influence over her husband's manners and morals.[44]

How a woman was able to transform a traditionally submissive role is evident in the arguments Stowe invokes to justify her criticism of her husband. Early in her marriage, she called on her husband to join her in "an earnest attempt to correct & reform all in us that needs reforming & to 'working out our own salvation.' " In a home conceived as a means to sanctification, a husband might become dependent on his wife's support if he was to achieve salvation. Harriet Beecher Stowe acknowledged that she did not believe in the possibility of achieving perfection in this life, but she told her husband that they both might attain "a baptism of the spirit" if they could learn to suppress their "murmurings, pinings, and discontents, and wishings that we were somewhere else and longings for an easier life." Marriage, in other words, could provide an anticipation of divine life, but only if her husband were willing to undergo an intensive struggle to discipline his will and learn to resist temptation. Only if he would treat marriage with proper seriousness could it become a vehicle for achieving Christ's saving love, in which "his purity will be ours & all impure thoughts fall from us as would mud & filth from the bright feathers of the heavenly dove & no temptations would find a place in us." In the trials of domestic life, carnal love would be sublimated into sympathy.[45]

That this idealized image of marriage as a means of sanctification could be used by a wife to make a husband dependent on her is illustrated in a variety of ways. Thus, Stowe told her husband that all that was wanting in him "is that you put personal holiness in the first place," and then chose as her evidence of his present lapses his omission of family prayers and his devotion to the daily newspapers. So that he might concentrate his time on self-purification, she asked to be given responsibility for the family's finances. In her letters, marriage is transformed from an instrument of sensual gratification into a mechanism of self-discipline, and there can be no doubt that at times Stowe invoked this conception of marriage in order to achieve a respite from her husband's sexual demands.[46]

Yet, more important, what Harriet Beecher Stowe sought in marriage was that state of holiness and perfect love that she had longed for as a young girl contemplating her father's religion. When she described to her husband the kind of love she longed for in marriage, she drew an explicit analogy with the evangelical ideal of love of God. "Love to any human being," she lamented, "only contracts and limits the mind . . . love to a human being becomes absorbing selfishness, to Christ it becomes benevolence." What she wanted to achieve with her husband was that compassionate understanding that she held up as a religious ideal. As a young girl she had deplored the instability of her emotions, and now that she was older she continued to long for equanimity. When her husband was away, she noted, she felt an acute need for his love and could not help feeling "desolate & wasted & cheerless." And yet she knew that a short time after his return home their feelings were "all forced off into months of cold indifference." She was struck by the fact that conjugal love like "religion is still a matter of temporary gushes & swellings," and she concluded that the "moments of communion & tokens of affection" upon which people set so much store were of doubtful value. She sighed for "some more perfect state to be attained in this world," but she feared that she and her husband would only "again draw each other earthward."[47]

When the soul is burdened with intense religious doubts and confusions, and longs to abandon the realm of metaphysical abstractions and to find more practical goals, the mind might project religious needs and aspirations onto marriage, where impulses toward selflessness and sacrifice might receive tangible expression. To make marriage a means of sanctification was a practical way to give concrete meaning to the primary concerns of evangelical religion: the cry for idealism, the longing for a mission, the impulse toward self-sacrifice and self-denial. This

The Stowe Winter Home in Mandarin on the St. John's River, Florida. Under the oaks, right to left: Harriet Beecher Stowe, her husband Calvin Ellis Stowe, her sister Mary Beecher Perkins, and her daughter Eliza. Courtesy of the Stowe-Day Foundation, Hartford.

conception of marriage is sometimes known as the cult of domesticity, and such a feminine role gave many middle-class women an ampler sense of purpose and identity. What Calvin Stowe said about the stabilizing influence of his wife upon his moral character—that she was "a balance wheel" to his emotions—applied to other Victorian families, for according to the cult of domesticity a married woman was responsible for exerting an uplifting and reforming influence upon her husband. If, in one sense, marriage could be regarded as a closing off of freedoms enjoyed in girlhood, equally it could be seen as the providential means through which a husband's spirit is renewed and his soul redeemed.[48]

Against this background we can begin to understand how a Victorian such as Harriet Beecher Stowe conceived of marriage. It was a vehicle of self-denial and self-discipline through which a woman might help save her husband's soul. From here, it was

only a step to seeing marriage, in her words, as an "exemplification of religion" where individuals could bury their doubts by
engaging in a spiritual endeavor. This view of marriage is clearly
delineated in a letter written after eleven years of marriage. Taking a retrospective view of her marriage in 1847, she contrasted
the "unnumbered tenderness[es]" her husband had exhibited in
the early years of their marriage with "the morbid brooding &
jaundiced eye on my faults" he had since shown. The explanation for this change, she was convinced, lay partly with her
mother-in-law, who "constantly pointed out my faults & kept
up . . . [a] perpetual state of complaint and irritation." So she
proceeded to remind her husband that such exacting criticism
had no place within marriage, since it undermined trust and
sympathetic feeling. "You know as well as I," she told her husband, "when both parties begin to stand for their rights & to
suspect the other of selfish exaction there is an end of every
delicate & refined affection & a beginning of coarse & brutal
selfishness." What she is saying is that the compassionate understanding that marriage requires is not consonant with the assertion of patriarchal rights and claims. As for herself, she freely
admitted her faults: she was "constitutionally careless & too impatient & impulsive to maintain that consistency & order which
is so necessary in a family." And she called upon her husband
to display that same forgetfulness of self that she had shown.
By asking that every action, every word, that her husband made
conform to God's law of selflessness and benevolence, Stowe
had found a vocabulary that could be used to motivate her husband to act in the ways she desired. She told her husband that
she hoped he took her criticisms of his character with the spirit
and intention in which she said them. She could assure him that
she did not so much blame him for his egotism as pity him, and
not a shade of unkind "feeling remains in my mind or agitates
my feelings." She felt nothing but desire that he make "progress
in self government" and gain "the victory over" himself. When
the Christian life was defined to be a life of purity and self-
renunciation, then calls for the suppression of self-will and lax-

ness stood as the most potent tools for shaping and influencing behavior.[49]

To look into Victorian feelings about love and marriage is to gain a fresh perspective on that intricate and mysterious process that social scientists call "secularization." In recent years, social historians have described the late eighteenth and early nineteenth centuries as a period of wide-reaching "modernization," and traditionally modernization—or progress—has been associated with a falling away from religious belief. Histories of Victorian marriage have tended to picture nineteenth-century marriage in this way. Emphasizing the extension of civil marriage and divorce and the increasing civil regulation of marriage, these historians have tended to see developments in marriage much as novelist Thomas Hardy did—as symptoms of a loss of faith and of an increasingly individualistic society. But this view of unilinear change does little to help us understand what actual individuals felt about love and marriage. What historians have depicted in terms of secularization was regarded by Robert Louis Stevenson, George Eliot, and Harriet Beecher Stowe as the sanctification of love and the transformation of marriage into "holy matrimony."

A close reading of personal papers helps us to see how religious forms and symbols were "secularized" in love and marriage and how in the emotions of love a Victorian could find confirmation for abstract religious aspirations. Instead of conceptualizing secularization as a lapse of religious belief, the process might be better understood as a transfer, or displacement, of religious needs and aspirations onto other, secular objects. By transforming relations of love and marriage into means of absolution and redemption, Victorians such as Stevenson, Eliot, and Stowe sought to give tangible meaning to abstract theological doctrines. Reacting to similar anxieties and strains—problems of spiritual doubt, worries about their capacity for independence, and tension aroused by their constant concern with purity and holiness—these figures looked to love as an answer to spiritual distress and personal despair.

The values and associations that Stevenson, Eliot, and Stowe attached to love and marriage were colored by profound religious concerns that these figures had articulated in their youths, in particular, a desire to elevate Christ's gospel of love and forgiveness to a central place in religious life. In part, this shift in focus from God the Father to God the Son was compensation for a deep sense of personal and moral weakness. This desire to make Christ not a peripheral part of Calvinist religion but the representative of Christian teachings was a vehicle for anxieties over independence, individualism, and a disruption of family ties. Hence, references to Christ speak of his patience, leniency, and forbearance in the face of sin, weakness, and imperfection.

And yet, that Stevenson, Eliot, and Stowe identified with Christ the Child and not with God the Father is both psychologically and culturally revealing. Anxious in their personal lives to assert a degree of autonomy and personal independence, it was the suffering of Christ and not the authority of his Father that they attributed, consciously or unconsciously, to themselves. Incapable of sustaining a view of religion that emphasized the absolute sovereignty of God, the helplessness of man, and the arbitrariness of God's saving grace, they instead stressed Christ's gospel of love and mercy. To elevate Christ, and his teachings of purity and holiness, and to contrast this view of God with the stern and forbidding character of the Calvinist God, was a way of demonstrating moral independence from their parents and of making religion a more personal, egocentric experience. Moreover, by emphasizing the figure of Christ, love was identified as the essence of the Christian life, a palpable expression of Christian principles. Love made the attainment of Christian virtue a practical possibility.

CHAPTER 7

Sister and Brother

F EW subjects engaged the imagination of the great nineteenth-century novelists more strongly than sibling relations. Of course earlier works of literature, from the story of
Cain and Abel to *King Lear,* had also taken sibling rivalry and
conflict as a subject, but such works tended to focus on different
issues from those of their nineteenth-century counterparts.
Where earlier works had examined the conflicts that arose out
of tangible family interests or out of the tension between two
competing ideals of family ties—one view emphasizing the subordination of individual interests to the social and economic advantage of the family unit, the other stressing a more limited
view of sibling obligations—the great nineteenth-century novels
dealing with siblingship, such as *Sense and Sensibility, The Mill
on the Floss,* and *Little Women,* while also concerned with the
economic and religious vicissitudes that drove siblings apart,
tended to concentrate on the symbolic and psychological significance of the sibling bond.

The significance attached to the sibling bond in such novels
can be properly understood only when it is seen in relation to
larger social changes that raised profound questions of duty,
personal identity, and continuity. In an increasingly individualistic society, in which the individual household was more and
more cut off from broader structures of kinship and work, familial relationships acquired significance above all other social ob-

ligations. Disruptive moral and intellectual developments further enhanced the significance attached to the sibling bond. Indeed, in the most famous Victorian novels dealing with sibling ties, such as *Little Women* and *The Mill on the Floss,* the sibling bond is specifically upheld as the epitome of loyalty and selflessness, continuity and cohesion. In such novels what the sibling bond represents is a reconciliation of the forces that appeared to be tearing society asunder. An emphasis on sibling loyalty was a way to counteract the problems of generational discontinuity and the anarchy of individualism.

A concern with sibling relations was not confined to the pages of literature. As John Clive has observed, close emotional attachments were not uncommon among prominent nineteenth-century literary figures such as Wordsworth; Disraeli; Harriet Martineau; George Eliot; Harriet Beecher Stowe; and Henry, William, and Alice James. In seeking to explain the importance of sibling ties in the Victorian home, this chapter begins by pointing out a historical paradox. Social and economic changes in the late eighteenth century tended to reduce the overt functions of sibling relationships; yet at the same time, sibling status acquired subtle new psychological significance, particularly as a way of helping individual family members adapt to socioeconomic change. For Victorian parents, many of whom could not expect to live to see their children married and established in new careers, the motives for fostering intense sibling bonds are not difficult to explain. Such parents had a strong sense that children had to be taught to protect each other and to look out for each other's interests. For children, the motives for maintaining sibling solidarity, especially after the parents' deaths, were more complex. As we will see, bonds between siblings served important psychological and ideological functions as a means of deviating from parental expectations.[1]

In traditional settings, sibling status and birth order tend to play an active role in the family's pattern of behavior. Sibling status is directly tied to the preservation of family properties through inheritance customs by which children of a particular sibling status receive a specific allocation of property upon marriage or the parents' death. Elder siblings were often directly responsible for the care of younger children. Also, birth order played an important role in defining when females could marry. The effect of such factors was to link the economic fortunes of individual family members directly to those of their siblings.[2]

By the first decades of the nineteenth century, however, sibling status had become less important, at least in an overt and formal sense, in structuring family functions. Alterations in inheritance practices, marked by a shift toward bilateral inheritance (i.e., partible inheritance among all children, male and female), was only one of the changes that reduced the formal functions of siblingship. A sharp decline in birth-order marriages was an indication of the emergence of a society in which sibling status was unimportant in a formal sense in organizing family behavior. Siblings were increasingly able, in adulthood, to accept or reject the ties created by siblingship. A growing emphasis on the contractual nature of the bonds among family members in the middle-class home meant that sibling loyalties and responsibilities could be assumed or dispensed with on the basis of voluntary choice and self-interest.[3]

Yet, if by the nineteenth century sibling status was less important in a formal sense in the distribution of property and the functioning of individual households, less formal but still significant psychological functions were part of the sibling relationship. Indeed, it is a basic premise of this chapter that in a period of rampant change, fluidity, and self-seeking, the bonds between siblings acquired enormous symbolic significance as a tangible representation of duty, unity, and continuity.

As John Clive has suggested, the emotional significance attached to sibling bonds needs to be related to changes in social history, such as the economic pressures that encouraged a late age of marriage and the ethic of purity that discouraged early love affairs. In such a context, emotional impulses might be directed inward, toward other siblings. The pattern of education prevailing in certain Victorian homes buttressed sibling attachments. For children who received the bulk of their early education at home, their primary intellectual and emotional outlets

might be found among brothers and sisters. Had early education taken place outside the home, sibling bonds might have
been diluted by peer-group friendships. Even more important
than economic pressures and educational patterns in encourag-
ing intense emotional relationships among siblings was the nature of the life cycle. In the typical middle-class Victorian home,
the parents could not anticipate living to see their children se-
curely established as adults. Given this circumstance, parents were
intent on fostering sibling solidarity in childhood as a way to
provide their children with a network of support. Adding to
this concern with family solidarity was a widespread anxiety
about the number of middle-class daughters who were postpon-
ing marriage or not marrying at all. Whether this concern was
the result of an actual increase in the number of spinsters or was
due to the growing visibility of unmarried women when they
lived outside clear kinship structures is a subject in dispute
among historians. The essential point is that parents fostered
strong sibling bonds as a way of assisting these daughters as
they grew older. Such parental concern with providing for the
care of unmarried daughters may have been rooted in an intense
sense of personal responsibility. During the late eighteenth and
early nineteenth centuries it was common for parents to keep a
daughter at home to care for them in their old age, and these
daughters might find themselves too old to marry after their
parents' death. These unmarried women might focus their affections and emotional needs on siblings instead of on a mate. A
high proportion of unmarried daughters may have worked to
reinforce the intensity of the sibling bond.[4]

This chapter is an effort to explain why, at a time when the
economic fortunes of individual family members were no longer
directly linked to their siblings, sibling solidarity became a prevailing concern in the middle-class Victorian home. To answer
this question, we shall look closely at two families: Catharine
Sedgwick's, where the children attached enormous emotional
significance to sibling bonds; and Samuel Butler's, where a son
largely rejected the roles, loyalties, and identity furnished by his
family. These two examples suggest that sibling ties—like rela-

tions between spouses and between parents and children—were a focal point for larger cultural tensions and problems.

In a period of profound generational discontinuity, when many traditional institutions and beliefs were thrown into question, sibling ties became laden with potent symbolic meaning. A stress on sibling bonds provided a tangible symbol of connection to the past and a sense of membership in a cohesive group. The emphasis on sibling solidarity also helped to conceal the distance to which children had departed from the values of their parents' generation. In addition to helping to legitimate divergences from traditional beliefs, a stress on the selfless and dutiful nature of sibling relations created a set of values designed to counterbalance the materialism and self-seeking individualism of the market economy. For people who aspired to establish social relations on a more moral and voluntaristic basis, the bonds between siblings represented a crucial symbol of the harmony of interests and of voluntary cohesion. An emphasis on sibling bonds served other functions as well. In the isolated and restricted setting of the Victorian home, close sibling relations provided a vehicle through which children could experiment with adult roles. In a rapidly changing environment, where a father seemed inappropriate as a model for emulation, the bonds uniting siblings offered an alternate model of duty, legitimacy, and authority.

The domestic life of Catharine Sedgwick, America's most influential female novelist before Harriet Beecher Stowe, illustrates sibling solidarity in its most extreme form. A close reading of her personal papers will illuminate the needs and functions that close sibling attachments served and shed light on the factors that encouraged close personal ties between brothers and sisters. To understand the unusually close bonds that formed among the Sedgwick children, it is important to know about certain family circumstances that heightened the relationship among this group of siblings. Here, it is instructive to know that Theodore Sedgwick, her father, spent extensive periods of Catharine's childhood in Philadelphia, 280 miles away from the family home, as a Federalist party leader; that Pamela Dwight

Catharine Maria Sedgwick. From an engraving by G. Parker based on a painting by Charles Ingham. Courtesy of the National Portrait Gallery, Smithsonian Institution, Washington, D.C.

Sedgwick, her mother, was debilitated by protracted periods of mental depression, requiring the intensive care of the Sedgwick daughters; and that although Catharine briefly attended boarding schools, much of her early education took place at home.[5]

The outward circumstances of Catharine Sedgwick's life provided a setting that was conducive to the formation of close sibling ties. Her father's frequent absences from home during her early childhood appear to have intensified her emotional dependence on her siblings. Further, the need to care for an ailing mother helped create a sense of shared sacrifice that bound the Sedgwick children together. In addition, the unsystematic nature of Catharine's formal schooling meant that her education depended largely on the instruction of her father and her elder siblings. But these external circumstances only provided a context in which more important psychological needs encouraged strong sibling attachments.

As we look further into Sedgwick's life, it becomes clear that the emphasis she places on her relationship with her siblings does not stem simply from the amount of time the Sedgwick children spent together in childhood. It quickly becomes apparent that she regards her close ties with her siblings as an answer to deep personal needs and problems and also as a way to resolve certain central and compelling questions of religious authority and commitment. We cannot begin to appreciate the meanings that she attaches to sibling solidarity without a clear understanding of her conception of her family background, for her stress on the importance of bonds between siblings is intimately tied to her perception of the central problems of her time: the decline of the Federalist party and the growth of social democracy, mounting doubt about Calvinist orthodoxy, and deep anxieties regarding individualism.

In her "Recollections of Childhood," written to a niece when she was sixty-three, Catharine Sedgwick suggests the factors that led to an emphasis on sibling affections. The aspect of her youthful environment that impressed her most was a sense of "great ferment." Nothing could better describe the contrast between the world of her youth and of her adulthood than the figure of her father. To reflect upon her father was to return to another world, an era in which her father "habitually spoke politically of the people as 'Jacobins,' 'sans-culottes,' and 'miscreants.'" Her description of her childhood is revealing in her surprisingly ambiguous characterization of her father. On the one hand, he stands out as an enormously imposing figure, who devoted himself to "public life at every private sacrifice—at the expense of his domestic happiness, his home-life, which was his ruling passion." On the other hand, Theodore Sedgwick is depicted as a rather archaic figure of authority. His daughter stresses that even during his lifetime, the traditional framework of politics that he represented was breaking down: his well-ordered and like-minded Berkshire community was dissolving into political and religious contention; previously deferential groups of people, now "grasping, dishonest, and vulgar," were increasingly visible; older conceptions of politics, order, and stability were in flux.[6]

It is only within this context of ferment that one can understand the intensity of the Sedgwicks' family life. In the political arena changes of the most profound kind were disrupting older notions of authority, deference, and community. To the Sedgwick family, this condition of change was deeply disturbing, both on a personal and on an ideological level. Elder and younger Sedgwicks were acutely conscious of the danger of sailing rudderless through the stormy seas of social and political change. It was imperative, in such circumstances, to find a source of order and stability to counteract the divisive influences of the outside world. And Sedgwick remembered how, in the midst of social and political convulsions, the love that pervaded her family's household had represented a potent antidote to the disruptions and divisions surrounding it. What is most striking about this idealized picture of her childhood home is not its extreme sentimentality but rather the meaning she attached to domestic harmony. In a world in which radical political and social changes were challenging and transforming older conceptions of authority and order, the home became a place of stability and a refuge from individualistic values. The idealization of the home was related here to democratizing pressures that appeared to be disintegrating all conceptions of harmony, order, and community. "Neither the power of despots nor the universal legislation of our republic can touch" the love of the family, which was necessary to stabilize social change by inculcating respect for harmony, order, and other domestic virtues.[7]

An element of romanticization is central to Sedgwick's de-

scription of her girlhood home, a characteristic that is important in helping us reconstruct the meanings and functions she
attached to her relations with her siblings. The central images
in her picture of her natal home are threefold: of the dominat-
ing presence of Theodore Sedgwick, who through "nothing
short of a self devotion to his country's good" left his wife and
little children, winter after winter; of a mother suffering from
recurrent illnesses; and of the children, who had been entrusted
by their parents with the care and maintenance of the household. For Catharine, this idealized image of her childhood home
is laden with significance: her father is explicitly identified with
the "image of Him" who is God; her mother represents the
selflessness, submission, and piety that constitutes true sanctification; and the children are associated with duty, sacrifice, and
selfless devotion. Thus, the central themes in Catharine's idealized picture of her girlhood home center around domestic harmony, renunciation of self, and dedication to an object of selfless duty. What this suggests is the way the Sedgwick girlhood
home consciously is upheld as a counter to the divisions and
disruptions of the outside world. The family is here made a
symbolic representation of divine love and duty, a tangible
manifestation of divine reality. When these themes of harmony,
selflessness, and duty are taken together, they reconfirm that the
emphasis on family ties is viewed as an antidote to major cultural problems: fears of fragmentation, deep anxieties about her
capacity for independence, and an intense yearning for a calling
to which she might selflessly devote herself.[8]

The years 1808 and 1809 dealt Catharine a double blow. In
her recollections, the death of her mother when she was eighteen and the remarriage of her father the next year stand out as
decisive turning points in the children's lives, marked by the
first appearance of jealousy, estrangement, and conflict within
the family circle. For many children, the loss of a mother and
remarriage of a father create resentments directed at the new
stepmother. What is interesting about Catharine's resentments
is the language she used to describe her stepmother. The stepmother is portrayed as possessing a "sort of frittering dissipa-

tion incident to a single woman's social life in a fashionable town circle." Deeply distressed at seeing such a superficial woman in her mother's place, the stepmother emerges in Catharine's comments as an example not to be imitated, "a languid valetudinarian, petulant and annoying to the last degree." The new mother "fluttered gracefully enough through the inanities of town drawing rooms" but "knew nothing of the business" of the higher moral life. In her references to her stepmother, two themes are intertwined: a contempt for the weakness and ineffectuality of fashionable women and a resentment against the disruption of the domestic circle. Sedgwick's grievance against her stepmother is a double one: not only did the stepmother break the family's unity and harmony, but she also is a symbol of a kind of woman—the superficial social butterfly—that Catharine condemned most severely. Indifferent to fundamental questions of morality and religion, equally oblivious to the duties and responsibilities entailed by a moral life, the stepmother represents those frivolous ladies of fashion who ignore the higher purposes of life.[9]

Sedgwick's recollections are as revealing in what they omit as in what they tell. It is noteworthy that she fails to draw any connections between the estrangements that accompanied her father's remarriage and the intense family conflicts over religion that erupted simultaneously. In what she tells us about these religious conflicts several themes stand out as carrying special significance. First is Catharine's conviction that orthodox Calvinism is a fetter threatening to shackle her and her sisters. She describes her sister Eliza as suffering "from the horrors of Calvinism," as being cast into a deep slough by her strict faith, a gloomy depression that seemed to have contributed to their mother's insanity. What is most remarkable about Catharine's comments is her perception of orthodox Calvinism as a force limiting women's role and influence, leaving them "elevated and unseen." In her references to the "cruel doctrines of Geneva," Catharine associates Calvinism with coldness, despair, and otherworldliness, factors that in her view tended to limit women's duties and responsibilities. What distressed her most about orthodox Calvinism was the morbid and unnatural sense of helplessness and alienation inculcated by the creed. In attacking the austere Hopkinsian version of Calvinism in which her family was raised—which held that Christ had died to manifest God's wrath against sin, rather than the strictly Calvinist doctrine that Christ's death was a vicarious atonement for men's sins—we might conjecture that Catharine was able to give voice to a rejection of the "incubus" that oppressed and burdened women's lives. Significantly, she concludes her comments by saying that redemption from Calvinism brings "a true apprehension of the filial relation to God."[10]

A second theme that emerges from Catharine's disclosures about religion is her intense sense of personal weakness and isolation. Although hostile to aspects of Calvinist orthodoxy, she remained caught up in the grip of the aspirations her religion prescribed. Eager to attain a life of perfect holiness and selflessness, she was never able to free herself from the feeling that she was preoccupied with the self. In her words, we can detect a strong note of ambivalence that surrounded her questioning of her family's religion. "If there is any thing that pervades my whole character," she notes disparagingly, "it is the love of freedom that 'leaveneth the whole lump.'" In much the same way that Eliot and Stowe deplored their uncontrollable sense of ambition and love of self, Sedgwick too was tormented by the sufferings of conscience. What was most upsetting to her was her "utter destitution of any 'claim to reward'"; her "entire helplessness as it regards any merit of" her own; her "entire dependence on mercy, mediation, and atonement." She could never rid herself of the feeling that her heart was devoid of the reverence required by a Supreme Being and, after intensive self-examination, felt herself to be without fixed beliefs on the most material points of religion. Even more disturbing was her consciousness that any "change of scene or society" was enough to induce her "to shake off" interest in serious matters "as fetters that constrained my vitality." What we see here is the profound sense of despondency that repeatedly wracked the evangelical conscience. Deeply divided between an ideal of perfect selflessness and holiness, and constant struggles with temptations to sin, she was terrified by the thought of losing "the precious anchor" that stabilized her emotions. Heavily burdened by the weakness and mutability of her deepest emotions, she, like Eliot and Stowe, desperately desired a mission in which she might selflessly submerge her identity.[11]

As we enter into her letters further, a theme that becomes evident is her intense yearning for a calling to which she could devote herself passionately. In response to her father's remark that when people grow old, their friends and relatives must resign themselves to their passing, Catharine, then eleven, writes excitedly: "Do you think, my dear papa, that I could leave my dear parents in their old age?" She proceeds to tell him that she could never leave them voluntarily and that her highest hope was to serve them in their old age, in order to "reward them for all their kind care." What we hear, in her letters, is an ardent desire for a feminine mission that might in some way be a match for her father's accomplishments. She writes that she has closely observed her father's life "to find some rules of action to apply to my own." She admitted to feeling the "disappointment that the humble architect of a cottage" has when surveying a palace, but continued to regard him as an appropriate model for emulation. "You may benefit a nation, my dear papa, and I may improve the condition of a fellow-being." Her life might be confined to "the limited routine of domestic life," but it could still be dignified by the same characteristics that distinguished her father's accomplishments: a dedication to usefulness and a desire to serve others selflessly.[12]

As the preceding paragraphs indicate, the problem that Sedgwick confronted most directly in her early life was a problem of "replication." What is constantly present in her letters is an uneasy recognition that she faces a very different social situation from that of her parents and that she will not be able to replicate her parents' lives, particularly her mother's. She longed intently for a feminine mission, one that would be "serious," "selfless," and "useful," but she felt an absence of suitable role models for emulation. In a period of transition, when discontinuity in

Theodore Sedgwick (1746–1813), father of Catharine Sedgwick. From a portrait by Gilbert Stuart. Courtesy of the Museum of Fine Arts, Boston.

personal experience is extreme, parents who represent older ways can no longer be easily accepted as models for succession. From her account, we know that she deeply admired her father but felt that his imposing and autocratic manner was inappropriate in an increasingly democratic era. What she has to say about her stepmother is filled with scorn; she describes her as lacking the earnestness and fixity of purpose necessary for a Christian life. Perhaps the most interesting portrayal in Sedgwick's recollections is that of her mother. Although Catharine adopted an attitude of worship toward the memory of her mother, exalting her as a model of "submissive piety," her comments are double-faced: her mother emerges as lacking the mental and physical strength to carry "the terrible weight of domestic cares." Her account of her parents and stepmother serves an important purpose. What it tells us is that the profound social changes of the late eighteenth and early nineteenth centuries could be experienced on an intensely personal level in terms of generational discontinuity.[13]

As we explore Sedgwick's life, we will observe the way that she sought to conceptualize continuities in her life. What we will discover is the way the family itself provided an answer to the problems of discontinuity and rootlessness of an increasingly individualistic age. The family was used as a psychological resource through which she and her siblings were able to respond to profound changes in their lives. The most important symbol of these changes in Catharine's life was the death of her father in 1813. His death, when she was twenty-four, seemed to symbolize broader fragmentations. With the death of her father, she became acutely conscious of her isolation and separation. She, like Eliot at the same moment in her life, felt a poignant fear of dissipation and uselessness and was alarmed that the loss of her father's authority would signal the disintegration of her moral character. Having lost her only social duty, of caring for her aged parent, she now feared the loss of all "counsel, protection, and love." As if these personal agonies were not enough, Catharine also experienced intense religious doubts. She cries out in her letters about the weakness of her moral character and fears that she will never be able to meet the requirements of her Heavenly Father. Fearfully lonely for her deceased father, stricken by deep spiritual doubts, she reached out to her brothers and sisters for fellowship and moral support. She called out for her siblings to recognize the "sacredness in the love of orphan children" and announced that it was their duty now to serve her "as the representatives of my father." [14]

For Catharine, the loss of her father was a shattering experience that disclosed the precariousness of all love and affection. Yet what is notable about her fears following her father's death is the way they mirror earlier religious anxieties. Long before her father's death she had voiced acute concern that her heavenly prospects depended entirely on the "indulgence" of her holy Father and that without the guidance and support of him her future would be gloomy. What emerges from both her father's deathbed comments and her religious doubts is an expression of a deep ambivalence about her capacity for independence and of her longing for a guardian who will counteract her feelings of weakness and despair. In her expressions of spiritual despondency and loss at the death of her father, Catharine provides us with valuable clues to the sources of her passionate desire for strong sibling bonds. Sibling bonds become a way of symbolizing unity, harmony, and continuity in the midst of disruptive change. Sibling ties also suggest a structure of reciprocal duties and obligations that she had found earlier in serving Theodore Sedgwick. [15]

Immediately following the death of her father, Catharine felt a compelling urge to write to her siblings about the subject of marriage. She announced that she was "satisfied, by long and delightful experience," that she could "never love any body better than my brothers." Furthermore, she had no expectation of ever finding their match. Her brothers should not be alarmed, she continued; she was not on the verge of a vow of celibacy, nor did she have "the slightest intentions of adding any rash resolutions to the ghosts of those that have been frightened to death by the terrors of maiden life." Still, she emphasized, "notwithstanding the proverbial mutability of a woman's inclination, the probability is in favor of my continuing to stamp all the coin of my kindness with a *sister's* impress."[16]

For Catharine, this declaration of sibling love served multiple functions. Most directly, the emphasis Catharine attached to sibling bonds was a response to a fear about the breakup of her own family following her father's death, when she became acutely conscious of her isolation. But we might speculate that her feelings of separation and loneliness were also a response to larger sources of strain and estrangement. Her quest for the security, wholeness, and warmth of the sibling bond may well have been accentuated by the disruptive changes occurring in the outside world. In a rootless, democratic society lacking the possibility of genuine "communion" with others, only the family remained as an agent of continuity, as a symbol of a tangible past, and as a stabilizing force. In a period of rampant change, the family acquired symbolic significance as a shelter from the world of bewildering change and as an antidote to individualistic aspirations. We might hypothesize that Sedgwick's mood of weakness and despair had its roots in painful personal loss and was also attributable to the consciousness of isolation that accompanied the growing rationalization and differentiation of life. Whatever its sources, this sense of isolation and despair could drive an individual to seek in family bonds a model of coherence, harmonious unity, innocence, security, and a symbol of selflessness and unifying belief.

That Sedgwick was convinced that her relations with her siblings should be those of an unmarried sister had its roots in a deep personal ambivalence toward marriage. Like Eliot and Stowe, she had an ardent desire to achieve perfect holiness and purity and, like those writers, recoiled from the temptations to selfishness she associated with marriage. It was the admonition of the apostles, she was convinced, that people had to learn "to possess not." To live as a true Christian required a person to learn that "it is good, to be left alone," and Catharine regarded marriage as a key symbol of all the forces that kept her from achieving moral perfection. In her private journal she wrote of her earnest longing to "rise more above the world" and to attain that state of purity "where self may lose some of its engrossing power"; and she was deeply troubled by the thought that marriage would multiply her worldly ties. To reject marriage was a way to renounce self and to resist temptation and to strive to shape the character into the image of Christ. Then, too, Catharine shrank from marriage because of a perception that marital ties often resulted in unhappiness. All around her she saw the "rapid decay of matrimonial love," and she regarded marriage itself as "very meddling and impertinent." [17]

Once again we see how a vocabulary taken from evangelical religion could be used by a woman to give voice to aspirations and desires that otherwise lacked social sanction. An emphasis on the evangelical ideas of holiness and purity provided a language that helped reconcile conflicting values. Evangelical Protestantism has two very different sides—one of which stresses the individual conscience and another that is preoccupied with self-renunciation and sacrifice—and Sedgwick reveals how these two sets of ideals could be invoked by a woman seeking to assert a measure of personal independence. Marriage, she implies, was one of those human relationships that arouses the base impulses of selfish individualism and possessiveness; celibacy becomes emblematic of purity and self-transcendence. Yet at the same time that the evangelical ideal of holiness could rationalize the motivations for electing not to marry, the language Sedgwick employs also suggests an element of self-doubt, particularly in regard to her capacity for independence. Her personal journal states unequivocally the theme that she must resign herself to the fact that her life is denied true earthly happiness. "My life is a good deal like that of the Israelites," she notes dejectedly. She is "but a sojourner" passing through this world. Here, we see that evangelical values could cut two ways: if the evangelical emphasis on absolute purity and holiness could provide a woman with an indirect way of criticizing dependency-generating relationships, the value attached to self-renunciation and sacrifice could also result in a profound sense of guilt over assertions of independence. [18]

For a conscientious soul such as Sedgwick, eager to find an

object to which she could dedicate herself, devotion to siblings became a tangible way to overcome spiritual despondency and self-doubt. As she remarks in her recollections of her childhood, she could "conceive of no truer image of the purity and happiness of the equal loves of Heaven than that which unites brothers and sisters." Essentially the same message was made in a series of letters to her siblings: "If ever I attain any adequate conception of the purity, and peace, and intensity of heavenly affections, it is from that I feel for you." The extravagance of Catharine's romanticization of sibling love was shared by her brothers and sisters. Sibling affection is celebrated as a higher form of love, " 'shuffled of all mortal coil' of earthiness . . . perfectly spiritualized, and yet . . . [retaining] its power of contact with every part of its subject." Sibling love is emphasized as a purifier of man's carnal nature, as a counterbalance to the everyday preoccupation with worldly ambitions. This is an affection that "has an irresistible power to improve and elevate, to lift above low attachments, to separate from unworthy associations."[19]

All these descriptions of sibling affection entail the same meaning: that the bond between brothers and sisters is preeminently pure, selfless, and spiritual. Catharine herself goes so far as to contrast the purity of the sibling bond with the marital tie. A yearning for exclusive love, she declares, is merely a sign of "selfish weakness," and she hoped dearly that her heart was strong enough to surmount the earthly desire to possess another person's love wholly. Trying desperately to achieve absolute purity and self-denial in her own life, Catharine dedicated her emotional energies to her siblings. Here was a supreme object to which she could dedicate herself totally. The intensity of this commitment can be seen vividly in the anguish she suffered upon the decision of her brothers and sisters to marry. Although Catharine was only seven when her sister Eliza married, she remembered this incident intensely "as the first tragedy of my life." She continued to think of the groom as a "cruel usurper." Her sister Eliza in turn portrayed Catharine as her "sister—mother—child—friend." The marriage of her brother Robert, when she was thirty-three, brought a similar sense of loss and disruption. To a sister she confided how she had "tasked myself to the duty of resignation." She acknowledged that she ought to express "gratitude" in gaining a new sister-in-law, so that each "repining thought" brought "the sting of guilt with it." Her brother showed touching sensitivity to her feelings. In a letter, he observed that "it is a very common sentiment that a sister must give up her place in a brother's heart when his wife takes possession of it." But he assured his sister that in his case this would not be so: "If this were so," he added, "I should be sorry to see you ever reconciled to my marriage." [20]

In what Catharine discloses about her anguish over her siblings' marriages, the major theme that stands out is her view of herself as an outcast from her father's home. Here, one suspects her comments are not merely idiosyncratic but may reflect the needs and insecurities of a particular class of people—isolated spinsters who felt themselves barred from productive lives. As Catharine noted, "the great disadvantage and the only reproach of a single life is, that we poor spinsters are generally condemned to uselessness." Throughout her correspondence she says that the great problem for a spinster is to resign herself to the vicissitudes of beginning life as "the primary object of affection to many" and then "to come by degrees to be first to none." Expanding on this observation in her personal journal, she reminded herself that such diminution of affection "is the necessity of a solitary condition, an unnatural state." On the basis of her personal experience, she would not advise any woman to remain unmarried. Her experience had been singularly happy: her feelings had not been embittered by the slights and taunts the repulsive have to endure. There was no moment in her life when she might not have married respectably, and her fortune was adequate to support her in leisure. Yet the result of all this happy experience was "that there is no equivalent [in her life] for those blessings which Providence has placed first, and ordained that they should be purchased at the dearest sacrifice." This passage is significant because it provides us with a rare glimpse into the sense of anxiety and alienation that even a highly

successful unmarried woman could experience during the nineteenth century.[21]

The decision to remain unmarried was not fully Catharine's.
Significantly, in 1827, when Catharine was thirty-eight and a well-
known author, her siblings responded severely to rumors of her
possible engagement. Her eldest brother, Theodore, articulated
the family's objections to a marriage. His sister's present situation was "certainly a singularly happy one"; she must not, on
light grounds, change it. Her brothers and sisters were dependent on her for her wise counsel and moral support and would
be unhappy if she changed her marital status: "The sincere, tried,
devoted affection of all the older members of the family, the
tender and filial reverence and attachment of the younger . . .
serve to bind you to that spot and confine you within that circle
in which these blessings are enjoyed." Such sisterly affection was
something that the family could "not willingly anticipate any
contingencies which may deprive us of it." This statement is as
remarkable for its invocation of the values of "self-denial" and
"sacrifice" as it is for its presumptuousness. Not a word of criticism is directed at Catharine's possible future husband, nor is
there a hint that selfish motives might lie behind the arguments
opposing the marriage. Instead, Catharine is simply asked to
sacrifice her personal pleasure for the higher good of the family.[22]

As we probe further into Sedgwick's life, it becomes apparent
that her family's emphasis on sibling loyalty and affection was
not only a way to deal with personal emotional needs for support but also a way to deal with fundamental religious problems. In an era of bitter religious controversy, when traditional
religious dogmas were being called into question and the influence of the clergy appeared to be eroding, domestic relations
became a model for divine love. To a barren and lifeless theology, the intimate relations of the family provided fresh symbols
of selflessness, sacrifice, harmonious union, and continuity. For
Sedgwick, the dutiful relations within a family became a prototype for the relations of God with his children and Christ with
his sisters and brothers. Thus, the Sedgwicks' conception of re-

ligion was shaped and influenced by their perception of their own family.

In what Catharine tells us about her family's religious life, one incident stands out as carrying particular importance: her father's deathbed profession of faith. Theodore Sedgwick's decision to publicly profess his religious faith on his deathbed stood as a potent symbol to his children. According to his daughter, he had deferred making a public statement of faith from a very unworthy motive: he had feared giving pain to his neighbors by joining any other church than theirs. When the elder Sedgwick finally felt prepared to assert his faith, he asked that the liberal Boston minister William Ellery Channing administer the sacrament (this occurred before Channing became involved in the "Unitarian controversy" that split New England Congregationalism over the question of man's capacity for moral improvement). In his children's eyes, this incident was significant for three reasons: it revealed their father's desire to transcend theological controversies, to be released from the dominion of sin, and "to repose himself entirely on the merits and atonements" of Christ. Once performed, the sacrament, in Catharine's view, had a transforming effect on her father's character: its administration seemed "to remove the bar of reserve that opposed the flowing out of papa's heart," and "the Word of God" he now "listens to with unremitting interest." The lesson of Theodore Sedgwick's profession of faith was simple and clearcut: it represented the triumph of religious liberalism over Calvinist orthodoxy.[23]

The relationship between the father's deathbed profession of faith in 1813 and his children's conversion to Channing's Unitarianism in the early 1820s is unclear. What is interesting psychologically, however, is the way the children sought to rationalize their conversion so that it did not seem to involve a break with their family's religious traditions. For the Sedgwick children, the conversion to Unitarianism was a way to remain faithful to their father's example. What we see is the way people sought to conceptualize continuities in their lives during a period of profound change. For the Sedgwicks, the movement away from

Calvinist orthodoxy was accompanied by a subtle shift in language. What they asked for from religion was the love that would serve the functions that, they believed, their own family had fulfilled: to provide guidance, protection, fellowship, and moral support. A focus on a religion of love and consolation helped to obscure the degree to which the children were in fact departing from the world of their father.

After their father's death, the Sedgwick children experienced an intense sense of loss and grief and expressed a great hunger for "purity, and peace, and intensity of heavenly affection." But religious discussions within the family brought only pain and contention. Inevitably, in Catharine's words, "the disposition to be convinced did not yield to the pride of producing conviction." Despite their religious differences, the children agreed on what they wanted—the "confidence and obedience that we are no longer outcasts from his family." This statement is important because it illustrates the functions that the children wanted religion to serve: to furnish the sense of relatedness and the emotions of love and selflessness they had found within their own family. Writing a year after her father's death, Catharine observed that the consolation of religious faith was "the incalculable comfort resulting from it—that simplicity of confidence that a little child feels in the presence of a parent where he is assured that nothing will harm him." In Catharine's letters, the figure of God is made analogous to her own father; her image of Christ is modeled on her conception of her own brothers and sisters. The purity and benevolence of family relations are explicitly identified with the characteristics of divine love.[24]

When Catharine finally broke with orthodox Calvinism during the winter of 1821, to join a Unitarian church, she declared that her primary objection to the orthodox creed was that it disrupted families, whereas the "purer and more rational faith" of Unitarianism tended to bring families together: "While those of the orthodox faith are . . . forsaking brethren and sisters," liberal religion taught a doctrine of love and sympathy. The Calvinist conception of a distant, awe-inspiring God tended to induce "habits of listfulness and indifference," while the doctrines of election and innate human depravity served to instill a morbid sense of helplessness and isolation. What she longed for was a religion that exhibited the confidence, support, and love she associated with her own family. As older theological dogmas gave way to feelings of doubt and despondency, and as traditional beliefs came into question, Sedgwick could find in her ties with her siblings a potent symbol of purity, innocence, and harmonious union. "There I have located my heaven," she wrote, and in an age of bewildering change and nagging doubt, her words show how a Victorian could grasp the more closely to sibling bonds as an anchor within a sea of loneliness and confusion.[25]

We are now in a position to decipher the symbolic meaning that Unitarianism carried for Sedgwick. To this woman, feeling by moments stricken by doubts, loneliness, and an overpowering sense of weakness, Unitarianism was a "religion of brothers" that makes "known to us the Father's love." She describes in a letter the great appeal of liberal religion to her: it has shown that "the mysteries of life, death, and immortality" are immediately and tangibly present in the intimate relations of the family. And of Channing, who had brought Catharine and her siblings into the Unitarian fold? He had shown "not merely the confidence of a child to the father, but the tenderness that is commonly felt to the mother," and had reassured the Sedgwicks of their holy Father's affection.[26]

The problem Sedgwick confronted repeatedly during her life was to find a way to adapt the values of authority, deference, and discipline she identified with her father to a radically changing social environment. Fearful that her father's death would signal the dissolution of other moral and familial bonds, she clung the more tightly to her siblings as a way to resist the atomizing, individualizing pressures surrounding her. For Sedgwick, as for many other Victorians, the disruption of the public world greatly intensified the attraction of sibling solidarity. In a period of enormous flux and fluidity, when older conceptions of community and kinship were cast aside, and further undermined by the erosion of certain traditional beliefs, the sibling bond stood as a island of stability, harmony, and continuity in a world of change. In an increasingly individualistic age, sibling bonds provided a tangible example of selflessness and voluntary cohesion—an ideal that would exert a strong influence on religious aspirations. The meaning attached to sibling bonds is a double one: if an emphasis on sibling ties was a vehicle for expressing anxieties over individualism and the disruptions accompanying social change, sibling relations also provided a set of values—of self-denial, sacrifice, and continuity—that helped individuals such as Sedgwick adapt to this world while obscuring the distance to which she and her siblings had moved from the world of their father.

Samuel Butler, author of *The Way of All Flesh,* was acutely conscious of the subtle ways that society disguised cruelty and manipulation behind a smoke screen of duty, self-sacrifice, and pious sentiments, and in his great novel on Victorian family life he sought to illustrate the moral pretensions of the Victorian family by quoting from a letter his mother had written to him when he was six. In 1841, when Fanny Butler wrote this letter, she lay weak in pregnancy, certain that death was near. Two thoughts pressed heavily upon her as she inscribed a last note to Samuel and a younger brother. Her first thought was that her sons be mindful of the sorrow that was soon to fall upon their father. Young children, she observed caustically, quickly forget the loss of a mother; but a father would find his only earthly consolation in his children. Fanny Butler's other concern was for her children's "everlasting welfare." "Snares and temptations from within and without" would beset her sons as they grew older, and she exhorted the boys to work together to resist evil and to gain the victory over self. She reminded her sons that their father had striven selflessly to promote their eternal happiness, and she urged the boys to reciprocate these sentiments by being obedient, attentive, and self-denying.[27]

In her final words, Fanny Butler made another entreaty to which she attached special significance. She told her sons that

"Family Prayers." A painting by Samuel Butler, 1864. Courtesy of the Master and Fellows of St. John's College, Cambridge.

they carried "a name which must not be disgraced" and emphasized that they were descendants of a grandfather and father of whom they must "shew themselves worthy." She called on them to "be true through life to each other—love as only brothers should do," for in the divisions and fragmentations of life it was vital that brothers provide each other with moral support. Finally, she reminded her sons that as elder members of the family they carried special responsibility for their sister, especially if she were to remain unmarried or their father were to die prematurely.[28]

Butler quoted this letter because it illustrated the most detestable form of moral pretense in the Victorian home: the pretension of parents to being more pious and more moral than they actually were. Yet there was a deeper reason for citing this letter. It epitomized the almost obsessive preoccupation of Butler's parents' generation with family continuity and solidarity. A demand that children live up to their family's name was a powerful tool for shaping character in the Victorian middle-class home. Not only Butler, but numerous other Victorians learned the importance attached to family continuity. When Charles Darwin recorded the details of his life, he recounted that one of his most vivid memories was of being told that his conduct and attitude made him a disgrace to his family name. Similarly, Henry Adams notes in his autobiography that the most trying moment of his life was when he was chastised by his grandfather for failing to live up to the name of Adams.[29]

The example of Sedgwick is important because it indicates how the disruptive social and intellectual changes of the early nineteenth century could heighten the appeal of family solidarity. Butler's life is useful in illustrating the intensely ambivalent emotions that accompanied the increased stress on family continuity and solidarity during the nineteenth century, especially as variants on Darwinism added to the meaning of such concepts as family identity, heredity, and inheritance. What Butler's life poignantly illuminates are the ceaseless conflicts that arose from a nagging sense that blood ties exert a real influence and obligation on an individual's life combined with a conviction that family duties are an illegitimate burden. This was a topic that engrossed Butler's attention in his scientific work, but it also dominated his private correspondence. On the one hand, Butler was struck by the unbridgeable gap that seemed to separate biological generations; on the other hand, he was also convinced of the existence of important continuities and identities between parents and children. For Butler, this issue was not simply a theoretical question. In his own life, he tried repeatedly to test the terms of his relationship with his parents and sisters, to clarify the nature of his responsibilities and obligations to his family, and to examine what it was that his family transmitted across generations.

Of the pictures of Butler that have engaged the popular imagination most vividly, the best known is that of the iconoclast who readily subjected family relationships to close critical scrutiny. Nowhere does this stereotypical image find more acute expression than in Butler's notebooks where Butler wrote acidly of what he believed to be the source of more personal unhappiness than anything else. He referred to the attempt to prolong family connections unduly and to make people stick together artificially. He was haunted by the pain that such unnatural associations had caused in his family. He was sure that his great-grandfather did not look forward to meeting his father in heaven, for his father had cut him out of his will. Nor could he imagine that his grandfather had any great longing to rejoin his great-grandfather, who was a worthy enough man but for whom nothing ever prospered. He was certain that his father, after he was forty, did not wish to see Butler's grandfather anymore. And speaking for himself, he had "no wish to see my father again."[30]

In his notebooks, Butler attributed the battle of sons against fathers to three sources. First was the pretension of fathers to supreme moral authority. Convinced that he was acting for his child's own good, certain that he was motivated only by the purest moral sentiments, a father easily mistook his personal preferences for the will of God and believed himself entitled to unreasoning obedience. Second, the father-son relationship was further complicated by the lack of clear obligations, responsibilities, and expectations between the parties, which led a father to exercise his prerogatives capriciously. Here was a relationship based neither on affinity nor upon any clear understanding between individuals. Then, too, Butler thought the conflict between a father and son reflected a larger biological conflict in nature, in which a new generation sought to adapt to changing conditions and to free itself from the iron grip of its predecessors.[31]

In marked contrast to this stereotypical image of Butler as hostile to all bonds based on consanguinity is another picture that emerges from one of his last works, a two-volume life and letters of his grandfather and namesake, Dr. Samuel Butler. No doubt, Butler set out to write this book in part to vex his father, who disdained the grandfather, and to annoy the followers of

Dr. Thomas Arnold of Rugby, who, the grandson believed, had appropriated his ancestor's accomplishments. But for anyone aware of Butler's reputed hostility to family bonds what is striking about this biography is the way he emphasizes the continuities and identities existing between grandfather and grandson. The picture that emerges from the biography resembles no one more closely than Samuel Butler himself. Like his grandson, the elder Butler attached the greatest significance to reforms that promoted "greater adaptability to changing circumstances hereafter." His religious views, too, anticipated the younger Butler's; in the grandson's words, "he recognized the fatuousness of the attempt to stereotype once and for ever the creed of any nation." Butler expressed "fascination" about this forebear who, unlike his father, was "ready to make all charitable allowances for others who differed widely from himself," and we might see in this biography Butler's effort, late in life, to prove indirectly that he had remained loyal to his family's traditions.[32]

To reflect upon the preceding discussion is to get a sense of how important a role family traditions could play in the psychological life of a Victorian. Even a person like Samuel Butler, who was acutely conscious of the plain discrepancies between the Victorian mythos of the family and family realities, felt a deep sense of family identity. The characteristics that arise most vividly from an examination of Butler's letters is a sense of paradox and contradiction: his letters are colored with a note of contempt and scorn toward his family; yet, he continued to keep close personal contact with his father and sisters.

An account of the genesis of Butler's highly ambivalent attitudes toward his family must begin with a heated personal conflict that erupted between father and son in 1859, when Butler was twenty-four, over the son's choice of a profession. Contention first surfaced in March, when Butler returned to Cambridge University, after preparing for ordination by serving for six months as a lay assistant in a London parish. Butler returned to Cambridge ostensibly with the goal of preparing for fellowships, but to his father, his motives were unclear, and Canon Butler asked, by letter, to know what his son intended to do with his life. He told Samuel that he had no special desire that he follow in his footsteps and be ordained, nor did he want to press his son into becoming a schoolmaster, but he definitely did want him "to do *something* for your living for your own sake." If Samuel were to say that he was content simply to remain at college, and would prefer to live on his allowance in order to improve his mind, then his father would not countenance this and threatened to decrease his allowance. Canon Butler's goal was not to force his son into any particular profession but simply to insist that he pursue some career. This letter provides us with an important clue to the nature of strains within the Butler household: a father attaches tremendous importance to his son's achieving personal independence but cautions that such independence not lead toward indecisiveness or self-indulgence.[33]

Butler's reply was to say that if his father insisted that he leave Cambridge, the only direction congenial to him would be to emigrate—to Liberia, perhaps, where he could promote cotton growing. Only indirectly did Butler indicate why he preferred to stay at the university or to emigrate abroad. He stated ambiguously that "a person when once he adopts ideas out of the common way, whether he be right or whether he be wrong he is done for here." Evidently, Butler was hinting to his father that his reasons for not remaining as a lay cleric stemmed from spiritual doubts. That this was the case is apparent in a letter written the next day to his mother. In his note, Butler heartily repented "having trusted my feelings to letter," for he feared that his words had resulted in misconceptions about his religious views. To his mother, Butler added that he could readily understand the hurt and vexation his father suffered to see his son sponging off of him and not finding a career as speedily as possible. But with words tinged with a certain bitterness he proceeded to say how galling he found it that his father had raised "the threat of 'docking one's allowance' (as if I had done something scandalous)." His first inclination, he wrote, was to do without the allowance altogether, but he decided against this course of action after becoming convinced that "it would only be cutting my own nose to spite my face." The pattern of thought illustrated in this letter is revealing: although Butler hoped desperately to free himself from his father's advice and to assert his independence, he continued to regard his father's authority as legitimate. Butler's indignation, at this point, was directed entirely against his father's threat to cut down his allowance—a permissible argument, because it was aimed only at an illegitimate mode of paternal influence.[34]

In his next letter, Canon Butler sought to correct misimpressions his earlier letter had evoked. He began by assuring his son that he had no desire to drive him into a line of life that he would find uncongenial. He added that he had no objections to his son remaining at Cambridge temporarily. But he then leveled two criticisms against his son. The first was that his son had failed to be candid and had concealed his actual motives for returning to Cambridge. The father decried his son's failure to state openly that he "had become some way or other discontented with the notion of taking" holy orders, and declared that his son's lack of openness indicated a lack of trust. The father's second charge was that the son's letters revealed indecision and vacillation. The idea of emigrating to Liberia "was the wildest conceivable vision"; as for the plan of raising cotton, Canon Butler observed that his son knew "less of farming than even I do." The father emphasized that all he wanted from his son was some sign that he had found some direction in his life. Butler senior wanted "a path," but what he found instead was "nothing but tangled brambles."[35]

It is difficult to read these early letters without developing a degree of sympathy for Canon Butler. What he was seeking from his son was some sign that he had developed a capacity for self-government and self-direction. As long as his son was unable to demonstrate this capability, however, he felt morally bound to exercise his paternal authority for his son's own good. Far from displaying contempt for his son's scruples, the elder Butler was simply asking his son to prove the strength of his moral character.

What began as a mild family dispute over a son's vocation

quickly escalated into a heated debate over the parents' moral authority. The father interpreted his son's indecision as a symptom of a broader moral flaw: as a rebellion against the whole ethos prescribing deference to authority, self-denial, and respect for religious and social proprieties. The son, in turn, came increasingly to believe that his father confused his own desires with the voice of duty and confounded his own position with the authority of God. The explanation for this escalating conflict is that both parties more and more saw the dispute as involving fundamental issues of legitimacy, authority, and moral duty. To the son, the contest involved nothing less than freedom of conscience. To the father, the issue that was raised was whether his son would acknowledge obedience to any authority, social or intellectual.[36]

It seems likely that Canon Butler's anxious concern for his son's future was not simply idiosyncratic but was closely connected with the circumstances of a particular class and culture. Behind his stress on self-direction and decisiveness lay a deep-seated fear that weakness of moral character would result in both economic and moral disaster. Canon Butler's letters indicated an intense concern that he lacked "the capital to be sunk in some overwhelming" failure on his son's part. He was particularly anxious lest his son "fall into a class not likely to be congenial" to the family. This fear of financial failure was intimately related to a fear worse than loss of money, a fear for his son's conscience and character. A father could understand a son's objections to entering the church. But what moral objections, Canon Butler asked, could a son have to entering, say, the bar? "Still," he insisted that he did not quarrel with this refusal: "but it rests with you," he told his son pointedly, "to find a substitute."[37]

To the modern reader there is something distinctively Victorian in the language and style of thought father and son exhibit in their letters, in particular, the emphasis on duty, self-sacrifice, hypocrisy, and obedience. In the father's letters, it is clear that a large part of his unhappiness stems from a feeling that his son treats his "just remonstrances as a letter from an equal." His son seemed to be unwilling to acknowledge the legitimacy of paternal authority and the need for filial submission. The son disputed this view and contended that if only his father would allow him a degree of self-determination, he would "secure a willing obedience . . . in the place of a sullen acquiescence." His father would have not simply external conformity to his wishes but obedience that was truly inward. In his reply, Canon Butler questioned whether this would truly be "willing obedience." An offer of "willing obedience to the very course you desire and we disapprove is [hardly] any great self-sacrifice on your part." What defines this exchange as emphatically Victorian is that it is based on a series of characteristically nineteenth-century juxtapositions: behavior is actuated either by moral principles and kindly sentiments or by selfish emotions; obedience is either passive acquiescence or it is based on active consent. This stress on duty, self-sacrifice, and inner motives can be traced intellectually back to the influence of the Scottish moralists and the Evangelical Revival. Yet the Victorian emphasis on such concepts as duty, self-renunciation, and willing obedience was also related to a more general social problem of maintaining deference to authority in the absence of traditional social controls. Unable to take for granted unquestioning obedience even within the family, Victorians looked to various internalized self-restraints to provide a substitute for external forms of discipline. Duty, self-denial, and self-discipline were to lay the foundation for voluntary submission and noncoercive order.[38]

Given the emotional misery that the contention between Butler and his father aroused, the family conflict ended surprisingly amiably. By the end of July, Samuel had expressed his willingness to give in to his parents' wishes and to undertake a career in the law. He still professed a strong dislike for this alternative and feared that the project would result only "in disappointment" for his parents "and unhappiness" for himself, and so he humbly asked his father's consent to a single year of instruction in art. Failing this, he requested permission to emigrate to New Zealand, where he might support himself raising cattle or sheep. In his letter, Samuel sought to turn his father's statements to his own purposes. He noted that he had heard his father "often

The Butler Family. Standing, left to right: Samuel Butler; Mrs. Thomas Butler, II; Thomas Butler, II; Canon Butler. Seated, left to right: Harriet Butler; Mrs. Butler; May Butler. Courtesy of the Master and Fellows of St. John's College, Cambridge.

say that you would never force a lad into a profession against his will," and that if a person was "sufficient fool to choose a profession" contrary to his abilities, the only way he will "get wisdom is by experience," and asked that these sentiments be applied to himself. With words exhibiting uncharacteristic diffidence, Butler concluded by emphasizing that no matter how differently he and his father might think, a son had "no right to treat" his parent without respect. The father also sounded chastened. He wrote that he was now anxious to meet his son's "desires as far as they seem not likely to be injurious," consented to his son's decision to emigrate, and promised financial aid.[39]

What is particularly striking when one shifts from Butler's letters to his father to his letters to his siblings is that they exhibit the same paternal tone as his father's letters to him. This is interesting because it parallels a pattern that we already saw in the letters of Robert Louis Stevenson. Despite his bitter personal conflict with his father, Stevenson virtually recapitulated his father's behavior and attitudes in rearing his stepson. Butler, too, adopted the same pose of moral authority in addressing his siblings that his father revealed to him. What we see in these letters is the way that adulthood ideas of love, authority, and dependence were deeply colored by relationships with the father. The relationship between father and child—which was the most emotionally intense and psychologically loaded relationship in these people's lives—became a prototype for later adulthood relationships. This meant that emotions of love were always associated with authority and dominance, dependence and submission.

Nowhere is this more evident than in Butler's censorious behavior toward his own brother. Thomas Butler II, two years his junior, was the real misfit in the Butler household. Although he attended Cambridge, he failed to take a degree, married a poor Welsh girl, abandoned her with four children to support, and took to living with a Brussels prostitute. At pains to deny any resemblance between his earlier revolt against his father and his brother's behavior, Butler wrote that he was "completely of a mind" with the rest of the family concerning Tom. Butler, in fact, exhibited a far deeper sense of disapproval than other family members: although he admitted to feeling *"very* sorry" for his brother, he was convinced that it was the family's solemn duty, under the circumstances, to cut off Tom Butler. Wholly oblivious to any similarities with his father's behavior toward him in 1859, Butler now declared that the family "should not recognize Tom, except as a disgrace to us all who is to be put aside once for all, and with whom no words are to be bandied." It is not presumptuous to draw a connection between Butler's critical and harshly punitive attitude toward his brother and his perception of his father's earlier treatment of him. His cold, highly intellectualistic indictment of his brother seems to be in part a reaction against his own unconscious guilt at his revolt against his father.[40]

What strikes one most vividly on turning to Butler's lifelong correspondence with his youngest sister May is a similar pattern of ambivalence: a mixture of contempt and scorn combined with a strong sense of personal identity. May Butler, six years his junior, was the only one of Butler's three siblings to make her home with their parents. After their mother's death in 1873, it was May who managed their father's household and served as his "comfort," the sole person to whom he could pour out his "worries and anxieties." Both symbolically and in actuality May was the intermediary between father and son. What seems certain is that Butler's letters to his sister give expression to deep internal tensions: isolated from his father and other Victorian thinkers by intellectual differences, alienated from many of his family's values, Butler continued to feel a strong psychological need to demonstrate to his youngest sister that he still maintained something in common with his family. Whether he was prepared to admit it or not, Butler did have strong intellectual disagreements with his family; yet for a variety of compelling psychological reasons, he felt it necessary to insist that he remained loyal to them.[41]

Butler's letters, when addressed to people who were not members of his immediate family, exhibit a striking degree of disdain for his sister. A letter to his sister-in-law, written in 1882, when Butler was forty-seven, is illustrative: he said that he "could hardly say how much" he disliked and distrusted May. For years past, he continued, she had never once invited him to visit her and their father, or said she was glad to see him, or asked him to visit again. His bitterest accusations against his sister, however, were to charge her with covertly sympathizing with his brother Tom and with aggravating tensions between himself and his father. "All is done in a quiet way," he noted. "For the present I . . . avoid a rupture by all means in my power, but if I survive my father times will change." What Butler meant by these remarks almost certainly was to assign a degree of blame upon his sister for the conflicts that arose between father and son. In his words we can almost hear the emotional pain that his intellectual differences with his father cost. Because he viewed his father's authority as morally legitimate, he felt free to deviate from his father's expectations only to the extent that he was able to deny responsibility for his behavior.[42]

To shift from Butler's comments about May to his forty-seven-

year-long correspondence with her is to catch a glimpse of man
who contrasts sharply with his fictional self-image in *The Way
of All Flesh*. As one reads these letters, it is difficult to ignore
Butler's repeated efforts to emphasize his loyalty to his family.
What would a reader of *The Way of All Flesh* make of Butler's
effusive outpouring of emotion upon learning that his mother
was seriously ill? There is much to be learned about the psychological meaning of sibling ties in Butler's remarks about his
mother's last illness. Before examining Butler's words, however,
it is necessary to place his remarks in context. In March 1873,
Butler informed his parents that he was the author of *Erewhon*
and that he planned to publicly acknowledge this fact in the
book's second edition. Shortly later, he learned that his mother
was gravely ill and that his father blamed his authorship of
Erewhon for his mother's failing health. His father told the son
never to visit the rectory at Langbar again and, at the mother's
funeral, said that it was the son's declaration of authorship that
had killed her. Butler said nothing to his father, but he let out
his emotions to his sister May. He wrote that he "could not
think of . . . going about" his daily affairs while his mother
was "lying perhaps at the point of death." Why, his sister was
surely asking, had he ever written *Erewhon*? His only answer
was to admit to a great error. His mistake was "in thinking that
the very great success which the book has met with would make
his father and mother proud of my having written it." Had he
only known that his mother's health was fading, he would certainly have kept knowledge of his responsibility for the book
"more quiet." In reading Butler's letter, it is hard not to con-
clude that he protests too much. He cannot help "being thor-
oughly vexed and alarmed": "he wracks his brains in vain" to
think of anything he could do to alleviate his mother's pain. He
describes himself as a "prisoner" suffering from ailments of his
own, only to add, "but what is this in comparison with what
you yourself must be witnessing!" Even in these words of grief,
Butler's message seems forced, conveying the tone of a man who
feels anxious and guilt-ridden over the injury he may have inflicted upon his mother. It is clear that Butler's words involve

something more than mere compensation. To experience deep religious doubt, to feel isolated from his family by an unbridgeable gulf of intellectual disagreements, left a Victorian like Samuel Butler longing for the warm, secure, innocent state represented by his family.[43]

The theme that sticks out most conspicuously from Butler's letters to his sister is his preoccupation with proving his fealty to his family. In 1878, for instance, his sister accused him of "forcing differences upon" his father by forwarding reviews of his books. Butler passionately denied this. His goal was quite the reverse: his aim was merely to demonstrate to his father "that disinterested third parties considered us in more substantial agreement than he was perhaps aware of." Butler said he believed this to be genuinely true: "indeed I am more and more sure of it every year." Precisely how far Butler deviated from his family's religious beliefs is a question still debated today. His relatives considered his attitudes nothing but a "parade of scepticism" (which his father said was "a not unnatural revulsion from Ultra Montanism [a revival of the Catholic doctrine of papal infallibility] on the Continent and its representatives in this country"), although recent scholarship has seen in Butler's stress on the role of design and mind in evolution an attempt to reconcile scientific knowledge and traditional religious principles. However far Butler diverged from his father's religious beliefs, the essential point is that he felt impelled to disguise and camouflage, even from himself, the extent to which he had broken intellectually with his family. This point is notable because it suggests how important psychologically it was for Butler to be able to assert meaningful continuities with the past.[44]

As we have already noted, in 1882 Butler had announced that his father's death would signal his final break with his sisters. Yet in fact succeeding years would see their relationship grow closer and more intense. He increasingly discovered in the sibling bond an emotional importance that he had not acknowledged before. The explanation for this growing stress upon the sibling bond seems to be linked inextricably to his work on *The Way of All Flesh*. His letters seem to indicate that as he proceeded to write his novel he was tormented by spasms of guilt. One letter is especially revealing. In 1873, when he was writing the keenly satirical portions of the book dealing with the childhood experiences of his fictional counterpart, Ernest Pontifex, he explicitly told his sister May that he was not working on a book "in which I have introduced my father." Fearful that she would hear rumors of his book, he stated unequivocally that he had not "the faintest conception what the present report can allude to."[45]

By any fair interpretation, Butler was lying. Yet even lies can point to underlying truths, and Butler's refusal to acknowledge that his novel was a direct attack upon his father may help illuminate Butler's own conception of his work. Without seeking to enter the protracted scholarly debate on Butler's intentions in writing *The Way of All Flesh*, it does seem worth emphasizing that for all the hostility and resentment that Ernest Pontifex has for his father, the novel lays much of the blame for Theobald Pontifex's harshness on the way he was treated by his own father.

As we examine Butler's letters, other evidence accumulates that also suggests the painful sense of guilt Butler felt as a result of his differences with his family. When his sister May fell ill in 1883, he quietly confessed that his "conscience smites me concerning her." When his father, too, fell ill the following year, he acknowledged that his only comfort sprang from his eldest sister Harriet's decision to reside with his father for the rest of his days. To a friend, he wrote that he was "in some measure sustained" by the very thought of his sisters. "What a thing it is to have sisters after all." It was after penning these words that he ceased work on his unfinished study of the deviousness of Victorian family life and placed *The Way of All Flesh* in a drawer. He issued instructions to his literary executor that his novel was not to be published until his sisters had died.[46]

Butler's classic description of a son's revolt against his father, *The Way of All Flesh*, stands out in Victorian fiction for its graphic description of the process through which a Victorian youth came into conflict with his parents' authority, worked through his feelings of resentment and rebellion, achieved an understanding of the poignancy of his parents' lives, and ultimately succeeded in winning a measure of self-respect and genuine independence. Butler's family correspondence reveals another, equally affecting side of this process of self-discovery and emancipation. What his letters to his father and sister give voice to is the immense sense of guilt and isolation that accompanied his questioning of traditional beliefs. Wracked by a deep sense of loss and loneliness, Butler looked the more intently upon family loyalties as a source of order and stability. Here was an emotional resource he could draw upon in his intellectual confusion.

In his personal notebook, Butler sought to account for the strains that tore apart Victorian families. Whenever he was able to get behind the veils of propriety he found a deep gulf separating generations. The instinctive antagonism between the old and the young was far too general, he believed, to be explained on the ground of defect in the older or the younger generation. The young of one generation became the old of the next, and both old and young always seemed to be good sorts of people to everyone except their own near relatives. The antipathy within families, he felt sure, could be understood only when it was viewed as part of a broader antipathy within nature between an incipient species and the "unmodified race" from which it was evolving. The first thing a new life form sought to do was to supplant and eliminate its predecessor. The older life form, knowing this, therefore did its best to prevent the new from arising. This biological conflict between generations also helped to explain the tensions that divided brothers and sisters. The "least modified" young men and women—the ones who were most nearly facsimiles of their parents—inevitably came into conflict with those siblings who represented newer ways of life.[47]

What strikes a reader most forcefully about these remarks is the way Butler sought to depersonalize the sources of strain within families and to reduce domestic conflict to a product of an impersonal biological conflict within nature. Here, as in his family letters, he attempts to diminish his personal responsibil-

ity for family quarrels by attributing causation to broader forces
and pressures lying outside his personal control. Yet we, too,
with the advantage of hindsight, can also see that the personal
family conflicts that plagued the Butler household were not
merely idiosyncratic.

The tragedy that divided the Butler household was not a
mundane and commonplace struggle of temperament and personality but a profounder drama. The conflicts and problems
that wracked the Butler family reflected broader tensions within
the general culture. Thus, Canon Butler might be firm and sensible in guiding and disciplining his son and still find his authority ineffective. This was because his authority lacked the
broader reinforcement of his culture. He lived in a society that
rewarded independence and self-reliance and that tended to isolate domestic ideals—of deference, obedience, and loyalty—from
basic religious, economic, political, and philosophical values. For
the child, too, the conflict with the father embodied larger cultural tensions and contradictions. The central paradox for the
son was to reconcile the contradictory demands for independence and self-government and for deference, loyalty, and obedience to authority.

In his pioneering attempt to trace the connections between
individual psychological development and social and cultural
transformations, Freud, in *Totem and Taboo,* laid out an analysis
that helps to illuminate the psychological dynamics of the Butler
and Sedgwick households. Freud was concerned, in the most
general sense, with the psychological effects of the drift away
from traditional hierarchy, prescribed authority, and ascribed
status. The killing of the "primal father" symbolized the de-
struction of boundaries of all kinds—psychological, religious,
political, and economic. In an effort to overcome the divisive
forces unleashed by this overleaping of social and psychological
boundaries, and to mitigate the excesses and uncertainties of
freedom, Freud argued that people responded by attaching
enormous stress to the importance of fraternity and the associ-

ated values of self-denial and voluntary submission. Various voluntary self-restraints, internalized in the depths of individual personality, would replace older conceptions of authority, obedience, and discipline by ensuring a basis of duty, deference, and individual responsibility.[48]

What we have seen in the Butler and Sedgwick households is the way that family ties—particularly the bonds between siblings—served as a source of continuity that helped ease deviation from traditional values. In a period of profound discontinuities, when public symbols, values, and institutions were being challenged and reconstructed, the approval and emotional support of a brother or sister could provide a child with a sense of legitimacy and continuity that helped him to depart from an older world without excessive guilt or anxiety. As the example of Sedgwick indicates, the family could function in almost quasi-religious ways, furnishing symbols and values that could help to shape religious ideals and aspirations. As the example of Butler illustrates, the family name could be invoked as a powerful instrument in shaping behavior and character. Historians who have studied the laboring classes during the early industrial era have found that migration, poverty, and integration into the market economy were often accompanied by a strengthening of ties based upon family and kinship. What has not been adequately recognized is that for more affluent families, too, the family unit also increased in importance, not solely as a material resource, but as a psychological, emotional, and ideological resource that helped ease the transition from one world of values to another.

Conclusion

THE gradual growth of historians' interest in the family, which is partly a reaction to recent demographic, economic, and ideological trends that have impinged upon the contemporary family, also reflects a major redefinition of historical scholarship, away from a preoccupation with public events toward a heightened concern with social history. Making use of new sources of data—particularly aggregate data derived from manuscript censuses, divorce and probate records, and parish registers—and drawing upon theoretical concepts and frameworks borrowed from the social sciences, this new social history of the family has sought to reconstruct the complex texture of family life in the past. The exciting breakthroughs in family history have depended on the testing and application of conceptual tools and methods of analysis taken from other disciplines. From ego psychologists, historians have gained insight into the power of a social and cultural context to shape the nature, timing, and particular form of problems of individual development. Demographers have increased historians' understanding of the importance of quantitative materials in calculating changes in household size, family structure, kinship organization, and the developmental cycle of domestic groups. From social anthropologists, historians have learned much about the relations among individual households, inheritance systems, and kinship structures.[1]

Unfortunately, the profound reshaping of our understanding of social history has so far had only a minimal impact on our theoretical understanding of family change or upon more traditional conceptualizations of history. The great challenge confronting social historians is to find productive ways to integrate their findings into more conventional accounts of history, while also subjecting to close critical scrutiny the constructs and theoretical frameworks of the social sciences. In this conclusion, we shall examine the ways in which this study fits into our understanding of family history and how it alters our understanding of the Victorian family and society.

First let us examine the implications of this study for our understanding of family change. In seeking to find useful ways to describe family change during the late eighteenth and early nineteenth centuries, social historians have tended to borrow many of their theoretical assumptions from such structural-functionalist sociologists as Talcott Parsons and David Riesman. Structural-functionalist sociology has bequeathed three major legacies to the social history of the family. First, structural functionalism has offered a description of family change in terms of specialization of roles and differentiation of functions. The distinguishing feature of socioeconomic modernization in the public realm was specialization and differentiation in the interests of increased economic productivity. Differentiation and specialization also transformed the middle-class family, but with different implications. The family, having lost control of many of its earlier productive functions—such as transmitting property and skills, arranging marriages and family alliances, and caring for dependent kin—increasingly specialized in a narrower range of psychological and ideological functions, in particular, instilling children with a capacity for self-control and self-direction and helping individual family members adapt to the strains of social and economic change. Differentiation and specialization had another effect on the family. Structurally, the family unit was increasingly isolated from broader kinship and occupational structures. This structural isolation, in turn, tended to increase the psychological isolation and intensity of family life.[2]

A second legacy of structural-functional sociology is a highly normative description of the direction of change in the patterns of middle-class family life. The history of the family, according to this perspective, involves a shift toward a family characterized by a more egalitarian distribution of power between spouses and parents and children. This perspective sees parental control over marriages giving way to marriages based on love; marriages arranged in the material interests of the natal families being supplanted by marriages in the interests of the spouses; and socialization, which had been conceived of in terms of breaking a child's will and instilling respect for the inviolability of authority, being replaced by a new nonauthoritarian style of childrearing, involving a rejection of physical force and a stress on government by consent.[3]

The third legacy of structural functionalism is a tendency to see a close coincidence between changes in family dynamics and organization and more general changes in politics, economics, religion, and philosophy. Thus, the transformation of patterns of socialization, emotional relationships, and authority relationships is seen as closely reflecting a larger transformation of cultural attitudes toward authority, progress, liberty, and sin. An emphasis on the mother's role in childrearing, the persuasive powers of influence, and a more egalitarian distribution of power in the family mirrors a broader shift in cultural values—such as the rise of more liberal religious doctrines that reject the notion of original sin and regard salvation as a gradual process in which the natural and supernatural join together; of "enlightened" philosophic notions stressing the malleability of human nature and the shaping influence of the environment; and of individualistic sentiments, evident in religious doctrines stressing human will and ability; economic dogmas emphasizing individual opportunity and responsibility; and a new political language built around concepts of consent, liberty, and equal rights.[4]

The most perceptive works in family history have gone far toward correcting the most glaring deficiencies of a crude application of a structural-functionalist model of family change. Philip J. Greven, Jr., and Lawrence Stone, for example, have identified the weaknesses of crudely linear, Whiggish views of family change, which characterize the evolution of the family and society in terms of a unilinear movement from patriarchal to egalitarian relations, from hierarchical to more democratic distribution of power, and from authoritarianism and prescription to consent and permissiveness. Other historical studies, such as those by Michael Anderson and Michael Katz, have demonstrated that the early industrial era saw continuing ties with the broader kin group and prolonged residence of children with parents that helped to compensate for the growing structural isolation of the family. The writings of Christopher Lasch have shown that the language of structural functionalism—built around dichotomies of instrumental and affective relations, authoritarian and permissive styles of socialization, and prudential and affective motives for behavior—is too rigid and schematic to capture the nuances and complexities of family interactions. Kathryn Kish Sklar has described the inconsistencies and contradictions as well as the convergences between domestic ideology and the ideals purveyed through politics, religion, economics, and philosophy. Other scholarship, informed by the concerns of feminism, by such historians as Nancy Cott, Carl Degler, Linda Gordon, and Daniel Scott Smith, has emphasized that the reorientation of the family toward narrower, more specialized functions had differential effects on the activities, status, and self-perception of the sexes. The discussions of Smith and Gordon, in particular, have reminded historians that they must see the family, not only as an integrated system of socially derived beliefs, but also as an arena of conflict and adjustment.[5]

And yet, for all that has been learned about the formal structure, developmental cycle, and demographic characteristics of individual families, much remains to be uncovered, particularly about the intricate and often tortured dynamics of family life and their relation to larger cultural problems of authority, legitimacy, discipline, and responsibility. As Philip J. Greven, Jr., has masterfully shown in his studies of the seventeenth- and eighteenth-century New England family, it is important for historians not to reify the concept of family but to locate studies of the family very precisely in a specific social structure and cultural context and to examine in detail the ways that cultural tensions and value conflicts are internalized and struggled with inside individual households. As his studies remind us, the problems of particular families can never be isolated from the more general problems of a particular social and cultural grouping. That goal represents the fundamental aim of this book.[6]

It began by tracing the development of new patterns of middle-class family life in the eighteenth and early nineteenth centuries, decisively different from the patterns that had existed earlier. Changes in the patterns of famiy life took place on a number of different levels. One dimension of change was demographic, evident in a marked decline of infant and child mortality; a gradual drop of fertility within marriage; a lengthening of life expectancy, particularly for mothers; a growth in the duration of marriages; a more rigid and uniform timing of the life stages; and a prolonged residency of children with their parents. These abrupt shifts tended to make the middle-class family a less transient, more psychologically intense arrangement than in the past.

A second dimension of change involved a rapid decline in the economic self-sufficiency of households, signaled by a dramatic decline in domestic industries in which married women and their children had directly contributed to the family's economic productivity. One implication of this development was to further enhance the psychological isolation of the household from the world of wage work. Closely related to the development of a "separate sphere of domesticity" were profound changes in middle-class women's roles and status. These changes were manifest in an increase in the number of women attending schools and working temporarily before marriage, as well as in the rising number of women who either delayed marriage or who did not marry. The insulation of married women from the world of wage work helped contribute to the image of women as exerting a superior moral influence over manners and morals. Yet another dimension of change involved a weakening of material reinforcements that had supplemented family discipline in the past, such as older systems of apprenticeship and fostering out of older children. The significance of these developments was contradictory: if structurally the middle-class household was more isolated than in the past, it was also cut off from earlier sources of support; if the family had become a more private institution, its functions were increasingly oriented toward public ends.

Demographic and socioeconomic changes in middle-class family patterns are inadequate to account for the immense psychological and ideological responsibilities attached to the nineteenth-century middle-class family. To understand the burdens and responsibilities invested in the middle-class family it is necessary to turn to a distinctive configuration of attitudes and expressive symbols—here called "literary culture"—that formed the basis for a transatlantic connection in the early nineteenth century, linking together an influential coterie of ministers, moralists, writers, and reformers in Britain and America. Responding to similar problems and tensions—such as the decline of deference, the diminishing influence of the clergy, and the dissolution of ordered and homogeneous communities—a small number of writers on both sides of the Atlantic looked to the family, and to internalized self-restraints instilled through various persuasive forms of moral and psychological influence, to counteract the anarchistic pressures of democracy and self-seeking individualism. Drawing intellectually upon the Evangelical Revival, with its stress on duty, domesticity, and self-denial, and indebted to John Locke and the Scottish moral philosophers of the eighteenth century, the literature on "family government" was also closely related to specific social problems, such as the problems of balancing aspirations for improvement with concerns about order and continuity and reconciling democracy with deference. Self-discipline and self-government, instilled within the family, were to make increased individualism safe.

It is important to our understanding of the specific Victorians studied in this book to know that they shared a common vocabulary and frame of reference that can be traced to "literary culture." It is also significant that the five subjects of this book came from families that were acutely conscious of their position in the vertical hierarchy characteristic of the patronage and dependency-based society of the eighteenth century. Such families entered the nineteenth century with a strong sense of their own gentility and of the need for authority, deference, and subordination. Descended from families with a tradition of civic or communal responsibility, the figures examined here inherited a strong sense of personal mission. Their sense of public calling, however, differed in fundamental ways from their parents', being more psychological and less rooted in a specific locality or set of religious beliefs.

Such figures turned almost naturally to the role of writer. Their childhood upbringing was felt in the high valuation they attached to the written word, which was regarded in their homes as an instrument for education, self-improvement, and recreation. Art and literature were conceived of as serving quasi-religious functions: shaping moral standards, elevating the sensibilities, and training and disciplining the emotions. For such individuals, self-improvement through literary culture was in many respects a secularized drive for salvation. Each of the subjects of this book experienced doubt in religious orthodoxy; in their adult lives, each dealt with primary issues of identity, belief, and authority, not in the realm of religion, but in the realm of language and literature.

In the first four chapters we sought to locate the lives of five Victorian authors against a backdrop of social and cultural history, in order to understand the demographic, social, and intellectual influences that impinged upon their lives. Such a glance at the social and historical setting of their lives was essential for providing a meaningful context against which we could understand the basic issues and problems confronted in personal life. In the last three chapters, we were concerned with the ways that domestic lives embodied larger cultural tensions and conflicts. The danger with this organizational structure is that it runs the risk of setting up too sharp a dichotomy between individual lives and social context. This is a problem that can be dealt with here by attempting to summarize and reemphasize the connections we have drawn between family dynamics and broader social and cultural transformations.

In seeking to reconstruct the emotional and psychological dynamics of the parent-child relationship, we discovered that relations within the Victorian families we studied took on a distinctive pattern of filial rebellion and accommodation. What we found was the filial rebellion directed against a father at the onset of adulthood, far from signaling a lack of identification between family generations, was a vehicle for the transmission and internalization of cultural patterns between generations. What was striking about this pattern of generational conflict within these homes was the reluctance of the children to directly challenge the legitimacy of their fathers' authority or to directly question the canon of values that emphasized parental authority and the need for filial submission. In attempting to assert a measure of personal independence and self-determination, the Victorians we examined tended to direct their hostility against religious orthodoxy. For these individuals, it was evangelical religion—with its stress on selflessness, individual responsibility, and personal holiness and its insistence on the importance of shaping the character in the image of Christ—that provided a symbolic language through which they could protest against illegitimate assertions of paternal authority, while at the same time demonstrating, through certain self-administered tests of character, a capacity for internalized discipline and self-denial.

This pattern of filial rebellion and accommodation was closely related to some of the main social and cultural problems of the Victorian era. Deeply ambivalent toward individualistic and egalitarian values, deeply disturbed by the fears raised by Thomas Hobbes and in a different form by Calvinist orthodoxy—that the centrifugal pressures of individual self-interest would erode all conceptions of order, stability, and Christian morality—Victorians of widely differing persuasions emphasized the stabilizing influence of the family as an antidote to individualistic and democratizing pressures. The Christian family, by inculcating respect for the legitimacy of authority and setting firm limits to children's behavior and expectations, offered a solution to some of the fundamental problems of the time: the dissolution of cultural and ethical homogeneity, the weakening of the disciplinary role of religion, and the decline of deference and fixed social orders. In this context, social harmony depended primarily on the government of the family and on the father in particular, since it was the father who was responsible for ensuring that a child developed a capacity for self-discipline.

This burden of responsibility was compounded by changing social and economic circumstances. For men who were losing their ability to directly transmit their "status position" in society, a central issue of childrearing was to ensure that children developed the qualities—particularly the ability to regulate and control their own behavior and sensitivity to the judgments and approval of other people—that were supposed to be necessary for success in an increasingly fluid and individualistic environment. Then, too, we saw fathers exhibiting a kind of ineffectiveness in exercising authority that was related to shifting economic, political, and religious values. A father felt his authority undercut by the intrusion of liberal values, stressing self-reliance and independence, and found that his firm and sensible appeals for filial obedience failed to influence the child's behavior. What emerges is a picture of the family increasingly cut off from more general social and religious values, and the father's authority isolated from larger cultural sanctions and supports.

For a child there were different problems to solve: to retain emotional bonds with parents while overcoming economic dependency, to convert emotional bonds into acceptable adult forms, and to demonstrate a capacity for self-government through certain symbols of internalized discipline. For the child, the personal family conflict with a father was not simply a private matter but a generational struggle against what the father represented. The conflict between a father and a son or daughter absorbed a wide range of other issues. This conflict provided a symbolic revolt against older conceptions of authority resting on hierarchy, prescription, and rigid subordination. For a child, the struggle to assert a degree of self-determination in the realm of conscience gave voice to larger concerns with personal freedom, individual responsibility, and self-government. It signaled a shift toward a new conception of authority and discipline, in which the legitimacy of authority depended on some form of consent, and in which the exercise of power was linked to the use of various persuasive forms of moral and psychological influence. In seeking to understand why the filial revolt was directed against the father, and not the mother, it is important to note that it was the father who represented public and external conceptions of authority; who furnished a model of instrumentality in contrast to the mother's affectivity; and who was the chief disciplinary figure, and moral and intellectual authority, in the home. Different kinds of tensions would characterize the twentieth-century home, where the mother would partially replace the father as the chief symbolic antagonist. Insofar as the mother succeeded in achieving an oligopoly over the domestic sphere, she would become the target of antitrust.

In exploring Victorian attitudes toward love and marriage, great emphasis was placed on the way that ideals of love, like relations between father and child, were closely connected with some of the deepest needs and problems of the age. Relations of love were emphasized as an answer to some of the central cultural conflicts of the time: as an antidote to positivistic and materialist conceptions of man, which appeared to drain life of meaning and to reduce people to mere mechanisms; as a reaction against competitive and impersonal market values; as a remedy for apprehensions about independence; and as a resolution to religious anxiety and confusion. To be able to exalt love as something pure and selfless, modeled on Christ's saving love, and to be able to sanctify marriage into "holy matrimony," was a way to give immediate and tangible expression to religious ideals and aspirations. When traditional beliefs were being questioned, one might turn from logic to feeling for comfort, and find in the heart a source of morality and feeling that were lost in a world dedicated to competitive individualism. Weary of religious controversy and contention, a Victorian could find in love a model of selfless devotion, sympathetic feeling, and ideal sentiment, an objective correlate for religious aspirations.

Evangelical religion was central in shaping attitudes toward love and marriage. A complex of symbols and ideals adapted from evangelical religion not only colored aspirations and ideals in marriage but also served to conceal cultural value conflicts and to provide a set of sanctions that could be used within marriage to influence and shape behavior. By adopting abstract evangelical notions of Christian "sympathy," "love," and "freedom," Victorians were able to reconcile ideals of marriage as essentially a hierarchical arrangement and as preeminently a spiritual relationship between equals; they were able to picture marriage as justified not only by its roles in rearing children and as a focus for emotions but also as a means of absolution and redemption, a school for heaven.

The explanation for this deification of marriage lies in part in social history, which reshaped the psychological significance of marriage, particularly for women. Not only did marriage mark, in new ways, a closing off of freedoms enjoyed in girlhood, but by the middle of the nineteenth century a woman's personal identity was linked, to a greater extent than in the past, to her future husband. It seems likely, under these circumstances, that marriage would become a more difficult transition than earlier in time. Given the elevated expectations of many middle-class women for self-fulfillment, by virtue of increased educational and employment opportunities prior to marriage, evangelical religion played a crucial role in furnishing the ideals of self-renunciation, duty, and self-discipline that helped women adjust to the obligations and constraints imposed by Victorian marriage.

Any attempt to explain the importance attached to sibling solidarity and family continuity during the Victorian era must begin by confronting an apparent paradox. Long-term changes in inheritance practices and rates of geographical and economic mobility, a gradual decline in patronage based on kinship, and the rise of ideologies emphasizing individual opportunity and achievement over ascription would seem to point in the direction of a weakening of family unity and continuity. Yet, as Alexis de Tocqueville noted in his classic *Democracy in America,* a decline in tangible family interests and obligations was not inconsistent with a heightened emphasis on sibling and family bonds.

The explanation for this inconsistency is attributable partly to compensation—a reaction against the pressures of social change, self-seeking individualism, and fluidity—all of which seemed to be eroding earlier conceptions of order, continuity, and stability. In an era in which individuals of diverse backgrounds felt cast adrift in a morass of intellectual perplexity, the sibling bond acquired new symbolic significance as an emblem of continuity and stability, a model of warmth, security, and innocence. Yet the importance attached to sibling solidarity represented something more than compensation. In a period of disruptive social and intellectual change, the bond between siblings symbolized an ethic of values emphasizing reciprocal duties and rights, organic and harmonious union, and voluntary acceptance of responsibilities. The bonds of loyalty and affection between siblings was symbolic of a larger cultural ideal—of harmonious, voluntary, and noncoercive unity that would not depend on authoritarian discipline.[7]

The familial patterns that emerged from this study can best be understood not as simply personal or idiosyncratic but as reflections and embodiments of more general religious, demographic, social, and economic developments and problems of a particular class, culture, and historical era. As we have seen, social, cultural, and historical factors shaped these individuals' lives in a variety of ways: demographically, in structuring age relations in their households and the timing of the life stages; psychologically, in limiting the number of sources of identification for children and reducing the role of the peer group in individual development; economically, in increasing the children's financial dependence on their parents and delaying the age at which they could achieve independence. Far from being idiosyncratic, the expectations these individuals attached to marriage, the emphasis placed on paternal authority, and the definition of the family as a moral counterforce to individualism and a locus of order and stability—all were shared by people who accepted the norms and values of "literary culture." By locating a series of Victorians in a specific social and historical setting, we can see that the basic concerns and preoccupations of their families—with instilling a high degree of self-discipline, with cultivating respect for the legitimacy of authority, and with developing sensitivity to the expectations and feelings of other people—constituted a response not solely to individual family needs but also to the larger problems of a particular culture: of adapting older traditions of deference to an increasingly individualistic age; of providing women and children with a measure of independence without undermining the structure of domestic authority; of nurturing, intensifying, and stabilizing individualistic aspirations. The family dynamics that are typically termed "Victorian" were a product of a central cultural concern: with counterbalancing individualistic and democratizing pressures through the voluntary acceptance of various internalized self-restraints and limits.

APPENDIX

A Note on the Use of the Term "Middle Class"

THE definitions of the term "middle class" are diverse, and with the growth of interest in social history the term has often been loosely used. The concept has been applied to groups as varied as intellectuals, professionals, small independent producers, retailers, tradesmen, artisans, and salaried white-collar employees. It has been used as an analytic construct to differentiate between social groups sharing a common economic experience and status relationship with other groups; it has also been used as a cultural construct to refer to individuals sharing common moral ideals, norms, and behavioral standards. Use of the term has been plagued by problems of understanding the different implications the concept carried in distinct social and historical contexts, and the difficulty of distinguishing social class from such related concepts as status groups, interest groups, and occupational groups.

If a concept such as "middle class" is to be used rigorously, careful distinctions need to be drawn between the various meanings of the term. In this appendix, we will seek to identify some of the major ways the concept has been defined. An economic category, a measure of relative social position, a perceived economic relationship—the term "middle class" has been used in each of these ways. Yet although the meanings of the term are many, in fact historians have tended to treat the concept from a small number of distinct perspectives. Here we will try to differentiate among some of the basic approaches taken by historians and suggest how the concept can be useful to our study of certain specific Victorian families.

One common way to conceptualize the category "middle class" is simply to group together all those individuals who are neither members of the aristocracy, the gentry, holders of large amounts of property, inheritors of substantial amounts of wealth, nor part of the laboring classes. The problem with this omnibus approach to the middle class, as R. S. Neale has suggested in his important study, *Class and Ideology in the Nineteenth Century* (London, 1972), is that the category that emerges is not meaningful in either economic or social terms. In an attempt to remedy this defect in the omnibus definition of the middle class, historians have tended to follow either Marx and seek to define "middle class" in predominantly economic terms, or Max Weber and define the concept in essentially social and cultural terms. In practice, the definitions that have emerged from these two perspectives sometimes closely resemble each other, conceiving of the middle class, not in terms of specific occupations or amounts of income, but as a social and cultural formation embodying distinctive economic, political, and ideological characteristics. Recent scholarship has placed special emphasis on the idea that the middle class is not necessarily a homogeneous formation.

There is another way to approach the concept of middle class. That is to treat the concept as a historical construct that developed as a result of broader intellectual, social, and historical processes. The term first gained widespread currency in the early nineteenth century to replace such earlier terms as the "middle ranks" or "strata" of society. A historical approach to the concept of middle class views the emergence of the term at once as an index of broader social transformations and as a perceptual lens through which individuals sought to make sense of social change. The precise ways in which this concept of class that arose during the early nineteenth century differed from earlier conceptualizations of the hierarchical divisions in society is a matter of some controversy, but recent scholarship has tended to emphasize three characteristics that distinguished this concept from its predecessors. The first is that the newer term "class" characterizes a society in which essentially horizontal social antagonisms tend to surpass predominantly vertical conflicts between traditional economic interests as a source of social and ideological conflict. Then, too, the growing use of the term "class" is a barometer of a heightened belief that social status is something that is acquired, not inherited, and therefore a signal of the declining importance of vertical loyalties based on patronage and dependence. Finally, such earlier terms as "order," "rank," "degree," and "estate," unlike "class," divided society hierarchically according to the respect, honor, and dignity attached to particular social functions not directly connected with economic roles.

Among the advantages of adopting a historical perspective on the development of the concept middle class is that it focuses attention on the social divisions that contemporaries regarded as crucial in defining their society and that it provides a sense of historical development that more static definitions of the concept lack. A shift in grammar is instructive in suggesting how a historical understanding of the concept can provide fresh insight into the way social change was perceived. Up until the 1840s, contemporaries tended to use the plural form "middle classes" instead of the singular "middle class." Such phraseology suggests that during the early industrial era contemporaries were acutely conscious of certain important socioeconomic divisions within the more comprehensive classification "middle class," divisions that were obscured during the heated political battles of the 1840s.

A historical understanding of the evolution of the concept middle class is particularly helpful in locating the subjects of this book in their social structure and understanding why their families were so sensitive to issues of deference, authority, legitimacy, and discipline. Their families were members of a social stratum that differed from other segments of the middle class in fundamental respects: in their sources of income, in their dedication to ideals of public and communal service, and in their genteel status antedating the nineteenth century on the basis of education and place in the local hierarchy of status and privilege. In certain respects, their backgrounds were conducive to an acute concern with order, stability, and community. Conscious of coming from areas where the older vertical bonds of patronage and dependence persisted well into the nineteenth century in a relatively homogeneous society, such individuals were highly sensitive to the gradual dissolution of the social bonds characteristic of the preindustrial social order and the disintegration of ethically homogeneous communities. And yet, in other important respects, the environment in which these figures grew up was unusually individuated, privatized, and hostile to earlier conceptions of authority and submission. Reared in households where they were physically and emotionally isolated from people not of their immediate families, strongly encouraged to develop a capacity for independence, profoundly influenced by the evangelical religious ideals of personal purity and perfect holiness, such individuals teetered uneasily between two worlds of values: the values of a deferential, patronage society based on bonds of dependence and the values of an increasingly individualistic, nondeferential society based on the values of personal responsibility and internalized self-restraints.

Notes

CHAPTER 2: THE VICTORIAN MIDDLE-CLASS FAMILY

1. John Pope Hennessy, *Robert Louis Stevenson* (New York, 1974), 23–24; Vanessa Parker, *The English House in the Nineteenth Century* (Historical Association pamphlet H.78, Truro, 1970), 4, 26.

2. Hennessy, *Robert Louis Stevenson,* 23–24; Barbara M. Cross, ed., *The Autobiography of Lyman Beecher* (Cambridge, Mass., 1961), XVII; Peter Gregg Slater, *Children in the New England Mind* (Hamden, 1977), 148–64.

3. The quotations are found in Barbara M. Cross, "Harriet Beecher Stowe," in *Notable American Women,* Edward T. James, ed. (Cambridge, Mass., 1971), III, 393. On the Victorian conception of the father's role, see Howard R. Wolf, "British Fathers and Sons, 1773–1913: From Filial Submissiveness to Creativity," *Psychoanalytic Review* 52, no. 2 (Summer 1965), 53–70; Bruce Mazlish, *James and John Stuart Mill: Father and Son in the Nineteenth Century* (New York, 1975); and Lee Krenis, "Authority and Rebellion in Victorian Autobiography," *Journal of British Studies* 18, no. 1 (Fall 1978), 107–30.

4. Arnold Silver, *The Family Letters of Samuel Butler* (Oxford, 1962), 32; Malcolm Muggeridge, *Samuel Butler* (London, 1936), 8, 49.

5. The quotation is from Leslie Stephen, *George Eliot* (London, 1902), 14.

6. This description is drawn from the account given by Richard E. Welch, Jr., *Theodore Sedgwick, Federalist* (Wesleyan, 1965), 250–51.

7. The literature describing the boom in historical studies of the families is vast. Recent examinations of this literature include Christopher Lasch, "The Family and History," *New York Review of Books,* November 13, 27, and December 11, 1975; Sylvia Junko Yanagisako, "Family and Household: The Analysis of Domestic Groups," *Annual Review of Anthropology* 8 (1979), 161–205; and Michael Anderson, *Approaches to the History of the Western Family, 1500–1914* (London, 1980).

8. The statistic on household membership is cited in Anderson, *Approaches,* 24. A similar point is made by Bernard Bailyn, "Europe in the Wilderness,"

in *The Great Republic*, Bernard Bailyn et al. (Lexington, 1977), 86–89, 104–8. On shifts in language see Raymond Williams, *Keywords: A Vocabulary of Culture and Society* (New York, 1976), 108–11; and Anderson, *Approaches*, 41–42.

9. The increasing isolation of the conjugal unit is described in James A. Henretta, *The Evolution of American Society, 1700–1815* (Lexington, 1973), 213–14. On prolonged residence of children in their natal home see Anne Foner, "Age Stratification and the Changing Family," *American Journal of Sociology* (1978 supplement), S 349. The expulsion of apprentices from the middle-class home is vividly illustrated in Paul E. Johnson, *A Shopkeeper's Millennium: Society and Revivals in Rochester, New York, 1815–1837* (New York, 1978), 43–48, 59.

10. Foner, "Age Stratification," S 345; Carl Degler, *At Odds: Women and the Family in America from the Revolution to the Present* (New York, 1980), 178–80, 155, 393–94; Joseph F. Kett, *Rites of Passage: Adolescence in America, 1790 to the Present* (New York, 1977), 14–37; Michael Katz, *The People of Hamilton, Canada West* (Cambridge, Mass., 1975), 303; W. A. Armstrong, "Mid-Nineteenth Century York," in *Household and Family in Past Time*, Peter Laslett, ed. (Cambridge, England, 1977), 213–14.

11. Katz, *People of Hamilton*, 304–5; Kett, *Rites of Passage*, 86–108, 144–72; Johnson, *Shopkeeper's Millennium*, 43–48, 59.

12. Foner, "Age Stratification," S 356–57; Tamara K. Hareven and Maris A. Vinovskis, Introduction to *Family and Population in Mid-Nineteenth Century America* (Princeton, 1978), 17; W. A. Armstrong, "Mid-Nineteenth Century York," 213–14.

13. Williams, *Keywords*, 108–11; Harold Perkin, *The Origins of Modern English Society, 1780–1880* (Toronto, 1972), 44–48.

14. On changes in the economic roles and status of women in England see Patricia Branca, *Silent Sisterhood* (Pittsburgh, 1975), passim; Ivy Pinchbeck, *Women Workers and the Industrial Revolution, 1750–1850* (New York, 1930); Margaret Hewitt, *Wives and Mothers in Victorian Industry* (London, 1958); Louise A. Tilly and Joan W. Scott, *Women, Work, and Family* (New York, 1978); and Perkin, *Modern English Society*, 149–60. On America see Degler, *At Odds*, chaps. 1–4, 8–9, 15; Nancy Cott, *The Bonds of Womanhood: "Woman's Sphere" in New England, 1780–1835* (New Haven, 1975), passim.

15. The most comprehensive overview of these developments is Degler, *At Odds*, chap. 13.

16. Perkin, *Modern English Society*, 149–60; Cott, *Bonds of Womanhood*, chaps. 1–2.

17. Perkin, *Modern English Society*, 158–59; Cott, *Bonds of Womanhood*, 61–62.

18. Foner, "Age Stratification," S 348–50, S 352–54; John Modell, Frank Furstenberg, and Theodore Hershberg, "Social Change and Transitions to Adulthood in Historical Perspective," *Journal of Family History* 1 (1976), 7–32.

19. The increase of spending on the upbringing of middle-class children, particularly of boys, is described in J. A. Banks, *Prosperity and Parenthood: A*

Study of Family Planning Among the Victorian Middle Classes (London, 1954), chap. 11. Other sources that contribute to a picture of children becoming the objects of expenditures designed to increase their future productivity are Kett, *Rites of Passage*, 168–71, and W. J. Reader, *Professional Men: The Rise of the Professional Classes in Nineteenth Century England* (London, 1966), chap. 12. On changes in the legal profession see Gerard W. Gawalt, "Sources of Anti-lawyer Sentiment in Massachusetts, 1740–1840," *American Journal of Legal History* (1970), 283–307; Gary Nash, "The Philadelphia Bench and Bar, 1800–1861," *Comparative Studies in Society and History* (1965), 203–20; John M. Murrin, "The Legal Transformation: The Bench and Bar in Eighteenth Century Massachusetts," in *Colonial America*, Stanley N. Katz, ed. (Boston, 1971), 415–49; Milton M. Klein, "The Rise of the New York Bar: The Legal Career of William Livingston," *William and Mary Quarterly* (1958), 334–58. On changes in the age of marriage of professionals in England see Patricia Branca, *Silent Sisterhood*, 20, n. 12.

20. Lawrence Stone, *The Family, Sex and Marriage in England, 1500–1800* (New York, 1979), 46.

CHAPTER 3: LITERARY CULTURE AND THE NEED TO SHAPE CHARACTER

1. Richard D. Altick, *The English Common Reader: A Social History of the Mass Reading Public, 1800–1900* (Chicago, 1957), 139, 161; David Brion Davis, "Attempts to Shape the American Character," in *The Great Republic*, Bernard Bailyn et al. (Lexington, 1977), 524–25.

2. Ednah D. Cheney, ed., *Louisa May Alcott: Her Life, Letters and Journals* (Boston, 1889), 27, 29.

3. Altick, *English Common Reader*, 115–16.

4. Charles Edward Stowe, *Life of Harriet Beecher Stowe* (Boston, 1889), 25.

5. Clarence Gohdes, *American Literature in Nineteenth-Century England* (New York, 1944), is still the fullest guide to the flow of ideas between nineteenth-century America and Britain, and this and the next two paragraphs draw heavily on material collected by Gohdes. Edward G. Salmon, "What Girls Read," *Nineteenth Century* 20 (October 1886), 515–29, cited in Gohdes, *American Literature*, 28; and Gohdes, "The Reception of Some Nineteenth Century American Authors in Europe," in *The American Writer and the European Tradition*, Margaret Denny and William H. Gilman, eds. (Minneapolis, 1950), 114.

6. Gohdes, *American Literature*, 141.

7. Ibid., 2; Frank Thistlethwaite, *The Anglo-American Connection in the Early Nineteenth Century* (Philadelphia, 1959), 78–79.

8. Thistlethwaite, *America and the Atlantic Community: Anglo-American Aspects, 1790–1850* (New York, 1959), 40–43; G. D. Lillibridge, *Beacon of Freedom:*

The Impact of American Democracy upon Great Britain, 1830–1870 (Philadelphia, 1954).

9. William R. Taylor, *Cavalier and Yankee* (New York, 1961), 40–45; David D. Hall, "The Victorian Connection," *American Quarterly* 27, no. 5 (December 1975), 561, 564; Thistlethwaite, *America and the Atlantic Community*, 138–39.

10. F. W. Newman, "Marriage Laws," *Fraser's Magazine* (August 1867), 169–70, 172, 178, 179.

11. Three highly informative studies about changing beliefs on the rearing of children are Peter Gregg Slater, *Children in the New England Mind: In Death and in Life* (Hamden, 1977); Carl Degler, *At Odds: Women and the Family in America from the Revolution to the Present* (New York, 1980); and Bernard Wishy, *The Child and the Republic: The Dawn of Modern American Child Nurture* (Philadelphia, 1968).

12. The best introductions to the writings of the Scottish moralists on character formation are David Brion Davis, *Homicide in American Fiction, 1789–1860* (Ithaca, 1957), chap. 1; and Kathryn Kish Sklar, *Catharine Beecher: A Study in American Domesticity* (New Haven, 1973), 80–86.

13. Mrs. A. J. Graves, *Woman in America: Being an Examination into the Moral and Intellectual Condition of American Female Society* (New York, 1843), xiii–xiv; Heman Humphrey, *Domestic Education* (Amherst, 1840), 21–24.

14. ". . . in order to become good citizens in after life, children must be accustomed to cheerful subordination in the family, from their earliest recollection." Humphrey, *Domestic Education*, 21–24.

15. Horace Bushnell, *Discourses on Christian Nurture* (Boston, 1847), 26–28, cited in Davis, *Homicide in American Fiction*, 9.

16. Humphrey, *Domestic Education*, 45–48.

17. Ibid., 21–24; Catharine Beecher, *A Treatise on Domestic Economy* (Boston, 1842), 26.

18. Elizabeth Appleton, *Early Education*, 2d ed. (London, 1820), 21, 30–31, 34, 40, 42, 51, 72, 128, 176, 187. Cf. Timothy Dwight, *Theology: Explained and Defended in a Series of Sermons* (New Haven, 1839), ii, 316–17. Dwight recommends that reproof and punishment be administered in private: "The parent . . . will enjoy the best possible opportunity for reproving him freely, largely, pungently, and solemnly; without embarrassment, which will necessarily arise from the presence of others. In the presence of others, the child will feel his pride wounded, his character sacrificed, and himself disgraced." Punishment is not to be directed at the body merely but at the child's sense of self-esteem.

19. Lydia Maria Child, *The Mother's Book* (Boston, 1831), 22–23, 27; Beecher, *Treatise on Domestic Economy*, 50, 152. Cf. Isaac Taylor, *Home Education* (London, 1838), 2, 3, 29, 30: Taylor, who was perhaps the most important lay theologian in England after Samuel Taylor Coleridge, became an Anglican early in life but maintained close ties with Dissenters; he stressed that domestic discipline depended on the ability of parents to instill in children "the most

absolute confidence, and an unchecked good will." The childrearing techniques of Louisa May Alcott's father, Bronson, are almost a caricature of the
methods prescribed by other writers, to evoke guilt and to induce an intense
sense of psychological dependency on the parents' approval and dispproval.
He would have his children spank him, or when they were especially naughty,
he would go without dinner. See Martha Saxton, *Louisa May* (Boston, 1877),
84–90.

20. Harriet Martineau, *Household Education* (London, 1849), 2, 18, 20, 68;
O. S. Fowler, *A Home for All* (New York, 1854), 62–64.

21. Catharine Sedgwick, *Home* (Boston, 1841), 26.

22. Humphrey, *Domestic Education,* 53–55.

23. Ibid., 21–24.

24. Ibid.

CHAPTER 4: FIVE VICTORIAN FAMILIES

1. Quoted in Robert Kiely, *Robert Louis Stevenson and the Fiction of Adventure*
(Cambridge, Mass., 1965), 3–4.

2. The comparison between Sedgwick, Cooper, Irving, and Bryant is made
by Edward Halsey Foster, *Catharine Maria Sedgwick* (New York, 1974), 26.

3. Quoted in Barbara M. Cross, "Harriet Beecher Stowe," in *Notable American Women,* Edward T. James, ed. (Cambridge, 1971), III, 394.

4. Ibid., III, 396.

5. Foster, *Catharine Maria Sedgwick,* 26; Cross, "Harriet Beecher Stowe,"
III, 394.

6. Cross, "Harriet Beecher Stowe," III, 393.

7. Leslie Stephen, *George Eliot* (London, 1902), 6–7.

8. Foster, *Catharine Maria Sedgwick,* 27; Stephen, *George Eliot,* 2–3.

9. Stephen, *George Eliot,* 8; Robert Louis Stevenson, *Edinburgh* (New York,
1912), 25; Kathryn Sklar, *Catharine Beecher: A Study in American Domesticity*
(New Haven, 1973), 15–17.

10. Humphrey House, "Qualities of George Eliot's Unbelief," in *Ideas and
Beliefs of the Victorians* (New York, 1966), 158; Noel Annan, *Leslie Stephen: His
Thought and Character in Relation to His Time* (London, 1951); and David D.
Hall, "The Victorian Connection," *American Quarterly* 27, no. 5 (December
1975), 562–63.

11. House, "George Eliot's Unbelief," 158–60.

12. Janet Adam Smith, *Henry James and Robert Louis Stevenson* (London,
1948), 34–35; Cross, "Harriet Beecher Stowe," III, 394.

13. Leslie Stephen, "Mary Ann Cross," *Dictionary of National Biography*
(London, 1917), V, 221; J. W. Cross, *Life of George Eliot* (London, 1884), III,
375.

CHAPTER 5: SON AND FATHER

1. Barbara M. Cross, ed., *The Autobiography of Lyman Beecher* (Cambridge, Mass., 1961), I, xvi–xvii; Barbara M. Cross, *Horace Bushnell: Minister to a Changing America* (Chicago, 1958), 13–30.

2. W. L. Burn, *The Age of Equipoise* (New York, 1965), 250–51.

3. In his correspondence Stevenson refers to himself as being "on his back" when ill, a curious mixture of sexual, economic, and physical imagery. See RLS to Colvin, Summer 1879, 3033. All correspondence is from the E. J. Beinecke Collection, Yale University.

4. W. E. Henley, "R. L. S." *Pall Mall* (December 1901).

5. W. Archer, "R. L. S.: His Style and Thought," *Time* (November 1885), 585; V. S. Pritchett, "Books in General," *New Statesman,* March 24, 1945, 193. For Stevenson's personal connections with the aesthetes see Mrs RLS to Dora Williams, Spring 1882.

6. Graham Balfour to Margaret Stevenson, December 2, 1895, 3926.

7. RLS, *Memories and Portraits* (Scribner's ed.), 189–90; RLS to Trevor Haddon, April 23, 1884. Stevenson's use of the word "depressing" suggests the notion of "repressing," a need to hold in feelings by self-control.

8. Sidney Colvin to Margaret Stevenson, May 5, 1896, 4384; Colvin to Lloyd Osbourne, July 13, 1899; Osbourne to Colvin, July 8, 1899; Mrs. RLS to Dora Williams, December 1880.

9. Thomas Stevenson to Colvin, November 10, 1879, 5474; Colvin to Charles Baxter, December 22, 1879, 4175; Colvin to Margaret Stevenson, May 5, 1896, 4384. On Colvin's editing of the correspondence, see A. H. Charteris to Margaret Stevenson, September 15, 1896, 4163; Osbourne to Colvin, November 13, 1898, 5313; Colvin to Osbourne, August 23, 1899. For an example of expurgation of the correspondence see RLS to Colvin, January 1875, 3005, where references to family conflicts, clashes with friends, religion, and sex were deleted from the published version.

10. On still-life painting see John Russell, *New York Times,* April 6, 1975, ii, 29. On the theme of home as a secure anchorage see RLS to Colvin, 1879, 3034.

11. Walter Houghton, *The Victorian Frame of Mind* (New Haven, 1957), 343.

12. Robert Stevenson to RLS, 5698; RLS to Haddon, June 1882, 8034; RLS to Colvin, 1879, 3034.

13. Margaret Stevenson to Colvin, May 3, 1896, 5602.

14. Colvin to Margaret Stevenson, November 12, 1895, 4378; A. H. Charteris to Margaret Stevenson, October 31, 1896, 4164.

15. RLS to Robert Stevenson, November 17, 1868, 3553; RLS, *Memories and Portraits,* 137–38; Alison Cuningham Cummy's diary, 74; RLS to Margaret Stevenson, September 5, 1868, 3320.

16. *Memories and Portraits,* 142–43; Thomas Stevenson, *Christianity Confirmed* (Edinburgh, 1879), B, 2, 3, 16, 110.

17. Thomas Stevenson to RLS, August 30, 1877, 5761; September 5, 1877, 5762.

18. Ibid.

19. Thomas Stevenson to RLS, August 30, 1877, 5761; October 17, 1877, 5764; 1883, 5775.

20. RLS to Thomas Stevenson, November 12, 1863, 3312; RLS, *Fleeming Jenkin* (Skerryvore ed.), 128, 132; *Memories and Portraits,* 139.

21. According to his mother's diary, RLS's father was absent from home, for example, thirty-three days between January 1 and April 30, 1853. Margaret Stevenson's diary, February 17, 1856; Stevenson's baby book, January 12, 1854.

22. Thomas Stevenson to RLS, May 13, 1855, 5753; Margaret Stevenson's diary, April 8, 1871, 53; RLS to Frances Sitwell, 99 n. 8 (National Library of Scotland classification; all letters with this classification are circa 1873). On contemporary Scottish writers see J. C. Furnas, *Voyage to Windward* (New York, 1951), 31.

23. RLS to Frances Sitwell, 99 n. 4; RLS to Robert Stevenson, October 1872, 3557.

24. RLS to Margaret Stevenson, September 5, 1868, 3320; RLS to Robert Stevenson, October 1872, 3557. Note that Stevenson's ideal wife is not a flesh-and-blood woman.

25. RLS to Frances Sitwell, 99 n. 4; RLS to Baxter, February 2, 1873; RLS to his parents, December 24, 1873, 3487.

26. RLS to Frances Sitwell, 99 n. 4; 99 n. 8; Thomas Stevenson to Colvin, January 8, 1880, 5748.

27. RLS to Baxter, February 2, 1873; RLS to Thomas Stevenson, January 11, 1883, 3465.

28. RLS to Margaret Stevenson, 1877, 3366; RLS to his parents c. 1878, 3500; June 1884, 3537; RLS to Colvin, Spring 1874, 2993; RLS to Sitwell, Acc. 1947 2; Mrs. RLS to Dora Williams, September 1881; Mrs. RLS to Colvin, Spring 1886; Thomas Stevenson to RLS, November 5, 1882, 5773.

29. RLS, *A Family of Engineers* (Skerryvore ed.), 192, 195, 237, 240, 242; Margaret Stevenson to Colvin, February 14, 1896, 5596; RLS to Robert Stevenson, September 1894, 3567.

30. RLS to Robert Stevenson, September 1894, 3567.

31. Ibid.

32. Stevenson's letters are filled to references to inner warfare and conflict that echo his references to prunes. E.g., "I am in a sort of despair now; being hot, indigested, solitary and purposeless." RLS to Mrs. RLS, October 1, 1882, 3278. See also Stevenson's comments on tuberculosis: "Consumption! how I hate that word; yet it can sound innocent, as, e.g., consumption of military stores." RLS to Edmund Gosse, January 23, 1880. This image suggests inner warfare in contrast to the normal association of military stores with external warfare. RLS to Colvin, October 1878, 3029; RLS to Thomas Stevenson, March 20, 1885, 3476.

33. Robert Stevenson thought RLS's "religion is more a philosophy than a religion . . . it is about life and acts here only, and nothing about the real substratum." Robert Stevenson to RLS, January 1880, 5708. RLS to Frances Sitwell, 99 n. 88: "For I do cling a little to God, as I have lost all hold on right and wrong." RLS to Margaret Stevenson, December 26, 1880, 3082: "Faith is not to believe the Bible, but to believe in God." Charteris to Margaret Stevenson, October 31, 1896, 4164; Henry Moors to Merrit Farren, December 16, 1916, 5247; Mrs. RLS to T. H. Rearden, Fall 1880, 8149; RLS to Thomas Stevenson, November 5, 1884, 3474.

34. Margaret Stevenson to RLS, 1877, 5627; September 1883, 5638; Thomas Stevenson to RLS, May 13, 1855, 5753.

35. RLS to Thomas Stevenson, October 1863, 3443; RLS to Margaret Stevenson, April 9, 1882, 3387; July 1, 1887, 3423; November 1883, 3405.

36. RLS to Baxter, December 4, 1873; RLS to Sitwell, 99 n. 16; 99 n. 54; RLS to his parents, November 28, 1880, 3508; RLS to Robert Stevenson, November 17, 1868, 3553; RLS to Margaret Stevenson, 1883, 3399.

37. RLS to B. B. Baildon, January 30, 1894.

38. For an indication of Stevenson's earnings see Furnas, *Voyage to Windward*, 267, 420, 430. In his letters, RLS turned to sarcasm to express his uneasiness over the selfishness and self-indulgence implicit in the life of the artist. "I grow delirious over a woodland aisle," he wrote, ". . . not with the hearty admiration of a genuine man, but a utilitarian, Benthamatical desire to take it and hug it and use it." RLS to Margaret Stevenson, 1883, 3399. RLS to Margaret Stevenson, February 16, 1883, 3397; September 11, 1883, 3404; RLS to his parents, January 17, 1883, 3520; RLS to Edmund Goose, January 2, 1886; Colvin to Baxter, October 19, 1880, 4175. For an example of Stevenson's view of the pursuit of money as a test see RLS to Colvin, January 10, 1880, 3046: "You talk about lending me coin; you don't understand; this is a test; I must support myself."

39. Kathryn Sklar, *Catharine Beecher: A Study in American Domesticity* (New Haven, 1973), 6–9, 18, 21; Edmund Gosse, *Father and Son* (New York, 1963), 23–24, 30, 36–37, 83; John Clive, *Macaulay: The Shaping of the Historian* (New York, 1975), 24, 38, 51, 258.

40. Sklar, *Catharine Beecher*, 21, 27, 31–32, 54.

41. Ibid., 34, 39.

42. Ibid., 81.

43. Barbara M. Cross, "Harriet Beecher Stowe," *Notable American Women*, Edward T. James, ed. (Cambridge, Mass., 1971), III, 394.

44. Clive, *Macaulay*, 3, 27, 39, 51, 258.

45. Ibid., chap. 3, 93, 139, 235, 258, 262.

46. Ibid., 53, 217–18, 250, 258, 269.

47. Ibid., 273–74.

48. Gosse, *Father and Son*, 62, 79, 96, 121.

49. Ibid., 15, 17, 26, 42–45. On Macaulay, see E. M. Forster, *Marianne*

Thornton: A Domestic Biography, 1797–1887 (New York, 1956), 53–54; on RLS see Margaret Stevenson's diary, 1852–1855.

50. Gosse, *Father and Son*, 9, 58, 63, 96–97, 226, 232, 250.

51. This discussion of generational continuity is influenced by the work of Kenneth Keniston, *The Uncommitted: Alienated Youth in American Society* (New York, 1965), 228–31.

52. Stevenson's uneasiness regarding his "fitness for life" continued until his death: "now it begins to look as if I should survive to see myself impotent and forgotten." RLS to Baildon, January 30, 1894, 2635. RLS to Colvin, October 1878, 3029; March 1884, 3050; RLS to Frances Sitwell, 99 n. 29; 99 n. 60; RLS to Gosse, July 29, 1879; RLS to Robert Stevenson, September 1894, 3567; Mrs. RLS to Dora Williams, November 1881. Mrs. RLS's first husband, Samuel Osbourne, once secretary to the governor of Indiana, worked as a court stenographer in San Francisco. His marital infidelities were a source of much dispute, and RLS contended that he would "protect" Mrs. Osbourne by marrying her. But it is conceivable that one reason why Frances Osbourne married RLS was concern for the novelist's health. See Furnas, *Voyage to Windward*, chaps. 6, 7.

53. RLS to Baxter, January 2, 1888; RLS to Margaret Stevenson, 1883, 3399; Mrs. RLS to Dora Williams, May or June 1883.

54. Furnas, *Voyage to Windward*, 81.

55. Ibid., 143, 152, 154, 163, 169; RLS to his parents, June 1880, 3502; January 24, 1883, 3521; RLS to Robert Stevenson, August 6, 1879, 3561.

56. Mildred Howells, *Life and Letters of William Dean Howells* (New York, 1928), I, 332.

57. RLS to his parents, December 8, 1880, 3509; RLS to Baxter, February 2, 1890. Also see Mrs. RLS to Dora Williams, April or May 1885.

58. Mrs. RLS to Dora Williams, April or May 1885; December 1880.

59. Osbourne to Colvin, August 17, 1899, 5326; and n.d., 5328.

CHAPTER 6: LOVE AND MARRIAGE

1. RLS to Haddon, June 1882, 8033, 8034. For other evidence that reveals Stevenson's uneasiness about what he considered "our limping, semi-scientific way of seeing thing," see RLS to Robert Stevenson, Fall 1874, 3560; RLS to Thomas Stevenson, October 12, 1883, 3467. Stevenson correspondence is from the E. J. Beinecke Collection, Yale University.

2. RLS to Haddon, June 1882, 8033, 8034.

3. RLS to Thomas Stevenson, October 12, 1883, 3467.

4. This chapter's attempt to relate Victorian attitudes toward love and marriage to broader religious and cultural anxieties is heavily influenced by the pioneering work of Walter E. Houghton, *The Victorian Frame of Mind* (New Haven, 1957), chap. 13.

5. J. C. Furnas, *Voyage to Windward* (New York, 1951), 81.

6. RLS to Sitwell, 99 n. 7; 99 n. 17; 99 n. 57; 99 n. 83; 99 n. 95; Acc. 1947 2 (National Library of Scotland classification).

7. RLS to Sitwell quoted in Furnas, *Voyage to Windward,* 82–83.

8. RLS to Stitwell, 99 n. 7; 99 n. 17; 99 n. 57; 99 n. 83; 99 n. 95; Acc. 1947 2.

9. RLS to Sitwell, 99 n. 53; 99 n. 56.

10. RLS to Sitwell, 99 n. 53; 99 n. 55; 99 n. 57; Acc. 1947 2.

11. RLS to Sitwell, 99 n. 18; 99 n. 24; 99 n. 27; 99 n. 55; 99 n. 63; 99 n. 72; RLS to Sitwell, quoted in Furnas, *Voyage to Windward,* 94.

12. Ibid.

13. RLS to Robert Stevenson, September 1894, 3567; Furnas, *Voyage to Windward,* 81.

14. RLS to Sitwell, 99 n. 47; 99 n. 48. Stevenson's statement that it would "be a small thing to die" leads one to note that the phrase "to die" in Elizabethan literature means to have an orgasm.

15. Ibid.

16. RLS to Sitwell, 99 n. 53; 99 n. 55; 99 n. 57; Acc. 1947 2.

17. GE to Maria Lewis, February 8, 1840, Gordon Haight, ed., *George Eliot Letters,* I, 50; GE to Martha Jackson, October 20, 1840, I, 70.

18. GE to Maria Lewis, August 18, 1838, I, 6; September 17, 18, 1840, I, 65–66.

19. GE to Maria Lewis, February 18, 1842, I, 127; GE to Sara Hennell, June 4, 1848, I, 264; GE to Maria Lewis, October 15, 1841, I, 116; August 12, 1841, I, 102; GE to Mr. and Mrs. Charles Bray, December 4, 1849, I, 322.

20. GE to Maria Lewis, February 18, 1842, I, 127; GE to Sara Hennell, June 4, 1848, I, 264.

21. GE to Maria Lewis, October 16, 1841, I, 116; August 12, 1841, I, 102; GE to Mr. and Mrs. Charles Bray, December 4, 1849, I, 322.

22. Edward Shorter, "Female Emancipation, Birth Control, and Fertility in European History," *American Historical Review* 78 (1973), 605–40; Daniel Scott Smith, "Family Limitation, Sexual Control, and Domestic Feminism in Victorian America," *Feminist Studies* 1 (1973), 40–57; Lawrence Stone, *The Family, Sex, and Marriage in England* (New York, 1977), 56; Alexis de Tocqueville, *Democracy in America* (New York, 1945), II, 212–14.

23. Daniel Scott Smith, "Parental Control and Family Patterns," *Journal of Marriage and the Family* 35 (1973), 423–24; Philip J. Greven, Jr., *Four Generations* (Ithaca, 1970, 222–23.

24. GE quoted in Leslie Stephen, *George Eliot* (London, 1902), 25, 27, 36.

25. GE to Robert Evans, February 28, 1842, I, 128–30; GE to Mrs. Charles Bray, April 20, 1842, I, 138.

26. GE to Charles Bray, May 1849, I, 283–84; GE to Mr. and Mrs. Charles Bray, May 30, 1849, I, 284.

27. GE to Charles Bray, May 1849, I, 283–84; GE to Mr. and Mrs. Charles

Bray, May 30, 1849, I, 284; GE to Francis Watts, August 3, 1842; I, 143; GE to Mr. an Mrs. Charles Bray, December 4, 1849, I, 322.

28. GE to Sara Hennell, October 9, 1843, I, 162.

29. Charles E. Stowe, *Life of Harriet Beecher Stowe* (Boston, 1889), 42–44, 46–49, 67.

30. Margot Peters, *Unquiet Soul* (New York, 1975), 69, 70.

31. GE to Charles Bray, February 28, 1859, III, 27; GE to Sara Hennell, November 13, 1860, III, 358; GE to Mrs. William Smith, March 1, 1873, V, 381. Lewes quoted in Leslie Stephen, *George Eliot,* 48.

32. GE to Mrs. Richard Congreve, June 10, 1880, VII, 296; GE to Mrs. Elma Stuart, October 14, 1870, VII, 210; GE to Charles Lee Evans, May 21, 1880, VII, 283.

33. Gladstone, "The Bill for Divorce," *Quarterly Review* (1857), 253.

34. Ibid.

35. HBS quoted in Forrest Wilson, *Crusader in Crinoline: The Life of Harriet Beecher Stowe* (Westport, 1972), 242.

36. Charles E. Stowe, *Life of Harriet Beecher Stowe,* 37, 42–43, 44, 46–49. In a letter describing her reaction to a biography of Madame de Staél, Stowe addresses the problem of "American distinctiveness": "in America feelings vehement and absorbing like hers become still more deep, morbid, and impassioned by the constant habits of self-government which the rigid forms of our society demand. They are repressed, and they burn inward till they burn the very soul, leaving only dust and ashes" (67).

37. O. S. Fowler, *Love and Parentage* (New York, 1846), 58, 68–69, 86–87; Sarah Ellis, *The Wives of England* (New York, 1843), 124–25; A. B. Muzzey, *The Young Maiden,* 2d ed. (Boston, 1841), 191; William Alcott, *The Young Wife* (Boston, 1837), 358. The conflict between a contractual and a sacramental conception of marriage is an old one. Here one might contrast the English phrase "daughter-in-law" with its French counterpart, *belle-fille.*

38. Herbert Spencer, *Principles of Psychology* (London, 1855), 601–2; Alexander Bain, *The Senses and the Intellect* (London, 1855), 398; J. D. Morell, *An Introduction to Mental Philosophy* (London, 1862), 456; Joseph Haven, *Mental Philosophy* 2d ed. (New York, 1879), 444–45, 449, 450, 490, 495–96.

39. Mrs. L. G. Abell, *Woman in her Various Relations* (New York, 1851), 294–95; Margaret Coxe, *Young Lady's Companion* (Columbus, 1845), 193–94, 209; Mrs. John Farrar, *Young Lady's Friend,* 2d ed. (New York, 1849), 280–81.

40. Mrs. A. J. Graves, *Woman in America* (New York, 1843), xiii–xiv; *American Lady* (Philadelphia, 1839), 193; Fowler, *Love and Parentage,* 138, 142; Fowler, *Matrimony* (Boston, 1859), 62, 63, 311, 337, 412; Ellis, *Wives of England,* 125, 126.

41. HBS to Calvin Stowe, Stowe Papers, Schlesinger Library, Harvard University, January 1, 1847. My interpretation of Stowe owes much to Barbara M. Cross, "Harriet Beecher Stowe," in *Notable American Women,* Edward T. James, ed. (Cambridge, Mass., 1971), III, 393–402.

42. Ibid.

43. Calvin Stowe quoted in Edmund Wilson, *Patriotic Gore* (New York, 1962), 18–27.

44. HBS to Calvin Stowe, January 1, 1847.

45. HBS to Calvin Stowe, September 4, 1842; May–June 1844.

46. HBS to Calvin Stowe, May–June 1844. On the ways Stowe achieved respite from sex see Mary Kelley, "At War with Herself," *Woman's Being, Woman's Place* (Boston, 1979), 201–19.

47. HBS to Calvin Stowe, September 4, 1842; May–June 1844; August 1844; August 1844(?).

48. Tocqueville, *Democracy in America*, 222–25. Calvin Stowe quoted in Kelley, "At War with Herself," 212.

49. HBS to Calvin Stowe, February 20, 1847.

CHAPTER 7: SISTER AND BROTHER

1. John Clive, *Macaulay: The Shaping of the Historian* (New York, 1975), 273–74.

2. Brian Sutton-Smith and B. G. Rosenberg, *The Sibling* (New York, 1970), 1–2; Philip J. Greven, Jr., *Four Generations* (Ithaca, 1970), 222–23; Daniel Scott Smith, "Parental Control and Marriage Patterns," *Journal of Marriage and the Family* 35 (August 1973), 423–24.

3. Ibid.

4. Clive, *Macaulay*, 273–74; Lawrence Stone, *The Family, Sex, and Marriage in England* (New York, 1979), 40, 233, 243–45; Carl Degler, *At Odds* (New York, 1980), 158–65.

5. "Recollections of Childhood," reprinted in Mary E. Dewey, ed., *Life and Letters of Catharine M. Sedgwick* (New York, 1871), 28–29, 35–36, 43–48.

6. Ibid., 34–35.

7. Ibid., 48.

8. Ibid., 36, 37, 48.

9. Ibid., 38.

10. Ibid., 68, 86–87, 93; CMS to Mrs. Frank Channing, September 25, 1821, reprinted in Dewey, *Life and Letters*, 144. The Catharine M. Sedgwick Collection is on deposit at the Massachusetts Historical Society. Extracts from the correspondence, journals, and notebooks are reprinted in Mary E. Dewey, ed., *Life and Letters of Catharine M. Sedgwick* (New York, 1871).

11. CMS to Mrs. Frank Channing, June 4, 1821, quoted in Dewey, *Life and Letters*, 122; CMS to Mrs. Frances Watson, March 23, 1810, in Dewey, *Life and Letters*, 86–87.

12. CMS to Theodore Sedgwick, Sr., February 1, 1801, in Dewey, *Life and Letters*, 86–87.

13. "Recollections of Childhood," in Dewey, *Life and Letters*, 28, 29, 37.

14. CMS to Mrs. Frances Watson, February 15, 1813, in Dewey, *Life and Letters,* 95; CMS to Robert Sedgwick, June 7, 1813, in Dewey, *Life and Letters,* 96–97.

15. CMS to Mrs. Frances Watson, March 23, 1810, in Dewey, *Life and Letters,* 86–87.

16. CMS to Robert Sedgwick, August 15, 1813, in Dewey, *Life and Letters,* 98.

17. CMS to Mrs. Frank Channing, December 5, 1821, quoted in Dewey, *Life and Letters,* 145–47; CMS to Mrs. Frances Watson, May 25, 1825, in Dewey, *Life and Letters,* 174.

18. CMS to Mrs. Frank Channing, December 5, 1821, in Dewey, *Life and Letters,* 145.

19. "Recollections of Childhood," in Dewey, *Life and Letters,* 52; CMS to Charles Sedgwick, February 2, 1829, in Dewey, *Life and Letters,* 202; Robert Sedgwick to CMS, March 28, 1816, September 1816, in Dewey, *Life and Letters,* 103.

20. CMS to Charles Sedgwick, February 2, 1829, in Dewey, *Life and Letters,* 201–2; "Recollections of Childhood," in Dewey, *Life and Letters,* 69–70; CMS to Mrs. Frances Watson, February 1822, in Dewey, *Life and Letters,* 149; Robert Sedgwick to CMS, February 1822, in Dewey, *Life and Letters,* 149–50.

21. CMS to Frances Watson, March 25, 1816, in Dewey, *Life and Letters,* 102–3; CMS journal, May 18, 1828, in Dewey, *Life and Letters,* 197–99.

22. Theodore Sedgwick, Jr., November 1827, in Dewey, *Life and Letters,* 189.

23. CMS to Mrs. Elizabeth Pomeroy, January 15, 1813, in Dewey, *Life and Letters,* 94–95.

24. CMS to Mrs. Elizabeth Pomeroy, March 12, 1814, quoted in Dewey, *Life and Letters,* 99–100; CMS to Robert Sedgwick, July 2, 1813, in Dewey, *Life and Letters,* 97–98.

25. CMS to Mrs. Frank Channing, February 19, 1821, quoted in Dewey, *Life and Letters,* 116; CMS to Robert Sedgwick, November 1, 1824, in Dewey, *Life and Letters,* 162–63; CMS to Robert Sedgwick, November 12, 1819, in Dewey, *Life and Letters,* 109.

26. CMS to Rev. Orville Dewey, November 29, 1847, in Dewey, *Life and Letters,* 302; CMS journal, October 28, 1835, in Dewey, *Life and Letters,* 247.

27. Fanny Butler to Samuel and Thomas Butler, February 6, 1841, in Arnold Silver, ed., *The Family Letters of Samuel Butler* (Stanford, 1962), 40–42.

28. Ibid., 41–42.

29. Walter Houghton, *The Victorian Frame of Mind* (New Haven, 1957), 394–95; "The Autobiography of Charles Darwin," in Francis Darwin, *Life and Letters of Charles Darwin* (New York, 1959), 30; *The Education of Henry Adams* (Boston, 1918), 12.

30. *Selections from the Notebooks of Samuel Butler* (London, 1930), 31, 32.

31. Daniel F. Howard, Introduction to the *Correspondence of Samuel Butler*

with His Sister May (Berkeley, 1962), 17; G. D. H. Cole, *Samuel Butler* (London, 1948), 40; *Further Extracts from the Notebooks of Samuel Butler*, A. T. Bartholomew, ed. (London, 1934), 91; "Father and Son" (1887, revised 1898) *Butleriana* (London, 1932), n.p

32. Samuel Butler, *The Life and Letters of Dr. Samuel Butler*, in *The Shrewsbury Edition of the Works of Samuel Butler*, Henry Festing Jones and A. T. Bartholomew, eds. (London, 1924), XI, 443–47; Philip Henderson, *Samuel Butler: The Incarnate Bachelor* (Bloomington, 1954), 164–65.

33. Thomas Butler to Samuel Butler, March 9, 1859, *Family Letters,* 64.

34. Samuel Butler to Thomas Butler, March 10, 1859, *Family Letters,* 64–66; Samuel Butler to Fanny Butler, March 11, 1859, *Family Letters,* 66, 67.

35. Thomas Butler to Samuel Butler, March 12, 1859, *Family Letters,* 67–68.

36. The escalation of the conflict can be traced in the letters dealing with religion. Canon Butler bade his son to explain what specific objections he had to taking holy orders. Butler answered pointedly, stating the precise passages in the Articles of the Church of England to which he was averse. Two New Testament passages raised particularly strong doubts in Butler's mind—passages that held that despite baptism man is unable to achieve moral purity. Butler responded to these passages by adopting the Pelagian position denying original sin and holding that man has perfect freedom of the will and can be "Holy even as Christ was holy upon earth." Only when one realizes that the issue of the efficacy of baptism had divided the Church of England in the 1840s and early 1850s can a modern reader begin to sense the significance of what Butler was saying. More was at stake here than a minor disagreement over church dogma. Members of Butler's family were convinced that he had declared himself an antinomian, holding that the moral law of Christianity was of no obligation. An aunt explained the family's position. Her nephew, she asserted, admitted to no rule of duty beyond his own will and feelings. Butler interpreted the controversy in quite different terms. His letters stress the critical importance of human ability and personal responsibility in matters of religion. His assertion of the possibility of achieving a sanctified life seems to give expression to a profound yearning in his own life: to break free of earlier habits of obedience and to assert a measure of independence. What we see is how an abstract theological issue—the efficacy of baptism—could dramatize issues of personal development and how the tensions and strains of an individual family could be seen to involve more general question of religious authority. Anna Wormsley Russell to Samuel Butler, May 13, 1866, *Family Letters*, 114–15; Samuel Butler to Thomas Butler, May 9, 1859, *Family Letters*, 73–75.

37. Thomas Butler to Samuel Butler, April 7 or 8, 1859; May 19, 1859; August 3, 1859; *Family Letters,* 72, 84–85, 88–89.

38. Samuel Butler to Thomas Butler, July 28, 1859, *Family Letters,* 85–87; Thomas Butler to Samuel Butler, May 19, 1859; August 1, 1859; *Family Letters,* 85, 87.

39. Samuel Butler to Thomas Butler, July 28, 1859, *Family Letters*, 85–87; Thomas Butler to Samuel Butler, August 3, 1859, *Family Letters*, 88–89.

40. Samuel Butler to Thomas Butler, March 15, 1881; November 26, 1881; *Family Letters*, 181, 194.

41. Thomas Butler to Samuel Butler, October 5, 1879, *Family Letters*, 146.

42. Samuel Butler to Henrietta Butler, June 10, 1882, *Family Letters*, 211–12.

43. Samuel Butler to May Butler, March 24 (1873) *Correspondence . . . with His Sister May*, 61–63.

44. Samuel Butler to May Butler, March 27, 1878, *Correspondence . . . with His Sister May*, 70–71; Thomas Butler to Samuel Butler, June 12, 1872, *Family Letters*, 121; Frank M. Turner, *Between Science and Religion* (New Haven, 1974), 164–200.

45. Samuel Butler to May Butler, November 12, 1873, *Correspondence . . . with His Sister May*, 65–66; Howard, Introduction, *Correspondence . . . with His Sister May*, 29–30.

46. Arnold Silver, Introduction, *Family Letters*, 25–26; Cole, *Samuel Butler to E. M. A. Savage*, July 11, 1883; January 6, 1884; January 14, 1884; and note appended January 15, 1902; *Samuel Butler and E. M. A. Savage, Letters, 1871–1885*, Geoffrey Keynes and Brian Hill, eds. (London, 1935), 290, 317, 318.

47. *Further Extracts from the Notebooks of Samuel Butler*, 91; "Father and Son," *Butleriana*, n.p.

48. Sigmund Freud, *Totem and Taboo* (London, 1930).

CONCLUSION

1. Christopher Lasch, "The Family and History," *New York Review of Books* November 13, 1975, 13, 14; Lawrence Stone, "The Massacre of the Innocents," *New York Review of Books*, November 14, 1974, 25.

2. Lasch, "Review of Lawrence Stone's *The Family, Sex and Marriage in England*," *New Republic*, July 8 and 15, 1978, 36; David Riesman, *The Lonely Crowd* (New Haven, 1950); Talcott Parsons and Robert F. Bales, *Family, Socialization and Interaction Process* (Glencoe, 1955); Kenneth Keniston, *The Uncommitted* (New York, 1965), 273–310.

3. Lasch, "The Family and History," 14; "Review of *Family, Sex and Marriage*," 36.

4. Edward Shorter, *The Making of the Modern Family* (New York, 1976); Fred Weinstein and Gerald M. Platt, *The Wish to Be Free* (Berkeley, 1975).

5. Lawrence Stone, *The Family, Sex and Marriage in England* (New York, 1979), 407–28; Philip J. Greven, Jr., *The Protestant Temperament* (New York, 1977), 3–18; Michael Anderson, *Family Structure in Nineteenth Century Lancashire* (London, 1971); Michael Katz, *The People of Hamilton, Canada West* (Cambridge, Mass., 1975); Lasch, "Review of *Family, Sex and Marriage*," 35, 36; Kathryn Kish Sklar, *Catharine Beecher* (New Haven, 1973); Nancy Cott,

The Bonds of Womanhood (New Haven, 1977); Carl Degler, *At Odds* (Oxford, 1980); Linda Gordon, "Voluntary Motherhood: The Beginnings of Feminist Birth Control Ideas in the United States," *Feminist Studies* 1 (Winter–Spring 1973), 5–22; Daniel Scott Smith, "Family Limitation, Sexual Control, and Domestic Feminism in Nineteenth Century America," *Feminist Studies* 1 (Winter–Spring 1973), 40–57.

6. Philip J. Greven, Jr., *Four Generations* (Ithaca, 1970); *The Protestant Temperament* (New York, 1977).

7. Alexis de Tocqueville, *Democracy in America* (New York, 1945), II, 202–8.

Bibliographical Essay

WHAT follows is not intended as a complete list either of works cited or of works consulted in the preparation of this study. It is intended rather to provide a convenient guide to the vast literature on family history, the transatlantic connection of the nineteenth century, and the specific individuals discussed in this book.

Family History

The literature on the history of the family is growing at an explosive rate. The most recent and thorough bibliography on the social history of the family is Gerald L. Soliday, *History of the Family and Kinship: A Select International Bibliography* (Millwood, N.Y., 1980). Useful guides to the major themes and interpretations in the literature on the family are: Christopher Lasch, "The Family and History," *New York Review of Books,* November 13, 27, and December 11, 1975; Sylvia Junko Yanagisako, "Family and Household: The Analysis of Domestic Groups," *Annual Review of Anthropology* 8 (1979), 161–205; Michael Anderson, *Approaches to the History of the Western Family, 1500–1914* (London, 1980); and Mark Poster, *Critical Theory of the Family* (New York, 1980). For more detailed and comprehensive overviews of family change in Britain and America, one would do well to turn to such recent works as Lawrence Stone, *The*

Family, Sex and Marriage in England 1500–1800 (New York, 1977), and Carl Degler, *At Odds: Women and the Family in America from the Revolution to the Present* (New York, 1980).

Anyone interested in the history of childhood and childrearing practices might begin with R. W. Beales, Jr., "In Search of the Historical Child," *American Quarterly* 27 (1975), 379–98, which can be supplemented by Peter Gregg Slater, *Children in the New England Mind* (Hamden, 1977); Bernard Wishy, *The Child and the Republic* (Philadelphia, 1972); and Joseph F. Kett, *Rites of Passage: Adolescence in America* (New York, 1977).

For understanding the changing roles and status of British and American women, the indispensable starting points are two review essays in the journal *Signs: Journal of Women in Culture and Society:* one by Barbara Sicherman, *Signs* 1 (1975), 461–85; and another by Mary Beth Norton, *Signs* 5 (1979), 324–37. Also important are Kathryn Kish Sklar, *Catharine Beecher: A Study in American Domesticity* (New Haven, 1973); Nancy Cott, *The Bonds of Womanhood* (New Haven, 1977); Patricia Branca, *Silent Sisterhood* (Pittsburgh, 1975); and Louise A. Tilly and Joan W. Scott, *Women, Work, and Family* (New York, 1978). Significant information may also be gleaned from Anne Kuhn, *The Mother's Role in Childhood Education* (New Haven, 1947).

The best introduction to the "new" social history of the family are the essays in John Demos and Sarane Bocock, eds., *Turning Points: Historical and Sociological Essays on the Family* (Chicago, 1978). The family's developmental cycle and the individual's life stages are explored in Tamara Hareven, *Transitions: The Family and the Life Course in Historical Perspective* (New York, 1978). The subject of changes in household composition over time is well covered in Tamara Hareven and Maris Vinovskis, eds., *Family and Population in Nineteenth Century America* (Princeton, 1978); Tamara Hareven, ed., *Family and Kin in Urban Communities, 1700–1930* (New York, 1977); and P. Laslett and R. Wall, eds., *Household and Family in Past Time* (Cambridge, England, 1972). New directions in research on the historical family are suggested by the essays in the *Journal of Family History.*

Transatlantic Connection

Of older publications on this topic, Clarence Gohdes, *American Literature in Nineteenth-Century England* (New York, 1944), remains particularly valuable. More recently Frank Thistlethwaite, *The Anglo-American Connection in the Early Nineteenth Century* (Philadelphia, 1959) and *America and the Atlantic Community* (New York, 1959), has provided an especially thoughtful overall interpretation of the flow of ideas between nineteenth-century Britain and America, which can be supplemented by G. D. Lillibridge, *Beacon of Freedom: The Impact of American Democracy upon Great Britain, 1830–1870* (Philadelphia, 1955). An excellent guide to the literature on the mid-century "Victorian" network of transatlantic connections is David D. Hall, "The Victorian Connection," *American Quarterly* 27 (December 1975), 561–74. R. K. Webb, *Harriet Martineau: A Radical Victorian* (London, 1960), and William J. Sowder, *Emerson's Impact on the British Isles and Canada* (Charlottesville, 1966), are particularly sensitive to the social groups that were most attuned to the transatlantic connection. On political connections between Britain and America, a valuable starting point is Robert Kelley, *Transatlantic Persuasion: The Liberal-Democratic Mind in the Age of Gladstone* (New York, 1969). Other aspects of the Anglo-American connection can be traced in Rowland T. Berthoff, *British Immigrants in Industrial America* (New York, 1953); J. Iverne Dowie and J. Thomas Tredway, eds., *Immigration of Ideas: Studies in the North Atlantic Community* (Rock Island, Ill., 1968); Charlotte Erickson, *Invisible Immigrants: The Adaptation of English and Scottish Immigrants in Nineteenth Century America* (Miami, 1972); Robert O. Mead, *Atlantic Legacy: Essay in American-European Cultural History* (New York, 1969); and René Wellek, *Confrontations: Intellectual and Literary Relations Between Germany, England and the United States During the Nineteenth Century* (Princeton, 1965).

No discussion of the transatlantic connection would be complete that failed to mention six recent works in American history that point to an Anglo-American community of reform. As important in method as they are in substance, each of these books, in different ways, seeks to show that the way certain nineteenth-century people were brought up; the values that prevailed; and the dynamics that developed in their homes, shaped their relationship to, attitudes toward, expectations of, and behavior in, the public world. Ann Douglas, *The Feminization of American Culture* (New York, 1977), examines the evolution of Victorian conceptions of childhood, domesticity, and masculinity. Daniel W. Howe, *The Political Culture of American Whigs* (Chicago, 1980), focuses on the moral outlook, character traits, values, and ideological commitments of key figures in the Whig political party. Michael Rogin, *Fathers and Children: Andrew Jackson and the Subjugation of the American Indian* (New York, 1975); George B. Forgie, *Patricide in the House Divided: A Psychological Interpretation of Lincoln and His Age* (New York, 1979); Peter F. Walker, *Moral Choices: Memory, Desire, and Imagination in Nineteenth Century American Abolition* (Baton Rouge, 1978); and Lewis Perry, *Childhood, Marriage and Reform: Henry Clarke Wright, 1797–1870* (Chicago, 1980), through close textual analysis of personal papers, literature, and political rhetoric, trace intricate connections between issues raised in childrearing and marriage and broader religious and political controversies. Acutely sensitive to language, each of these authors is able to isolate connections between domestic ideology and political rhetoric, between conflicts within individual households and larger cultural symbols of dominance, authority, and control.

Robert Louis Stevenson

The starting point for research on Robert Louis Stevenson is the extensive collection of letters and manuscripts located at Yale University. Additional correspondence is deposited in the National Library of Scotland. Sidney Colvin edited *The Letters of Robert Louis Stevenson to His Family and Friends* (2 vols., 1899; 4 vols., 1911), but the texts are incomplete and unreliable. The official biography was written by Stevenson's cousin, Graham Balfour, *The Life of Robert Louis Stevenson* (2 vols., 1901). The standard modern biographies are J. C. Furnas, *Voyage to Windward* (New York, 1951); Jenni Calder, *Robert Louis Stevenson: A Life Study* (New York, 1980); and James P. Hennessey, *Robert Louis Stevenson* (New York, 1975). Other studies of note include Jenni Calder, *Stevenson and Victorian England* (New York, 1981); David Daiches, *Robert Louis Stevenson and His World* (New York, 1977); J. Herbert Slater, *A Stevenson Bibliography* (New York, 1974); and Roger G. Swearingen, *The Prose Writings of Robert Louis Stevenson: A Guide* (Hamden, 1980).

George Eliot

The basic source of information on George Eiot's life is the collection of Eliot letters edited by Gordon S. Haight, *The George Eliot Letters* (8 vols., New Haven, 1954–55), which can be supplemented by Haight's study of Eliot's early years in London, *George Eliot and John Chapman with Chapman's Diaries* 2d ed. (Hamden, 1969). The definitive biography is Gordon S. Haight, *George Eliot: A Biography* (New York, 1968). Among other useful biographical studies are: Rudy V. Redinger, *George Eliot: The Emergent Self* (New York, 1975); R. T. Jones, *George Eliot* (Cambridge, England, 1971); and Leslie Stephen's classic *George Eliot* (London, 1902). The literature on George Eliot's fiction is so vast that only a few of the most important titles can be listed here. Among the most useful are Henry Auster, *Local Habitations: Regionalism in the Early Novels of George Eliot* (Cambridge, Mass., 1970); Alan Mintz, *George Eliot and the Novel of Vocation* (Cambridge, Mass., 1978); and Bernard J. Paris, *Experiments in Life: George Eliot's Quest for Values* (Detroit, 1965). A guide to sources on George Eliot is Constance M. Fulmer, *George Eliot: A Reference Guide* (Boston, 1977).

Harriet Beecher Stowe

The manuscript collections of the Schlesinger Library, Harvard University, and the Stowe-Day Foundation of Hartford, Connecticut, are the basic sources of information. Forrest Wilson's *Crusader in Crinoline: The Life of Harriet Beecher Stowe* (New York, 1941) is the standard biography, which includes material omitted from the two official biographies, Charles Edward Stowe, *Life of Harriet Beecher Stowe* (Boston, 1889), and Annie Fields, *Life and Letters of Harriet Beecher Stowe* (Boston, 1897). A useful guide to sources is Jean W. Ashton, *Harriet Beecher Stowe: A Reference Guide* (Boston, 1977). Charles H. Foster, *The Rungless Ladder: Harriet Beecher Stowe and New England Puritanism* (New York, 1954), examines the moral and philosophical ideas in her works. Some of the most valuable material on Harriet Beecher Stowe can be found in biographical studies of other members of the famous Beecher family. *The Autobiography of Lyman Beecher,* ed. Barbara M. Cross (2 vols., Cambridge, Mass., 1961), which Harriet Beecher Stowe helped compile, sheds much light on her family background. Among other studies of value are Kathryn Kish Sklar, *Catharine Beecher: A Study in American Domesticity* (New Haven, 1973); Marie Caskey, *Chariot of Fire: Religion and the Beecher Family* (New Haven, 1978); Earl A. French and Diana Royce, eds., *Portraits of a Nineteenth Century Family: A Symposium on the Beecher Family* (Hartford, 1976); Milton Rugoff, *The Beechers: An American Family in the Nineteenth Century* (New York, 1981); and Lyman Beecher Stowe, *Saints, Sinners and Beechers* (Indianapolis, 1934).

Catharine Sedgwick

The correspondence, journals, and notebooks of Catharine Sedgwick can be found at the Massachusetts Historical Society. Mary E. Dewey, *Life and Letters of Catharine Sedgwick* (Boston, 1871), provides a detailed record of her personal life and her religious beliefs. The two standard studies of her life and work are Edward H. Foster, *Catharine Maria Sedgwick* (New York, 1974), and Sr. Mary M. Welsh, *Catharine Maria Sedgwick: Her Position in the Literature and Thought of Her Time Up to 1860* (Philadelphia, 1973). New departures in the study of Catharine

Sedgwick are suggested by Mary Kelley, "A Woman Alone: Catharine Maria Sedgwick's Spinsterhood in Nineteenth-Century America," *New England Quarterly* 51 (1978), 209–25.

Samuel Butler

The basic primary sources on Samuel Butler's life are twelve volumes of self-annotated correspondence in the British Museum and four volumes of notebooks on deposit in the Chapin Library, Williams College. The major published sources of information include *The Family Letters of Samuel Butler,* ed. Arnold Silver (Stanford, 1962); *Samuel Butler and E. M. A. Savage, Letters, 1871–1885,* ed. Geoffrey Keynes and Brian Hill (London, 1935); and *The Correspondence of Samuel Butler and His Sister May,* ed. Daniel F. Howard (Berkeley, 1962). The most thorough guides to writings by and about Butler are: J. A. Hoppe, *A Bibliography of the Writings of Samuel Butler* (London, 1925), and Stanley B. Harkness, *The Career of Samuel Butler 1835–1902: A Bibliography* (New York, 1956). The official biography is H. Festing Jones, *Samuel Butler, Author of Erewhon (1835–1902)* (London, 1919). Recent studies treating different aspects of Butler's life include: Martha R. Garnett, *Samuel Butler and His Family Relations* (London, 1926); Phyllis Greenacre, *Quest for the Father: A Study of the Darwin-Butler Controversy* (New York, 1963); Philip Henderson, *Samuel Butler: The Incarnate Bachelor* (Bloomington, 1953); Malcolm Muggeridge, *Earnest Atheist: A Study of Samuel Butler* (London, 1936); and Clara G. Stillman, *Samuel Butler: A Mid-Victorian Modern* (New York, 1932).

Index